CALIFORNIA LEGISLATURE

Tenth Report of the
Senate Fact-Finding Committee
On Un-American Activities

1959

MEMBERS OF THE COMMITTEE

SENATOR NATHAN F. COOMBS, *Vice Chairman*   SENATOR JOHN F. THOMPSON
SENATOR EARL D. DESMOND *   SENATOR JOHN F. McCARTHY
SENATOR HUGH M. BURNS, *Chairman*
R. E. COMBS, *Counsel*
MARY E. HOPE, *Executive Secretary*

Published by the
SENATE
OF THE STATE OF CALIFORNIA

LIEUTENANT GOVERNOR GLENN M. ANDERSON
President of the Senate

HUGH M. BURNS   JOSEPH A. BEEK
President pro Tempore   *Secretary*

* Deceased, 1958

LETTER OF TRANSMITTAL

SENATE CHAMBER, STATE CAPITOL
SACRAMENTO, JUNE 19, 1959

HON. GLENN M. ANDERSON
President of the Senate, and Gentlemen of the Senate;
Senate Chamber, Sacramento, California

MR. PRESIDENT AND GENTLEMEN OF THE SENATE: Pursuant to Senate Resolution No. 132, which appears at page 5111 of the Senate Journal for June 12, 1957, the Senate Fact-Finding Committee on Un-American Activities was created and the following Members of the Senate were appointed to said committee by the Senate Committee on Rules: Senator Nathan F. Coombs, Senator Earl D. Desmond,* Senator John F. McCarthy, Senator John F. Thompson, Senator Hugh M. Burns.

The committee herewith submits a report of its investigation, findings, and recommendation.

Respectfully submitted,

HUGH M. BURNS, *Chaiman*
NATHAN F. COOMBS, *Vice Chairman*
JOHN F. MCCARTHY
JOHN F. THOMPSON

* Deceased, 1958.

(3)

TABLE OF CONTENTS

Copies of previous Un-American Activities Reports may be available in California Public Libraries.

COMMUNIST ACTIVITIES IN CALIFORNIA

PERIOD OF OPEN ACTIVITY

Several years ago this committee received a crate of documents from an anonymous source. The papers were of such a nature that they were readily identified and authenticated as the records of a top-flight little group of Communists who were operating the party's cultural and political apparatus in southern California. They contained hundreds of names, both those of Communists and sympathizers who could be safely contacted. There were files of correspondence, the membership and mailing lists of front organizations, and minutes of Communist meetings.

We were especially interested in the minutes of a strategy meeting by five Communists, because they were discussing us, and agreed that the committee could never have accomplished the work of the past two years unless it had at least a quarter of a million dollars in addition to the sum appropriated to it by the Legislature.

Their statement, however flattering, was not so significant as the long-range strategy disclosed for future Communist activity on a statewide basis. The party was to concentrate on infiltration of politics, education, and trade unions, and was to do so as openly as possible. Aside from the fact that unforeseen circumstances have made it expedient for these plans to be conducted largely from underground positions, the program set forth in these documents has been meticulously followed.

This windfall of highly secret documents came from the Communist Party to the committee in a rather curious manner. Someone had discovered that the party intended to move several packing cases and filing cabinets of documents from one location to another. The transportation was to be done late at night by truck and the details concerning the arrangements were supposed to be known to a very limited few. Nevertheless, as one of the trucks containing the most critical filing cabinet started on its way from the old location to the new one, it rolled over a deep rut and that particular packing case was jarred off the truck and fell into the street. It so happened that an individual friendly to the committee was standing nearby and apparently had some inkling as to what was transpiring. He secured the documents and presented them to the committee.

At that time there was considerable Communist activity at the University of California in Los Angeles, and there had also been a good deal of activity among writers connected with the motion picture industry. At the university during 1943 a function was held called the Writers' Congress, which we have described in detail in an earlier report. This function was participated in by the Hollywood Writers' Mobilization, also exposed by the committee as a Communist-dominated organization. Many of the names mentioned in the documents that came to the committee's attention in the manner described above were those of faculty members of the university, students attending that institution, and prominent members of the Hollywood Screen Writers' Guild.

The committee had been exceedingly active in investigating the university and the Hollywood Writers' Mobilization, as well as various Communist front organizations that functioned throughout the southern part of the State from 1941 through 1945. A great many public hearings had been held at which Communist functionaries, officials of front organizations, faculty members from U. C. L. A., faculty members from the Communist school in Los Angeles, teachers in the Los Angeles City School System, and people who were working in the motion picture industry were all subpoenaed and questioned at great length.

We cite these matters to illustrate that from 1939 through 1955, Communist activity in the United States, and particularly in New York and California, was brazen, open, impertinent, and publicly flaunted for all to see. There were demonstrations in public offices and picket lines in front of public buildings. There were student demonstrations on the campuses and at the front gates of various universities throughout the State. There were party line pamphlets and reams of propaganda emitted by hosts of Communist front organizations that were flourishing from one end of the State to the other. There were motor caravans that advanced on the State Capital during sessions of the Legislature; there were open letters, public demonstrations of all sorts, and great strikes such as those at North American Aviation Company and Warner Brothers studio, led by Communists who disdained to conceal their open participation in these tiny revolutions and tests of the class conflict. It was, indeed, an era of open Communist Party activity in this State, and the committee reacted by holding many open hearings and amassing great volumes of testimony.

Since 1955 all of this has changed. There is no longer this defiant and brazen activity on the part of the Communists in this State. On the contrary, they have retreated by plan to carefully prepared positions and have insinuated their unknown members into strategic positions throughout our governmental and social structure. The front organizations formerly so useful to the party have now been abandoned, with very few exceptions. Consequently, the state committee has held fewer hearings and devised new techniques to meet the new challenge posed by this abrupt change in Communist Party operational techniques.

This transition from open to underground activity was undertaken because of excellent and logical reasons, all of which will be explained in detail hereafter. The party is working more feverishly than ever before, and we will show later in this report how successful the new technique has been when we reproduce statements from the Communist Party itself taking credit for some of the most momentous changes wrought for the protection of subversive elements in our country since the Communist Party began operating in the United States in 1919.

It is unfortunately true that too many people are inclined to gauge the success of the various governmental agencies investigating subversive activities by the amount of sensational headlines those investigations produce. During the early years of Communist activity publicity was necessary in order to combat the subversive menace and to break through public apathy and misunderstanding as to the real nature of the problem. That time has now passed. Much of the old apathy remains, but it is still no longer necessary to convince the average American citizen that Communism is indeed subversive, that the American Communist Party and every one of its members are subject to the complete disciplinary control of the Soviet Union, that the party is the great reservoir from which espionage agents are recruited for international Communism, and that the Communist Party is determined, at any cost, to destroy all non-Communist governments throughout the world and to establish in their place a world Communist dictatorship.

A great many uninformed individuals have a tendency to believe that since the Communist Party of the United States has recently shrunk in membership to an all-time low, that the Communist menace is now a thing of the past; that all committees should be disbanded, the F.B.I. should be emasculated, and that we should all return to our business of making the most of our political and economic opportunities. This naive attitude and this incredible ignorance concerning the Communist menace is international Communism's greatest weapon against us. Experts in the anti-Communist field have told us over and over again, that it is not the number of Communists about which we have to worry so much, it is the incredible facility with which they insinuate themselves into strategic positions from which they exercise a control far disproportionate to their numerical strength. At the height of its success the Communist Party of the United States comprised approximately 100,000 members; in 1943, there were about 3,000 known members in Los Angeles County alone. After considering all of the reliable sources available to it, this committee is convinced that the national strength of the Communist Party at the present time is between 15,000 and 20,000.

Communist Fallout

Let us, at this point, indicate a matter that has never been discussed before in this country, insofar as we are aware, but that has been mentioned briefly by a British writer, Mr. Colm Brogan, in an article which he entitled, "Beware the Ex-Communist." Every Communist Party in the world, with the exception of the party in the Soviet Union and those which lie behind the Iron Curtain, has an enormous membership turnover every year. Those members who climb to positions of authority or who are recruited for espionage purposes are not suffered to leave without a terrific struggle. But the rank and file members are continually coming in and out of the party organization. They do not, however, appear before any governmental body, confess the error of their ways, explain the matters that led up to their disillusionment and disaffection, and give their country or their state the benefit of their knowledge concerning a conspiratorial and subversive effort to gnaw away at the foundations of those governments. On the contrary, the ex-Communist usually leaves the party because he is mad at some superior functionary, because he is unhappy at an assignment that is distasteful to him, or because he disagrees with the current Communist Party line. After 18 years experience in this work, your committee is absolutely convinced that the overwhelming majority of rank and file Communists who leave the party are prompted to do so because in their opinion it is not strong enough and is not taking enough emphatic action in its unceasing efforts to subvert and destroy the State and nation. These ex-members are still Marxists, they are still Communists, and they have a peculiar choice of freedom as they are no longer bound by the inexorable ties of party discipline and the current Communist Party line.

On several occasions the committee has subpoenaed these former members only to find that they are more defiant than ever, more determined to show their old comrades that they are steeled fighters in the world class struggle; and we have even convicted them and sent them to jail, where they proudly served a term of 30 or 60 days and emerged more dedicated and more fanatic than before—proudly wearing the martyr's badge as a symbol of their Marxian determination and zeal.

During every normal year the American Communist Party has lost approximately 25 percent of its total membership for one reason or another. Most of the turnover is due to disaffection on the part of rank and file members as already stated, but there is also swift disciplinary action for the untrustworthy, the recalcitrant, the dissident, the troublemaker—those who stray from the path of rectitude and fail to toe the mark demanded by rigid party discipline. By this we can easily see what an enormous reservoir of former Communists has been created since the founding of the party in 1919, and we then realize that the Communist Party has a poisonous fallout of its own which is constantly increasing and which poses a far more deadly threat to our American way of life than the fallout that is emitted by the nuclear experiments which the Communist Party is so determined shall be stopped.

The Soft Hook

The Communist Party shifted its activities into high gear approximately 35 years ago and it should now be quite plain that a great many individuals who commenced as rank and file party members have since achieved such positions of strategic importance and prominence, both to themselves and to the Communist cause, that they resigned from the party to protect themselves in their exalted positions and to further the cause of world Communism by posing as sincere liberals. It is ironically true that a great many of these former Communists became honestly disillusioned with the party and sought to sever the last vestige of connection with it. They were suffered to do this by the Communist functionaries until the time came when their services were necessary for the cause. At that time it was quite a simple matter to remind these unfortunate hostages that the party still retained indisputable evidence of their former membership, and now that the individual was happily married, had several children, was secure in a remunerative and influential position, he could easily be destroyed if his former affiliation was disclosed. The usual technique is referred to by the Communist Party as getting the victim on "the soft hook." He would be asked to perform some trivial service for the party, such as permitting a party secretary to be employed in his office so that she could take his telephone calls, open his mail, arrange his appointments, monitor his speaking engagements, and channel her fund of strategic information into the right places. Once this had been done, the hook sank deeper and deeper. Finally, he would become so hopelessly enmeshed in party activities against his will that a complete break appeared to him utterly impossible without sacrificing his career, his position, his friends, and even risking the alienation of his family.

We have referred to this technique time and again in previous reports, and those who believe the Communist Party incapable of such unethical and immoral conduct are incredibly naive. Let us analyze a hypothetical case, but one which is predicated solidly on documentary evidence in the committee's files. Universities have been and always will be a principal target for Communist colonization and infiltration because they deal with impressionable young students studying to be lawyers, doctors, engineers, nurses, social workers, teachers, and to occupy other positions of leadership and prestige. Let us, therefore, use a mythical university as the scene for our hypothetical case.

Suppose we take the case of a student who is preparing himself to be a teacher of, say, economics. Naturally brilliant and hard working, this young man soon made an enviable reputation as a scholar. He graduated with honors in the midst of a severe depression but found work with one of the many agencies of the Federal Government, the National Economic Commission on Migratory Workers. Here he was surrounded by Communists, and soon discovered that unless he went along with the party program he would be out of a job. Every morning copies of the *Daily Worker*, the *People's World* and the propaganda pamphlets of the State, County and Municipal Workers of America and the United Federal Workers of America were scattered around the office, and the anti-Communists were ruthlessly eliminated regardless of their abilities, while those who remained neutral and passive were relegated to the more unimportant positions with no prospects of advancement. It eventually became evident that even the head of the agency in Washington was a Communist Party member, or at least an ardent fellow-traveler, so brazen were the activities of his employees.

Working in intimate association with party members, in an atmosphere where Communism somehow appeared to be fashionable, and where only Communists were rapidly advanced and accepted by the leadership, our young student was easily pursuaded to become a party member. He joined, not so much because of his ideological convictions but more as an expedient to hold his job under adverse circumstances and to further himself as much as possible. Thereafter he worked for one federal agency after another, his promotions came easily, and his circle of close association with leading Communists became ever wider. With a few he even formed genuine friendships, but after the war was over and the depression ended he lost interest in party affairs and went back to the university as a graduate student. He took his doctorate, secured a faculty position and settled down to achieve prominence in his field. Success came rapidly and he married, began to raise a family, took an active interest in university politics and the same qualities that had served him so well as an undergraduate, and as a federal employee, and as a professor, now made him an influential member of the academic world. He was a member of powerful committees through which new faculty members were being selected, and through which the university affairs were conducted.

It was at this point that one of his old comrades came to see him and asked him to do a little service for the party, first congratulating him on his fine family and his success at the university. There were no threats, no promises; none were necessary. Here was a chance to make a clean break but there would be an enormous price to pay. There were his wife and children, his colleagues, his job; everything he had worked for placed in sudden jeopardy. And it was really such a little favor, after all—merely to use a certain secretary who was already a capable university employee. She needed a better job, so his old friend said, and the party wanted to do something for her. In the end she got the job, and the barb of the soft hook was sunk fast. The new secretary began suggesting the names of applicants for faculty positions that would be acceptable to the party and insisted that others be rejected. Every evidence of resistance on the part of her employer met with hints of disclosure of his past.

As the years went by more secretaries were placed; faculty members in favor with the party were appointed to the most important committees, and were somehow enabled to rise rapidly in their several departments. The university had been awarded several vital and highly secret research projects for the Federal Government, and these in particular seemed peculiarly attractive to several of the relatively new members of the faculty and to some clerical workers who had been recommended by the party through its campus contacts. No amount of security screening could possibly prove them to be anything but extremely progressive as they had no documentable records of subversive affiliation or activity. That, of course, is why they were so carefully selected and why they were so useful.

Eventually our mythical university came to be run by its academic committees instead of by its board of trustees. Most of the trustees in institutions of this type are appointed because of their wealth and prestige and are never expected to actually supervise the running of the university anyway. Therefore it was quite simple for this vacuum to be filled by the faculty, and for it to take over and operate the institution by a complicated system of committees. Inevitably, the committees that exercised the most authority were composed of the most radically "liberal" professors, "manic-progressives," as Mr. David Boroff calls them. Thus was created a tightly-controlled clique of elite professors whose influence was far greater than one might expect. And how were they manipulated into these positions, and by whom were they controlled? Why, by a tiny, hard core of Communist functionaries who made a tool of a former party member by patiently waiting and watching until he reached a position of importance and had a family, and then they used the "soft hook" technique to blackmail him into total obedience.

And this, in brief, is how a few amoral Communist professionals can control a university, a labor union, and many other large and predominately non-Communist organizations. Does this seem a bit too lurid and sensational? Too farfetched? Too melodramatic? We can only repeat that while wholly hypothetical, it is based on solid evidence in the committee's possession. The Alberts case, the Laura Law case, the Hudson case, and the Abrams case seemed far more incredible until they were proven to be Communist murders; three of them in California.

Bearing in mind that in 1937 there were at least 3,000 Communists in Los Angeles County, that New York has always had a larger membership than California, and that the alltime high for the United States was some 100,000 party members, we may quite safely put the average number of persons subject to party discipline at 20,000 per year. And if there has been a membership turnover of approximately 25 percent, this would mean a 35-year reservoir constantly being supplied with ex-Communists.

Experience has demonstrated beyond all doubt that an extremely small percentage of these former Communists really sever their allegiance to the cause. As Mr. Brogan, British journalist, puts it:

> "When a man submits to some years of discipline and indoctrination, Communism *does* something to him, and it cannot be undone unless the man himself makes a painful and total reappraisal, not only of his political beliefs, but also of his whole approach to life. The men who leave the Party over a personal quarrel, a dispute over some particular issue, or for reasons of their own personal convenience, are quite unlikely to make this reappraisal. Yet these are the great majority of those who do leave. Ideologically, they are still more or less on call." [1]

[1] "Beware the Ex-Communist," by Colm Brogan. *American Opinion,* Nov., 1958, Vol. 1, No. 9, page 10.

We have seen how the Communist Party of the United States during its 35 years of.activity has left a poisonous fallout of former members, virtually none of whom have completely broken away from their old ideological ties and their dreams of a world Communist government. In addition, there is also a group of highly dedicated and specially trained individuals who comprise what is known in party parlance as the "sleeper apparatus." These individuals make regular payments of Communist Party dues in the normal manner, have never been permitted to attend party meetings, are instructed to pose an anti-Communist conservatives, and to insinuate themselves into the most strategic possible positions and lie dormant until such time as they are able to exert their influence for the party's benefit in a time of critical need. It is not appropriate at this place to mention the names and positions occupied by some of these people, but such a list will be given and supported by documentary evidence at a subsequent place in this report. There has always been a fairly large underground apparatus of the Communist Party— leaving on the surface for public view a propaganda machinery such as newspapers and magazines, the media through which these are disseminated such as the bookstores in San Francisco and Los Angeles, the Communist Party recruiting centers and educational institutions, such as the California Labor School in San Francisco and Los Angeles, and a smattering of Communist fronts that are used to attract the unwary non-Communist liberals and imbue them with the necessity for supporting the Communist Party line and possibly to recruit some of them as party members.

During the period that we are now discussing, the period of open Communist activity, the underground was relatively small and that portion of the party functioning above ground relatively large. As we shall see later, in 1955 and 1956 the entire Communist Party apparatus was submerged except for a tiny fragment that was left to operate the newspapers and the monthly ideologically magazine published by the National Committee of the Communist Party of the United States.

INFILTRATION OF STATE GOVERNMENT

The Communist Party of California has made two efforts to infiltrate the political structure of the State and exercise a profound influence on its government. The first of these efforts occured during 1938 and was carried through the election of 1940; the second effort occured in 1948 and was carried through the elections of 1950. Whether or not the party made a similar effort in 1958 remains to be seen. There is considerable pursuasive evidence to the effect that such an effort has already been made and will be intensified during 1959.

By the mid-thirties the Communist Party all over the United States was beginning to feel its strength. This was largely because its activity was not impeded to any appreciable degree, and no adequate intelligence work had been done for the purpose of collecting reliable information concering the identities of the leaders, the nature of the physical organization of the party, an analysis of its techniques and familiarity with its ideological background and its propaganda. Consequently, with the meeting of the Seventh World Congress of the Communist International in Moscow in 1935, and the institution of the so-called "United Front" tactic, each of the foreign Communist parties was ordered to discontinue its practice of functioning alone and independently and to adopt a program of subtly boring into all mass organizations for the purpose of switching them into conformity with current party line. In December, 1936, the Communist Party of California ordered its Political Commission to create a People's Legislative Conference, through which the trade unions, churches, peace groups, farmers organizations and the EPIC movement could be consolidated. There were 17 Communists appointed to this commission and they immediately opened offices in San Francisco and Los Angeles. They observed the new ground rules by manipulating several well-known non-Communist progressives into the new front organization as officers, and over their signatures a call was issued for a meeting to be held in Sacramento on January 16, 1937. More than 200 organizations were represented and the People's Legislative Conference was under way. The Communists carefully placed their own members in obscure but powerful jobs to keep activity under control, this responsibility being entrusted to five highly trained persons.

During the 1937 session of the Legislature 90 bills, all drafted by the Professional Section of the Communist Party in San Francisco, were presented by a group of Assemblymen who were organized by their Communist contact for this very purpose. The inauguration of this Legislative Conference was only the preliminary step. The party had perfected a much more elaborate and far-reaching plan. It wanted to inaugurate a California Labor's Nonpartisan League; to send members into the Democratic and Republican Parties; to replace conservative and middle-of-the-road Legislators with more liberal candidates and thus to write the laws, elect the executives—in short, to capture political control of the State. The plan almost succeeded, as we shall see.

On April 19, 1937, under the auspices of the San Francisco Central Labor Council, a mass meeting was held. Non-Communist labor leaders advocated formation of a nonpartisan league but the project got out of control and soon collapsed. But Communists do not give up so easily, and it was decided to have the People's Legislative Conference declared an affiliate of the league. Preparations were accordingly made, a meeting of 300 delegates convened at Santa Maria on June 20, 1937, and it was announced that henceforth the People's Legislative Conference would be known as Labor's Nonpartisan League in California. New officers were elected and while only one was a Communist, he was the secretary-treasurer and wielded enormous influence. In order to insure that there would be no possibility in losing control, however, a majority of the members of the State Executive Committee were under complete control of the Communist Party apparatus.

The drive to infiltrate and control the Democratic Party, in particular, was to be accomplished through a specially organized spearhead of seven members of the Legislature and two co-ordinators. By September, 1937, the new machinery was working smoothly and thus in less than a year the Communist Party of California had employed a group of politically ambitious liberals as tools in erecting a powerful political machine completely under Communist control. An organizing convention was held in San Francisco on December 11, and 12, 1937, and the first part of the operation was completed. The second phase consisted in the capture of the Democratic Party, if possible, and the planting of a powerful Communist nucleus in the Republican Party.

Labor's Nonpartisan League effectively consolidated the labor vote; it now remained to bring together the non-labor liberals and progressives. Accordingly, a second organization was formed, the California Committee of One Hundred for Political Unity. It eventually became the California Committee for Political Unity, directed by a Communist fraction of 14 people, each an experienced, tough, reliable party member.

Much of the foregoing information is taken from reports of informants who actually operated at high levels and in positions of authority in the organizations heretofore mentioned; their evidence has been carefully checked and corroborated, and in addition, the committee has taken considerable information from a book by Robert E. Burke, *Olson's New Deal for California,* University of California Press, Berkeley, California, 1953, as well as the testimony of the Secretary of the Communist Party of Los Angeles County, Jack Moore, and various Communist Party publications. The committee also referred to *The Politics of California,* by David Farrelly and Ivan Hinderaker, Ronald Press Company, New York, 1951, and various documents and records of the United Organizations for Progressive Political Action, Labor's Nonpartisan League, Statewide Legislative Conference, and other organizations.

One of the informant's reports concluded, "It is clear that in 1937 and 1938, the Communist Party in California transformed its traditional methods and forms of political work in accord with its United Front tactics. Statements made by William Z. Foster and Earl Browder indicate that the Communist Party intends to further develop its political activities so that it may play a decisive role in the 1940 elections."

Political Fronts

And this informant could not have predicted more accurately. Los Angeles County, with its enormous voting population, had been carefully cultivated. As a matter of fact, the Communists had, in 1935, created the United Organizations for Progressive Political Action with

35 constituent members. Meetings were held weekly in cafes and restaurants in the city, and by 1936 more than 70 organizations had been drawn into the UOPPA—all very progressive. Its organ, the *United Progressive News,* was published from 416 Bank of America Building, Second and Spring Streets, Los Angeles, by a staff of seven—all Communist Party members. United Organizations for Progressive Political Action tested its strength in organizing the campaign to recall Governor Merriam. This provided an excuse for obtaining the names and addresses of people who were sufficiently opposed to conservative politics and to the alleged reactionary policies of the Governor to sign recall petitions. This is an old Communist trick and was employed with astonishing success in 1932 and 1934 when petitions were circulated for the ostensible purpose of winning the Communist Party a place on the primary ballot in Los Angeles, and again by the Independent Progressive Party in 1948 to qualify that organization to participate in the statewide election. The real purpose of this device, however, consisted of obtaining thousands of names of liberal and progressive individuals from which to recruit new members for the party, or at least to enlist as many of them as possible as ardent fellow travelers and supporters of the Communist Party line. By June 23, 1936, UOPPA had endorsed a slate of 7 candidates for Congress, 19 for the State Assembly and 11 for the Judiciary.

The Communist Party Political Commission usually held its meetings at 3989 Denker Avenue in Los Angeles, and later met in various houses and downtown restaurants. A former member of the commission told our committee under oath:

"That our commission discussed ways and means of influencing various prominent persons in the Democratic Party—I recall in particular (name omitted)—and frankly discussed the past record, weaknesses and stupidities of such persons with a view toward controlling them; one of the tactics most frequently planned as a method of controlling a political figure was to invite him to a Communist Party fraction meeting, planning on revealing to him after he had been lured into the meeting, that he was sitting in an 'open' fraction meeting, and giving him to understand that this fact would be used against him unless he did the bidding of the Communist Party;

"At that time I realized that few Americans who had been reared to believe the best in their fellow man could withstand such Machiavellian cynicism in politics, and realized full well that such scheming, unprincipled political manipulators would be very successful in politics; at that moment I realized the true meaning of Georgi Dimitrov's 'popular front' speech; he meant that the Communists could accomplish more by devious indirection than they would by standing on a soap box and shouting revolution, as they had in the past; but by that time I also realized that there was no hope of finding honesty or frankness within the Communist

Party; heretofore I had put down much of the things with which I was dissatisfied to 'lack of development' and to the 'wrong interpretation of the Communist Party line;' now I knew that the higher one went, the worse the corruption;

"That the fates of many political figures were decided at meetings of the aforesaid commission, in view of the fact that the Young Democrats, the CIO, a large bloc of the motion picture colony, as well as the Democratic Party itself, could be manipulated by these Communist schemers; our Commission had the facilities to reach everyone of the supposed 3,000 Communist Party members in Los Angeles County with the directives—'musts'—and these individuals, in turn, because each one of them was as active or more so than myself, influential in several organizations, could multiply his influence by several hundreds; thus our Los Angeles County Political Commission of the Communist Party was determining a large part of the policies of Los Angeles City and County and the State of California."

In discussing the techniques that were employed to utilize non-Communists and the various Communist front organizations, the statement continued:

"Individuals who were 'liberal' merely because of their humanitarian impulses could be brought under the Communist Party political influence through such organizations as the United China Relief and the Friends of the Abraham Lincoln Brigade; the Jewish people could be influenced through their hatred of Nazis, through the Hollywood Anti-Nazi League; that Mexicans could be influenced through the Spanish Speaking People's Congress; that Negroes could be influenced through the National Negro Congress, and the Japanese-American voters through the publication *Doho*; women, especially housewives, could be reached through the League of Women Shoppers; and so on, to say nothing of the 21-year-old youths which the Communist Party tried to reach through its Youth Assemblies, which later became the California Youth Legislature, member of the national Communist-controlled American Youth Congress; I know from Communist literature and official Communist statements that all of the foregoing organizations were at that time controlled by the Communist Party;

"That we discussed some briefly, some at length, the role, in relation to Communist Party program, of the Los Angeles Newspaper Guild, the National Lawyers Guild, the Screen Writers Guild, the Screen Actors Guild, the Screen Directors Guild, the Teacher's Union, the International Alliance of Theatrical and Stage Employees Progressive Conference * * *; the CIO Council; the Musicians' Union; the Culinary Workers Union, as well as the Workers Alliance and the new-born Communist co-ordinating body for WPA, the Arts Unions Council;

"That those were our implements; our methods were described previously as basely cynical; the coating of idealism which was wrapped around the Communist Party plans when they were handed down to the more tender comrades with whom I had previously associated was now left off; without so much as a reference to the Communist 'enabling act,' that is, Lenin's statement that 'the end justifies the means,' this commission plunged into the California political field to build a secret, camouflaged, efficient political machine;

"That we probably had less than a thousand active Communist *cadres* (the Communist Party term to indicate a human unit, which is a 'thing,' not a being, in Communist thought) in the entire Southern California area who were adept enough in parliamentary tricks, smooth enough to camouflage the Communist Party line, daring enough to face and bluff out attacks, cynical enough to proceed on orders without idealistic justification, and who were tied, hand, brain and hide, to the Communist Party. We had to juggle them around, give each many roles to play, co-ordinate all work in order to make the Communist Party camouflage machine sound like a million volts. It required more than training, or even long experience, and even the cleverest and the slipperiest of American type political maneuvering. We had access to, and drew from, the Communist Party's Asiatic form of intrigue; the use of teamwork and a combination of brazen affrontery and sly-psychological tricks * * * "[2]

Communist Political Techniques

On February 6 and 7, 1937, a citywide conference was held in the Angelus Hotel, at Fourth and Spring Streets sponsored by a division of UOPPA, called the Youth Federation for United Political Action. Thirty-six sponsoring organizations sent delegates and 21 adult advisors; four of the observers were mature members of the Young Communist League, although there was very little for them to do as the affair was completely under Communist control from its inception.

Shortly before the Los Angeles City elections in the spring of 1937, a flood of propaganda gushed from the UOPPA office—postal ballots, sample polls, straw votes and lists of candidates endorsed by the organization. By this time the party, its friends, its network of front groups, its press, and its legion of fellow travelers, had become most active. If the Political Commission was successful in the municipal campaign, the apparatus could readily be expanded and shifted into an even higher gear for the 1938 state elections. Already the groundwork had been prepared, the situation seemed made to order for Communist Party strategy and the time was ripe to follow the direction of the Communist International and apply the tactic of the United Front.

[2] Affidavit of Rena Marie Vale, former member of the Communist Party Political Commission, November 23, 1942.

The Communists had already managed to slip many of its members into the Republican administration of Governor Merriam, and concentrated them in the State Relief Administration. This provided an ideal medium through which they were brought into close contact with applicants for relief, and afforded an excellent opportunity for the indoctrination and recruiting of a great mass of maladjusted and embittered people. Already the party had singled out Governor Merriam as a symbol of reaction, and clamored for his recall and defeat. Party propagandists mobilized to urge the election of a liberal administration and hoped to send more of its members to help the newly-elected officials spread the new "progressive" way of life throughout the State. It is hardly necessary to point out, as indeed the Communists have frankly admitted, that both major political parties have always been subject to infiltration—the obvious strategy being to "help" with every major campaign in the hope of manipulating undercover Communists into positions of political influence or other strategic importance to the party.

By March, 1937, the activity that preceded the Los Angeles City election had reached such a pitch that UOPPA moved to larger quarters in the Spring Arcade Building at 541 South Spring Street, and augmented its staff considerably. Not all of its candidates were elected in the spring of 1937, but enough success was achieved to encourage the Communist Political Commission to give its approval for an extended participation in an all-out effort in the state election of 1938.

While the United Organizations for Progressive Political Action was the pivot around which the Los Angeles municipal elections turned, so was Labor's Non-Partisan League the strategic center for the state election of 1938. At Santa Maria, on June 20, 1937, 300 delegates met to discuss the further activities of the People's Legislative Conference. Once again the Communist Party fraction which completely dominated the organization kept well in the background and arranged to have a large majority of non-Communists take the floor. The real purpose of the Santa Maria conference was to have the delegates pass a resolution authorizing the executive committee of the California People's Legislative Conference to "make formal application as soon as such application is possible on behalf of the conference for affiliation to Labor's Non-Partisan League." Already the Communist Party fraction had been in correspondence with the officers of the Labor's Non-Partisan League and it was agreed that the quickest way to firmly establish the league in California was to have it absorb the People's Legislative Conference. The party fraction also had in mind that if this plan was successfully accomplished, the Communist Party would continue to dominate the organization regardless of its name. In further preparation for party control when the conference would become Labor's Non-Partisan League, new officers were elected as was a new State Executive Committee of 28 persons. With one exception, all of the officers were non-Communists. The party felt, however, that the nominees would continue their co-operation, but as an additional precaution a large majority of the State Executive Committee were Communist Party members.

The minutes and report of Labor's Non-Partisan League, on the occasion of its California state convention, held in San Francisco, on December 11 and 12, 1937, indicate how completely the Communist Party controlled every activity of the organization. The credentials committee of six included five members of the Communist Party, and after a motion had been adopted that only delegates from the A. F. of L., the C. I. O., the Railway Brotherhoods and other branches of Labor's Non-Partisan League could be seated at the convention, on a subsequent recommendation of the credentials committee and the approval of the convention, the delegates from the Workers Alliance and the National Negro Congress were also seated. Both of these organizations were dominated by the Communist Party. The organization report on the structure of Labor's Non-Partisan League was given by its state secretary, Herbert Resner, a party member. Wyndham Mortimer, International Vice-President of the United Automobile Workers of America, and a member of the Central Committee of the Communist Party, and Louis Goldblatt, assistant C. I. O. Regional Director, and also a Communist, were given the floor and in detail outlined a policy regarding Labor's Non-Partisan League which, needless to say, fully represented the Communist Party position. Thus, for the first time in California, the Communist Party, through its control of this and other organizations, was in a position to exercise a predominant voice in a general state election, and it became equally clear that in 1937 and 1938 the party in California transformed its traditional methods in the form of political work in strict accordance with the new tactic of the United Front promulgated by the Secretary of the Communist International at the Seventh World Congress of that body held in the Soviet Union. Statements made by William Z. Foster and Earl Browder indicated that the Communist Party intended to further develop its political activities so that it could play a decisive role in the political affairs of the State.

The Communist Party achieved a greater success in the state election of 1938 than it did in the Los Angeles municipal election in the preceding year. It had endorsed the successful candidates for Governor, Lieutenant Governor and several members of both houses of the Legislature. Even before the election, arrangements had been made for the placement of Communists and fellow travelers in positions controlled by political patronage, and while jobs were parceled out to carefully selected people so that the liberals and progressives supported by the party would replace conservatives, anti-Communists and neutrals in the key positions of government, there were far from enough positions to go around. It was only natural that the most important positions be filled with relatively conservative men who figured most prominently in the *open* conduct of the campaign, but the Communists were not interested in these posts; they concentrated on office staffs, executive secretaries and, most vital of all, those departments of government through which they could contact masses of people: the Departments of Labor, Agriculture, Public Works, Social Welfare and Relief.

William Z. Foster, the head of the Communist Party of the United States, was quite aware of this patronage problem and he wrote in the ideological publication of the National Committee of the Communist Party, in 1939:

"The distribution of appointive jobs—municipal, county, state and federal—has always been a central foundation of the old Party's mass mobilization system. Whole groups of voters are clustered about each political job. Big machines are built on this basis, and the two parties are constantly torn with struggles over rich prizes.

"To overcome this evil, patronage practice will be a big but necessary task in Democratic front political foundations. Appointive political jobs will continue for an indefinite time yet, and the way to handle their distribution is for the Democratic front party to take firm responsibility, and not the leave them to the control of political overlords." [3]

And, speaking of the role to be played by the Communist Party during this period of its open activity, Foster concluded:

"* * * the whole matter of improving the system of political mass organizations should be carefully studied and its lessons applied diligently and with dispatch. In this task the Communist Party, with its Marxian training, militant spirit and wide mass following, bears a great responsibility." [4]

Another prominent official of the Communist Party, Paul Cline, the Los Angeles County Chairman, had also written some material for *The Communist* in the edition for November, 1938, in which he corroborated to a large extent the statements made under oath by Rena Vale, the former member of the Political Commission. He said:

"Within the brief space of two months the federation was able to secure the affiliation of over 400 organizations and groups with an aggregate membership of nearly 300,000 people. Participating * * * were the biggest Methodist churches in the city, Labor's Non-Partisan League, the Federation for Political Unity, the Motion Picture Democratic Committee, scores of A. F. of L. and C. I. O. unions, large numbers of women's groups, Negro groups, and youth organizations. In composition, the federation [Federation for Political Unity], represented a true cross section of the people of Los Angeles. Most significant was the fact that the high-standing Methodist church leaders and conservative businessmen

[3] *The Communist*, February, 1939, page 138.
[4] "New Methods of Organization," *The Communist*, op. cit., p. 146.

* * * were ready and able to find a common ground of action with representatives of left-wing groups like the I. L. D. [International Labor Defense] and the I. W. O. [International Workers Order].

"The Communist Party, as a vital element in the great Democratic front movement that is rapidly surging forward in California, will continue unreservedly to devote itself to this end." [5]

William Schneiderman, during the campaigns in 1937 and 1938, and for a number of years both before and after these events, was the head of the Communist Party for the State of California. Writing with considerable authority, he also corroborated the statements made by Miss Vale when he wrote:

" * * * the organization of the Democratic front for victory in the elections is not an easy and simple task, due to the extremely complicated political situation and the many factors which will stand in the way of the unification of the Democratic forces. We Communists are keenly aware of the responsibilities we bear to bring about this unity. We have become an important factor and a recognized force in the labor and progressive movement, the progressive forces are beginning to appreciate and understand the role we are playing in the building of the Democratic front."

And writing about the 1938 campaign, he said:

"* * * Today this movement is gathering around its support for Senator Olson, the leading progressive for the Democratic nomination for Governor in the August primary. * * * The Non-Partisan League has conducted an energetic campaign for political unity of labor." [6]

After the primaries Schneiderman said:

"The Communist Party in California is participating in the election campaign with the aim of contributing its part for the unification of all democratic forces for the defeat of reaction. * * * The Party is becoming a recognized force for unity in the labor and progressive movement, and as such is receiving even greater support of progressive-minded people who appreciate the role of Communists in helping to build the Democratic front. We are conscious of our task; that out of this election struggle must come, not only a progressive victory, but a stronger, mass Communist Party capable of fulfilling *still greater responsibilities in the struggles to come.*" (Committee's italics.) [7]

[5] *The Communist*, November, 1938, pp. 1021-1027.
[6] *The Communist*, July, 1938, pp. 663, 664.
[7] The Election Struggle in California," by William Schneiderman. The *Communist*, October, 1938, pages 919 and 926.

Governor Olson was not a Communist, but he was a sincere and dedicated liberal in the true sense of the term. Shortly after he had assumed office he declared:

"We are determined to oppose equally the despotism of Communism and the menace of Fascism.[8]

Being naive in matters subversive, it was therefore relatively simple to surround Governor Olson and a great many of his more important assistants with Communist Party secretaries and clerical workers. For example, shortly after the new Governor assumed his duties letters began to come out of his office over the signature of a woman who had formerly served on the Political Commission of the Communist Party of Los Angeles County, and who was now a trusted clerical worker in the Governor's Office.[9]

We now know something of the political techniques used by the Communists in California in two extremely important elections, one municipal the other statewide, and when the new administration took over its Governor was surrounded by party members. The State Relief Administration was heavily infiltrated during the Merriam regime; now it was saturated. John Jeffery, a Communist, headed a union known as the State, County and Municipal Workers of America, so utterly dominated by the party that it was more an integral part of the organization than one of its fronts. All Communists employed by the state were members of the SCMWA which rapidly grew into a powerful and arrogant pressure group. All of the key relief administrators were Communists; so were most of the case workers and other office employees. This afforded them contact with thousands of relief applicants who were herded into another union, the Workers Alliance, headed by Communist Alexander Noral. Here again the Communists exhibited their unfailing determination to undermine all outsiders and to help one another. Not only did they promote themselves, but so long as the relief recipients stayed in the Workers Alliance, dutifully attended its meetings and paid rapt attention to the speakers imported by the party, there was no trouble with their relief status. Their grievances were promptly taken up by Workers Alliance committees that conferred with their comrades in the SCMWA, and always to the satisfaction of the complainant. This, of course, was not too difficult because the Communist Party was operating both unions.

As their numbers grew, as they placed their members in more and more key positions, these young Communists became more brash. At first they were merely impertinent; now they were overbearing. Some members of the Workers Alliance got more than enough of being regimented into this union and made to listen while Communist organizers harangued them, under penalty of being deprived of the common necessities of life. In rural communities throughout the state, citizens resented this sudden invasion by groups of radical state relief administrators and began to take a hard look at this social phenomenon

---

[8] *Olson's New Deal for California*, op. cit., p. 24.
[9] 1943 report, Un-American Activities in California, affidavit of Rena M. Vale, p. 157.

masquerading under the guise of "liberalism." They found Communist papers and Communist propaganda freely and abundantly distributed in the relief offices, and immediately complained to their representatives in Sacramento. So indignant were the citizens, and so insistent were the demands that this ridiculous mess be cleared up, that an Assembly committee was appointed for that purpose. It investigated the situation in the State Relief Administration, reported that it was being operated by Communists, exposed the real nature of the Workers Alliance and the SCMWA, and handed its written report to the Assembly at the 1941 general session of the Legislature. Armed with the reliable facts concerning the situation, the Legislature acted. Communists were fired from the State Relief Administration, and the situation was alleviated. But the undercover party members still clung to the administration like barnacles, as stenographers, as secretaries, as office workers, and a very few in extremely important and sensitive positions. Particularly in the Departments of Labor, Employment, Social Welfare and similar agencies that were of strategic importance to the party, a concentration of Communists was found. For example, Dorothy Healey was employed by the Department of Labor in an important position that brought her into constant contact with masses of potential recruits to Communism. She is now the Chairman of the Communist Party of Los Angeles County; and there were others whose names have been mentioned through many of the reports previously issued by this committee.

Independent Progressive Party

Almost simultaneously with the beginning of American Communism, that young and lusty movement sought to infiltrate and take over the National Farmer-Labor Party. In 1922, there was a Conference for Progressive Political Action (the term which was to be borrowed by the Communist Party in Los Angeles some 14 years later) at Cleveland and from it the Farmer-Labor Party drew renewed vigor—enough to once more attract Communist attention. Accordingly, the Communists sent representatives to the Farmer-Labor Chicago convention in 1923, packing the hall with delegates from more than a dozen of its fronts all posing as separate and independent organizations. Having thus resorted to the device of packing the convention, the Communist minority easily seized control of a far larger non-Communist political party. An observer, Robert Morss Lovett, declared that as invited guests the Communists "came into the house and carried off the ice cream." [10]

Having obtained control, the Communists sought to swell the ranks of the Farmer-Labor Party by widespread appeals for additional members. But, instead of attracting workers, the Communists repelled them.

[10] *The Techniques of Communism*, by Louis F. Budenz, Henry Regnery Co., Chicago, 1954. See also, *American Communism, a Critical Analysis of Its Origins, Development and Programs*, by James O'neal and G. A. Werner. E. P. Dutton & Co., Inc., 1947.

The underhanded devices of the bold hypocrisy, the utter ruthlessness and the complete disregard for truth or ethics or the welfare of others were hardly characteristics that could attract non-Communist membership. Soon the ranks were depleted and only the Communists and those who were under party control remained. So the first attempt to operate through a third party failed.

In 1947 a group of liberals decided to back Henry A. Wallace for President of the United States, and around this movement there developed a third independent political party, the Independent Progressive Party. Immediately the Communists saw an opportunity once more to use this ultra progressive movement for their own ulterior motives. Relying on the approved techniques for Communists in such matters, and profiting by experience, delegates from a wide array of front organizations were sent to actively participate in conventions and meetings throughout the country, but particularly in New York and in California.

When John L. Lewis started the C. I. O. and ran short of organizers the Communists provided them in abundance, and before Mr. Lewis found out what was *really* going on he had been eased out of his own organization and the Communists were in control. So it had been with the Farmer-Labor Party in 1923; so it had been with the California elections in 1937 and 1938, and so it was with the Independent Progressive Party in 1947 and 1948.

The Communist apparatus provided scores of eager and energetic precinct workers and propagandists. Their members staffed the offices of the I. P. P. all over the country. They provided the petition circulators, and the Communist press lambasted the other two major parties and sang the praises of the Independent Progressives throughout the campaign.

On July 7, 1947, the *Daily People's World*, the California Communist newspaper, announced that a Democrats for Wallace meeting would be held in Fresno on July 19th. In the issue for May 28, 1948, the Communist paper printed a list of Independent Progressive Party endorsements for Northern and Central California districts, accompanying the roster with the following statement:

> "Neither Henry Wallace nor presidential electors for him will appear on the ballot at the primary. He is to be nominated by a state convention of the Independent Progressive Party in August, for the ballot in the November general election."

And in the issue for June 3, 1948, an editorial in the Communist paper declared:

> "The June 1, primary was the opening round of the critical election struggle of 1948. It was not yet, however, a decisive test of the relation of forces in California or the Nation. It could at best give only the first indications of the political strength of the progressive forces and the Democratic coalition, expressed through

candidates supported by the new Independent Progressive Party, barely two months old.

The light vote was due primarily to absence of a contest in the presidential primary. Truman and Warren were unopposed in the Democratic and Republican primaries, and Henry Wallace was not entered on the primary ballot (his nomination to be made by a state convention in August). Thus, in a year when voters look upon the presidential race as all-decisive, the lack of a contest in the primaries resulted in a light vote.''

''* * * the elections have projected the new Party as a major force on the political scene in California. It is necessary to note, however, a number of weaknesses exhibited by Progressive forces in the election, which if overcome in time could have resulted in a more impressive result:

The split in the labor movement, caused by the A. F. L. leadership and right-wing leaders in the C. I. O., prevented the labor movement from playing a decisive role in this election. The split in the C. I. O. prevented the Political Action Committee from playing the major role it did in the past, although progressive C. I. O. unions made an important contribution to the support of progressive pro-Wallace candidates.

The pro-Wallace candidates who won the primaries did so on a basis of a broad coalition of labor and progressive forces in both the Democratic Party and the new Party. In the majority of cases, however, pro-Wallace candidates did not have such a broad coalition supporting them, and depended mainly on left-progressive forces in the campaign.

The progressive trade unions did not mobilize full support behind progressive candidates, showed some vacillations as a result of right-wing pressure, and in some cases gave only half-hearted support to progressive candidates.

Some pro-Wallace candidates, or their campaign committees, thought it 'smart politics' to tone down their identifications with the Wallace-forces, and in some cases were very weak in presenting the important issues in the fight for peace, labor's rights, and civil liberties.

All these questions deserve a fuller and more detailed analysis later, when the results in full are studied.

The main thing is that the new party movement has gotten off to a good start. The next step is to prepare for the presidential election struggle and to build a mass movement of support behind the Wallace platform and ticket, and elect the Progressive candidates for Congress and the Legislature that have come through the primaries.''

Some of the I. P. P. candidates for election to state and national positions were known party members, some were fellow-travelers, others were opportunists and a few were apparently too naive to realize that the Independent Progressive Party in California was nothing more nor less than a creature under Communist domination. The chairman of the Independent Progressive Party in California was Hugh Bryson, then President of the Marine Cooks and Stewards Union, which had been expelled from the C. I. O. because it was found to be Communist dominated, and who was later convicted and sent to a federal penitentiary for having lied about his Communist affiliations and activities.

Over and over again the committee has received indisputable evidence of the active Communist participation in the Independent Progressive Party in this state; another example of how a small, disciplined, highly trained and dedicated Communist minority can penetrate, manipulate and assume control of a much larger non-Communist body. Certainly the overwhelming majority of individuals throughout the country, and most assuredly in California, who voted for the Independent Progressive Party candidates, were themselves sincere liberals who were dissatisfied with the two major parties for one reason or another, and, as we have seen, a majority of those who participated in the Los Angeles municipal election of 1937 and the state-wide election of 1938, were not Communists but most decidedly were, consciously or unconsciously, following the Communist Party line and toiling in the Communist vineyard. An analysis of the techniques used by the party during these campaigns reveals much. It discloses a common political denominator that runs through all of the party's strategy in infiltrating and controlling operations of this type. It should be quite manifest that only by a familiarity with the successful techniques employed by the Communists in the past can we be adequately prepared to prevent them from succeeding in the future.

Let us now turn to 1958 and 1959 and see, if we can, what lies ahead so far as Communist political activity is concerned. Obviously, the best source is the Communist Party itself, and we are fortunate in having available some of the reliable party statements issued within the last few months that cast considerable light on its future policies.

Current Communist Political Activity in California

We have previously pointed out that only the incredibly naive and misinformed can possibly believe that after the death of Stalin, the accession of Khrushchev and the era of underground activity, that the Communist Party has suddenly become insignificant and no longer poses any threat to our way of life. The following quotations from the monthly ideological publication of the National Committee of the Communist Party of the United States should remove all doubt, even in the minds of the most skeptical, concerning the party's future political plans. In May, 1958, party member Albert J. Lima, Chairman of the Northern District of the Communist Party of California, and a member of its national committee, wrote:

> "The strength of labor and the minority (Democratic) conference, as well as the strong progressive trend among the club dele-

gates, made itself felt in issues and candidates. The attempt of the machine to steamroller support for the team of Attorney General Brown for Governor and Congressman Clair Engle for U. S. Senator, ran into stiff opposition. Brown had overwhelming support from all groupings, mainly because he was considered to be the most substantial candidate with a possibility of beating the Republicans.''

''* * * In another memo by Nemmy Sparks, the Southern California District dealt with the problem in the following manner:

'Are the Republican and Democratic Parties twin parties of Capitalism? Of course they are.

The state co-ordinating committee, representing both districts of the Party, considered the approach to individual candidates along the following lines: We stated that the main interest of labor and the people as a whole in this election lies in the struggle on issues; in the effort to develop a coalition among the forces of the people that will last and continue to grow after the election; and to defeat the major standard bearers of reaction.

It was proposed that any independent candidacy should be considered in relation to the above point. An independent candidacy with a base among the general Left, it was felt, could exercise considerable influence on the issues in public debate and counteract the pressures upon candidates to water down issues and to make concessions to reactionary opponents. The alternative to the above could be a Party candidate whose campaign would be much more limited, but who could present the Party's position on the issues of the election. Because of the ballot restrictions in California this might have to be in the form of a write-in candidate for the finals.

The above policy tends to be caught between extreme viewpoints. On one hand some say only candidates should be supported who can get the broadest kind of support. From this source, Left-independent candidates are strongly opposed unless they have substantial labor and liberal support. In the present uncertain political atmosphere and lack of organizational forms, candidates who could run independently and have support in labor and liberal circles are very reluctant to be candidates. The Left, therefore, tends to find itself confined to pressuring major party candidates on issues as the only form of electoral activity.'

''* * * The 1958 elections can result in a resounding rebuff to the Republicans and their plans for the 1960 election. It can also be the arena in which the Left begins to solve some of its problems.'' [11]

---

[11] *Political Affairs*, May, 1958, pp. 29-39.

Robert Thompson, national Communist functionary declared:
"* * * In a number of important unions, and in some area
union conferences, party forces as a part of a growing Left have
been able to play a tangible and constructive part in the shaping
of union programs and activities on the unemployment issues.
Another such area has been Party activities in the fight against
anti-labor, so-called 'right-to-work' legislation, particularly in California and Ohio.

* * * There are clear indications that both Labor and the
Negro people's forces are participating more actively and more
independently than has been true in recent years.

Labor's participation in the California primary campaign was
an outstanding example of this.

* * * Our Party is becoming more active in all of these situations. The presentation of a Party legislative program has been
helpful in this. Of greatest importance is the fact its electoral
policy is taking clear shape nationally and in various states.

Three propositions form the broad framework within which
this policy is developed. These were stated by Arnold Johnson in
his article on the 1958 elections in the June *Political Affairs:*

'(a) To do everything possible to influence the elections in
the interests of the people.

(b) To promote even greater independence of labor and its
allies and a broad people's coalition policy based on the workers,
and the Negro people, farmers, and all other democratic forces.

(c) To bring forward the Party and its program, strengthen
its influence and build it in the course of the campaign.' " [12]

Albert J. Lima, in his capacity as Northern District Chairman of
the Communist Party of California, had this to say about party participation in California politics in September, 1958:

"Of course the trade union leadership has always been part
and parcel of politics, but eventually the needs and demands of
the class transcend the tenuous political ties of the leadership with
corrupt bourgeoise politics.

Our Party had agitated during this entire period [1937-1950]
for a farmer-labor party and many unions adopted resolutions in
support of this demand. Nationally, Labor's Non-Partisan League
conducted vigorous campaigns on issues and candidates. Certainly
the stage was set for the U. S. labor movement to follow the path
established by labor of the countries in Europe—the forming of
their own political party.

However, the outbreak of World War II, and the flexibility
of the two-party system, plus some peculiar electoral methods
which retard the development of third political parties in our
Country, combined to head off this development.

---

[12] "On the Work and Consolidation of the Party," by Bob Thompson. *Political Affairs,*
August, 1958, pp. 37-52.

The next period in which the possibility of breaking with the political control of the monopolists emerged was 1947-1948. Once again there were many factors present which indicated the possibility of such a development. * * * The need was present, but the willingness and determination of decisive sections of the labor movement was not. The move toward a third party was premature and abortive and the two-party system was more secure than ever, because of the split in the labor movement and the expulsion of the progressive * unions from the C. I. O. From that point the decisive influence of the C. I. O. on the political and economical life of our Country began to wane.

Thus, we have examined the question twice before at 10-year intervals and it is being posed again. (Committee's emphasis.)

There is a definite trend which indicates the possibility of winning important sections of the labor movement to organize and act independently of the two major parties. For example, in California the labor movement is not relying on the Democratic and Republican Parties to guarantee the struggle against the right-to-work threat. It has plunged into independent political action in a major way and in a more aggressive manner than for many years.''

* * * for us, and for the entire Left, it is necessary to try to determine the potential and eventual outcome in order to map out strategy and tactics.

In other countries, where labor has formed an independent political party welfare issues are adopted as national laws. In our Country, the labor movement has pressed for 'fringe benefits' which embody many elements adopted as national laws in other countries. This has been particularly true in recent years and has been a further expression of the U. S. workers attempt to take up the slack of the lack of a political party of its own.

The International Longshoremen's and Warehousemen's Union on the West Coast has been discussing this question and formally adopted a general program for an independent political grouping. Their role in the right-to-work fight in California has been a positive contribution to the entire labor movement, while maintaining a sharp and critical attitude for the slowness of the top leadership of the A. F. of L. in California.'' [13]

It should be carefully noted that the line italicized for emphasis by the committee, ''Thus, we have examined the question twice before at 10-year intervals and it is being posed again,'' constitutes a complete verification of the fact that in 1938, when the Communist Party of California played a decisive role in our state election and in 1948 when it endeavored to launch a party of its own, both movements

---

* The CIO called them Communist-dominated.
[13] ''On Labor and Political Action,'' by Albert J. Lima, Northern District Chairman of the Communist Party of Ca'lfornia. *Political Affairs*, September, 1958, p. 58, et seq.

originated and were dominated by the Communist Party of this state. And not only does this verification come from an authority of unquestionable accuracy, but Mr. Lima also predicts that the time is now ripe, in 1958, for the California Communists to *again* engage in all-out political activity. Let us see why 1958 was selected as an appropriate time for this sort of action.

In 1938 several mass organizations were used separately at first, and then welded together into a potent political machine. The separate organizations were the United Organizations for Progressive Political Action, Youth for Political Action, and the California People's Legislative Conference. The organization into which they were amalgamated was Labor's Non-Partisan League.

In 1948, the impetus behind the Independent Progressive Party in California came largely from the Communist-dominated unions such as the United Mine, Mill and Smelter Workers, the International Longshoremen's and Warehousemen's Union, and the Marine Cooks and Stewards Union, as well as such potent fronts as the Civil Rights Congress and the Arts, Sciences and Professions Council. In addition there was the customary camp-following group of assorted leftists ranging all the way from genuine fellow travelers to naive do-gooders.

The Independent Progressive Party started with considerable furor but quickly lost its momentum. It had been suspect from the start. Hugh Bryson's record of Communist activity as president of the Marine Cooks and Stewards had already been made public by this committee.[14] When he was selected as statewide president of the newly-launched party, many of the California newspapers quoted from our report and there was very little excuse for anyone to plead a lack of knowledge concerning the subversive leadership of the IPP. Furthermore the organization immediately adopted the current Communist Party line and devoted about as much time to jamming through party resolutions disseminating party propaganda as it did to purely political matters. Another serious error made by the IPP was the contest of its own candidates against such liberal Democrats as Helen Gahagan Douglas and Chester Holifield, both of whom refused to co-operate with the new political party and scrupulously ignored it throughout the campaign. This mistake was recognized by the party strategists in October of 1948, but it was then too late to remove the names from the ballots and the belated withdrawal of the IPP candidates from all positions where liberal Democrats were running on the Democrat ticket simply made matters worse by focusing attention on an already bad situation.[15]

Strategic Errors Rectified

The major blunders committed by the Communist Party strategists in 1938 and 1948, are now quite evident. In the first campaign there was very little effort to conceal the fact that the Communist Party

[14] See 1947 report, pp. 194, 151, 160, 163-166.
[15] *The Politics of California*, by David Farrelly and Ivan Hinderaker. Ronald Press Co., N. Y., 1951, p. 100.

vas masterminding a great deal of the political maneuvers and after he campaign was over the impertinence of the young party members vho were staffing the State Relief Administration and some of the lder and highly indoctrinated Communists who held other state posiions, became so offensive that the California voters were aroused and wept the subversive elements out of state employment. In the second lection the Independent Progressive Party permitted itself to be iniltrated and captured by the Communists, led by a well-known Communist, and once again demonstrated the same weakness by using the novement as a vehicle of dissemination for Communist propaganda rather than operating it as a purely political organization.

In the 1958 election there was no separate autonomous organization, t being clear that the Communists could not support Knowland, who obviously stood little chance of winning from the outset; there was no third party for them to use, and there was no amalgamation of friendly organizations through which party strategy could be directed. Therefore, there was only one alternative and that was to throw party support to candidates who stood greatest chance of getting elected and striving to subtly infiltrate the new administration with undercover party members.

Most important of all, however, was the profound change in the Communist Party line that occurred in 1956, that signaled the commencement of the second United Front period throughout the world, and which served as a guide for the strategy of the Communists in this state during the 1958 campaign. We mentioned this change in our last report, but not in any political connection. Let us now see what practical effect it has had upon our political situation.

The Twentieth Congress of the Communist Party of the Soviet Union was held in Moscow during February, 1956. The open meeting was held early in that month, and a few days later a "secret" meeting was held and attended by hand-picked delegates who assembled to hear confidential remarks by Nikita Khrushchev. The secret was well kept until it burst like a bombshell from the American State Department into the pages of the American press. Even the *Daily Worker* of New York was obligated to carry the story, and since it purported to be a verbatim account of what transpired at this "secret" conclave, and was later authenticated by the Kremlin, we can be quite certain of its accuracy.

It was natural that the most sensational content of this second speech should be played up in the American newspapers, and this consisted of the castigation of the late Joseph Stalin, a condemnation of his ruthless practices, a repudiation of the purge trials that swept the Soviet Union in a blood bath from 1935 to 1939, downgrading of the Soviet Secret Police system, and assurances to the Russian people that they would henceforth have more freedom. The writers in the Soviet Union were assured that they would be able to express their thoughts without being censored or repressed by the Soviet hierarchy; Communist Parties abroad were told to pursue their separate ways to

eventual attainment of the Communist utopia in their own manner,
and in conformity with the environment in which they operated; citizens were also invited to express their criticisms of the existing regime
—all of these things being the ingredients of a newer and freer way
of life for the Communist peoples of the world.

The first book that appeared after this pronouncement was one by the
Russian author, Dudintsev called "Not by Bread Alone." It rocked
the Soviet Union from one end to the other, and immediately the
censorship of the Stalin era was again clamped down hard. Then in
Yugoslavia Milovan Djilas wrote a book called, "The New Class," and
he was immediately clapped into prison for daring to criticize the
Communist Party of Yugoslavia. And in China Mao-Tse Tung dutifully followed the dictates of the Kremlin by announcing that in
every field of flowers at least a hundred should rise and express their
criticisms of the Chinese Communist regime. That regime was almost
smothered beneath an avalanche of posies, which resulted in the blos-
soms being neatly severed from their stems by the sweeping sickles of
the Chinese Communist political police. Poland and Hungary took
Khrushchev at his word and started on their separate ways toward the
Communist goal by enthusiastically taking measures to get the Russian agents out of their countries. We now know what happened;
Anastas Mikoyan promising that everything would be settled by negotiation, lulling the counter-revolutionists into a false sense of security
by his solemn assurances, thus gaining time to marshal the tanks
and other armor and Soviet troops for the purpose of slaughtering so
many of the civilians that the revolution was wiped out in another
bath of blood.

But there was something else, an even more important content in
the Khrushchev speech that has not received much attention in the
press of our country, but which has exerted a profound effect on Communist strategy throughout the world, and particularly in the United
States. We have seen the result in California in unmistakable terms,
and it will assuredly determine the strategy of the party in endeavoring to move into our political situation during the next few years.

Khrushchev also said that henceforth it would be proper and desirable for foreign Communist Parties to make common cause with other
mass liberal organizations. This meant the launching of the second
United Front, and permitted the Communists to collaborate with the
Socialists, the Trotzkyites, and a whole array of ultra-liberal organizations. No longer would they operate through the intricate apparatus
of Communist front organizations, because this was no longer necessary.
Front organizations were being exposed to public view for exactly
what they were as fast as the party could create them. They were infiltrated by government agents, their rosters of members and their
mailing lists were obtained, their party line activities were analyzed,
and they were so mercilessly brought under the glaring light of public
scrutiny that they soon ran short of members. The only people they
could recruit were people who already had long records of Communist

collaboration, and they were so few in number that the front organizations began to wither away from lack of financial and popular support. The same thing, to a large degree, was true of the Communist-dominated unions. From 1948 through 1950, the A. F. of L. and the C. I. O., particularly the latter, conducted sweeping investigations that resulted in the expulsion of a number of these old Communist saturated unions and they, too, were exposed to public view so thoroughly that the party deemed it inexpedient to use them for political purposes on a wide front in this state.

Now it would be possible for the Communists to make common cause with the other organizations that have been heretofore mentioned, and they immediately proceeded to do so, commencing during the latter part of 1956, and continuing on an accelerated scale until the present time. In the 1957 report we pointed out that within a matter of weeks after Khrushchev's speech the California Communist Party was obeying this change in the party line by permitting its officers to meet with representatives of the Socialist Party, the Young Socialist League, and, what was far more astounding, with members of the Trotzkyite movement.

Those who read our report of subversive infiltration at U. C. L. A., will recall that in connection with the death of a student, Sheldon Abrams, we found among his papers abundant proof that such meetings were indeed being held in 1956; and moreover, that they were the first in the United States to implement Khrushchev's directive for the opening of the second United Front.

The testimony of Dr. Robert Neumann, of the U. C. L. A. Department of Political Science, was of great value in making clear what the United Front strategy was and how it was devised at the Seventh World Congress of the Communist International in 1935. It was this United Front tactic of working through other liberal groups and through a confusing complexity of front organizations with appealing names and carefully concealed Communist control that made possible the amazing success of the Communists in this country in their widespread penetration of our American institutions immediately thereafter. Labor unions, universities, the entertainment fields, the creative arts, and governmental agencies were the main targets—including of course the invasion of our state government in 1938 by the enthusiastic use of this United Front technique.

But such successes proved too heady a wine; the party became too defiant, too overbearing. The people reacted, the Legislature appointed a committee to find out what was going on and report the facts, and there then began an era of exposing the extent of the infiltration, a description of the front groups and the people who operated them from concealed positions—and, in direct proportion to the degree of exposure, the potency of the California Communist Party began to decline. It became extremely difficult to attract liberals to front organizations that had been thoroughly revealed as under Communist control. And so it was with the motion picture industry, the universities, the trade unions, the public utilities and the various departments of the state government. Once the people thoroughly understood the nature and imminent menace posed by the operations of the Communist Party, they reacted as might be expected of loyal and patriotic citizens and began to cleanse themselves of the undercover Communists who had managed to worm their ways into strategic positions by the tactic of the United Front.

The public utilities, instead of having only special agents who policed the institutions, thereupon began to employ men with F. B. I. or military and naval intelligence experience to help them get rid of the Communists already in their employ and lock the doors against continued infiltration. The universities began to co-operate in the same direction, as did the school systems, the trade unions and the entertainment fields. The Federal Bureau of Investigation then began gathering the evidence from its undercover agents and launched a series of prosecutions under the Smith Act that deprived the party of its leadership, and the Supreme Court consistently upheld the rights and prerogatives of legislatures in keeping themselves actively informed concerning subversive threats to state governments, upheld the convictions that were obtained by the Federal Bureau of Investigation under the Smith Act, and upheld convictions of contempt against defiant party members who adopted a practice of invariably invoking the Fifth Amendment when questioned about their subversive activities and affiliations and using the forums of the legislative committees and the courtrooms as media for the dissemination of violent Marxist propaganda.

Driven to underground positions and compelled to break the physical organization of the party into tiny units of three to five members; its means of communication and propaganda disrupted by reason of the long continued exposure and conviction of leaders, the Communist Party was becoming desperate. It then declared war on the Supreme Court of the United States in 1952, and devoted virtually all of its attention to the liquidation of legislative investigative committees and bringing about a reversal of the Supreme Court decisions that had enabled the committees and the government to operate so successfully in hamstringing the activities of the Communist conspiracy throughout the country. Then came the launching of the *second* United Front as a result of the Khrushchev speech at the Twentieth Congress of the Communist Party of the Soviet Union in February, 1956, and, as we have seen from its own documents, the party began to resume its old arrogant attitude, to emerge from concealment and participate in a political campaign in 1957 and 1958 in California. We shall see a little later how the party claimed the credit for bringing about a change in the decisions of the United States Supreme Court dealing with subversive matters, and how it created a new national front organization for the purpose of bringing about the liquidation of legislative committees and hampering the activities of the Federal Bureau of Investigation and other governmental intelligence agencies engaged in counter-subversive work.

This, then, was the background against which the party resumed its political activities in California in 1957 and 1958. We have already pointed out, and emphasize again, that the Communist Party expressed itself as completely dissatisfied with both of the major political parties, although it had infiltrated both to some extent. During the 1958 election it had no choice but to repudiate the conservative Knowland and endeavor to insinuate some of its older adherents into the administration of Governor Brown. The new Governor had made it abundantly clear that he wanted no cooperation from the Communist Party in California, or any other place, and he repudiated their support and was unalterably opposed to Communism. The Democratic Governor who preceded him 10 years earlier had also made clear his anti-Communist attitude when he declared: "We are determined to oppose equally the despotism of Communism and the menace of Fascism."[16]

One of the candidates for election to the office of State Superintendent of Public Instruction during the 1958 campaign was Holland Roberts, frequently but erroneously referred to as *Dr.* Holland Roberts. On March 6, 1958, this item concerning his candidacy appeared in the *San Francisco Call-Bulletin:*

"Ex-Labor School Head May Seek Office.

San Jose, Mar. 6, (AP). Dr. Holland Roberts, whose California Labor School was called 'an instrument of the Communist Party' by a government board, may run for State Superintendent of Public Instruction.

He took out nomination papers yesterday and has until March 28 to file petitions.

The Subversive Activities Control Board, set up under the McCarran Act of 1950, made the report concerning this school after a hearing in January, 1957. Dr. Roberts was director of the now defunct school.

He said last May that the school was closing because it lacked funds to fight the board's ruling in the courts.

Roberts, in taking out nomination papers, said he lived in Palo Alto and was an educator.

He had been an associate professor of Education at Stanford University in 1944, when he resigned to join the Labor School in San Francisco, becoming director in 1949.

Before a House Un-American Activities Committee, headed by Representative Harold Velde, (R.-Ill.), Roberts denied in 1956 that the school was subversive and that it had Communists and Communist sympathizers on its faculty."

In passing, it may not seem inappropriate for us to point out something that the newspaper article overlooked. The committee investigated the California Labor School, beginning in 1945, branded both it and its director Communist and subversive, and referred to the school in its reports for 1947, 1948, 1949, 1951, 1953 and 1955. We examined

---

[16] "Olson's New Deal for California," op. cit., p. 24.

Roberts under oath on several occasions, and he was identified as a Communist Party member by several witnesses, including a former member of the party who served as Mr. Roberts' secretary while he was director of the school in San Francisco. He also served as chairman of the American-Russian Institute in San Francisco, one of the few potent Communist front organizations still operating on a nationwide basis. Both the school and Dr. Roberts had been identified as subversive and Communist since 1945, and the fact appeared with monotonous regularity in the newspapers up and down the Pacific Coast. Notwithstanding this fact, Mr. Roberts did run for State Superintendent of Public Instruction in 1958, and polled more than 400,000 votes. The Communist press and all of its propaganda machinery worked feverishly in this campaign, and while even Roberts' most energetic supporters expressed the belief that he would be unable to prevail over the incumbent, nevertheless it is a demonstration of current Communist vote-getting ability and capacity for hard work that should not be overlooked or underestimated.

What, then, is the present situation concerning Communism in California politics? It should now be quite clear that we can learn much, and perhaps profit a good deal, by knowing something about the devices and general strategy used by the party in the past. In 1938 and 1948 there were many Communist fronts that were used to great advantage as entering wedges to force a way into the political field. Today there are only a few and these were thoroughly exposed almost as soon as they commenced business. But bear in mind that these fronts did not disappear because of any desire by the party. On the contrary, they were maintained as long as possible and often ran deep into the red. They collapsed because of exposure for what they really were, exposure by government agencies—certainly not because they were liquidated by the Communists according to plan.

Now we are in the era of the second United Front and we have secured ample evidence in California that the party has obediently been making common cause with other liberal organizations since April of 1956. It is also becoming more evident daily that the party is mobilizing a large group of so-called "sleepers"; that is, party members who have never been required to attend meetings, have never received any written evidence of affiliation, and who are instructed to pose as conservatives or at least mild liberals in order to avoid detection. Once they are called into service, however, they are useless to the party unless they follow the party line and promote party interests. Any such activity always makes them vulnerable to detection, exposure and elimination from sensitive positions. The American Communists are still striving diligently to form an independent and liberal political body of their own, and we can conclude this section with no better authorities than one from the leader of the Southern California District of the Communist Party of California and an official statement by the National Committee of the Communist Party of the United

States. Dorothy R. Healey, heretofore mentioned as having once been in the employ of the State Department of Labor, recently declared:

"Our district has attempted to provide leadership on some political fronts of immediate concern to the welfare of the people. The H-bomb campaign, Little Rock and the South in general, the struggle for Negro rights, *the 1958 election* (committee's emphasis) and the anti-labor drive in California were among the questions discussed at the district council, with a concrete program proposed to the club for action." [17]

The National Committee has informed us in unmistakable terms that the radical element in American labor, comprising such Communist dominated unions as the United Mill and Smelter Workers; the United Electrical, Radio, and Machine Workers; the American Communications Association; the International Longshoremen's and Warehousemen's Union, and the Public Workers of America—plus all ultra-liberal organizations—will be forged into one major and independent political party by the Communists, if their present plans materialize. Basically, it will be a "politically independent" labor force, with broad liberal affiliation and support.[18]

Since no written evidence of membership in the Communist Party has been used since December, 1947, since the party is extremely sensitive to counter-infiltration and is therefore functioning largely underground, since most of its front organizations have been forced out of existence, the only practical method that can be employed to combat Communist infiltration in politics and other fields of activities lies in a thorough understanding of Communist practices, a familiarity with the Communist Party line as it changes from time to time, and an accurate knowledge of what undercover Communists may be expected to do once they have managed to insinuate themselves into positions of political authority. Armed with adequate knowledge of these matters, it is possible to prevent the infiltration of sensitive political positions which is a manifestly simpler thing to do than to handle the situation once the infiltration has succeeded, as was most forcibly illustrated by the administration of Governor Olson.

INFILTRATION OF EDUCATION

Infiltration of our educational institutions has always occupied a high place on the Communist Party program. Originally the intent was to use this reservoir of impressionable young students for recruiting purposes. During World War II, and even to a larger degree thereafter, infiltration of our educational institutions has been used for another purpose because the government has allocated to many of our larger colleges and universities enormous contracts for conducting secret researches that are valuable to the defense of our nation.

---

[17] "On the Status of the Party," by Dorothy R. Healy. *Political Affairs,* March, 1958, p. 40.
[18] "A Policy for American Labor," by the National Committee, Communist Party of the United States. *Political Affairs,* Aug., 1958, p. 11.

.Consequently, it is desirable for the Communist Party to plant its undercover members in strategic positions so that they can have an overall picture of this highly sensitive research activity.

In order to get a proper perspective of present conditions in California regarding the infiltration of our educational institutions, let us examine it against the background of the last national convention of the Communist Party of the United States and the remarks made by the nation's outstanding expert on Communism, J. Edgar Hoover, regarding the convention and the program adopted by the party thereafter. Mr. Hoover explained how carefully the program was rigged to create the illusion that the American Communists would no longer obey the Kremlin but would henceforth go it alone, something like Tito; that party leaders were no longer trusted by the rank-and-file membership; that the party was torn asunder by internal dissention; that membership had dwindled so much that American Communism should no longer be regarded as a grim and serious threat but merely as a minor irritation.

Actually, this elaborate piece of misdirection was part and parcel of what we have termed "operation lullaby." This 1957 national convention of the party was rehearsed with all the meticulous attention to assigning the actors their various roles, to setting the stage, to arranging the lighting effects and the dramatic impressions that might have been devoted to a stage production. Indeed that is what the convention was, in accordance with Communist custom. Said Mr. Hoover:

> "The skillful Communist propagandist, Mr. Simon W. Gerson, sought to create several illusions in connection with the change in Party leadership and organization which has given a completely distorted and slanted view of what happened. To illustrate:
>
> Prior to the convention rumors were planted that Foster and Dennis were to be ousted. The convention did abolish all offices. This was slanted to convey the impression that the convention action was a slap at Stalinism. Actually, this strategy had been carefully charted at a two-day preconvention meeting in New York. The convention did create a new national committee of 60, 20 of whom were elected at the convention. In addition, an 11-member administrative committee was chosen to direct the day-to-day business of the Party until the National Committee could designate a Secretariat. Of the 16 members of the old National Committee not in prison, nine were elected among the 20 members-at-large. Others may be elected by the districts to fill the 40 additional posts in the near future. Several of the Old Guard, including Foster and Dennis, were elected to the Administrative Committee.
>
> The illusion was created that there was a break with the past since Miss Charlene Alexander of Los Angeles, aged 26, and no hardened Bolshevik, got the largest number of votes among the 20 members elected to the National Committee. This was the

Party's way of currying favor with the Negroes since seven of the 20 elected were Negroes, including Miss Alexander. Actually, the average age of the 20 elected was 45 years of age and their average length of membership in the Communist Party was 22 years. Gerson led reporters to believe after the convention that Gates had cemented his position and won out in his fight against the cult of the individual. There were headlines such as 'U. S. Reds Quit Foster, Kremlin,' and the press reported that the Party 'dumped' Foster and 'voted out of office' Eugene Dennis, who had been replaced with 'collective leadership.' Actually, the Communist Party had created a broad new national committee and a Secretariat in line with the new Soviet line of 'collective leadership.' Foster, who had been criticized as having developed his own 'cult of the personality,' was now a part of a 'collective' commit tee in Moscow style; in fact, this had already been decided prior to the convention.''

*   *   *   *   *   *   *

''This was a convention made up essentially of functionaries. In fact, one Party leader bemoaned the fact that few workers were there. In the balloting on February 12, 1957, for the National Committee only 13 votes were allotted to the entire Southern region, with 136 out of the 292 ballots allotted to New York State, 33 to California, 24 to Illinois, 20 to New Jersey, and other states and regions ranged from one to 12 ballots.

The fact is the Communists could not stand for the free press to observe their proceedings because they cannot long survive the truth. Norman Schrank, Executive Secretary of the New York State Communist organization, launched a verbal assault on news photographers and was observed to push a photographer aside which is illustrative of their attitude.

The Communist Party's 1957 convention was designed to hoodwing the public with a 'new look.' Its program is designed to enable them to develop a militant assault, to accomplish their 'historic mission' of wrecking and infiltrating this nation.''[19]

In July, 1955, Mr. Hoover had made a visit to California, and while spending a portion of his vacation in La Jolla issued the following statement:

''The Communist Party, U. S. A., today is concentrating tremendous effort in the State of California. Roughly 15 percent of all Communist Party members of the nation reside in California, ranking this State second only to New York in Party membership.

---

[19] Statement by J. Edgar Hoover, Director, Federal Bureau of Investigation, to the Subcommittee to Investigate the Administration of the Internal Security Act and other internal security laws, of the Committee on the Judiciary, United States Senate, Eighty-fifth Congress, First Session. "An Analysis of the 16th Annual Convention of the Community Party of the United States," March 12, 1957, United States Government Printing Office, Washington, D. C. 1957, pp. 9-10.

"The growing population, industry and strategic location of California has made this state a prime Communist target for years, and that is why the party is operating a highly efficient underground apparatus in California, as well as trying to increase aboveground operations."[20]

As California's population has continued to increase, so have the activities of the Communist Party in this state, one of the most important of those activities being the infiltration of our educational institutions and our trade union organizations. In previous reports we have described in detail the extent to which the party has managed to send its members into the educational institutions, both at the university level, in the high schools and, to some extent, in the grammar schools. In tracing the history of this infiltration we have shown that it reached its peak during the period from 1939 to 1944, and since 1944 has been steadily declining, although it is still a most serious problem.

Several years ago this committee established a co-operative plan with the administrative heads of most of the universities and colleges in the state and this plan is still in operation. It affords a system whereby representatives of the committee and representatives of the various colleges and universities can exchange information concerning problems; and it does not, and it never did, entail the maintenance of any organization of undercover investigators on any university campus or the employment of students as informers. Its purpose is simply to provide as much reliable and expert assistance as possible in aiding the various university administrators to devise practical means of preventing the infiltration of their several institutions by subversive agents. The committee can conceive of no legitimate objection to this sort of co-operative enterprise by anyone except the most ardent type of party member or fellow traveler.

Such a vociferous clamor was raised by the Communist Party and its subservient organizations shortly after this co-operative plan got under way, and such a determined effort was made to wreck it by sensational and widely-publicized accusations, that the committee was thereby afforded ample evidence that the system was eminently successful in disrupting the party's infiltration of our schools.

Confusion on the Campus

One reason that the academic world has not taken the problem of Communist infiltration more seriously may lie in the fact that far too many educators even yet fail to realize that Fascism does not change its character simply because it flourishes as a Soviet-directed conspiracy to conquer the world instead of being directed by Adolf Hitler. We once examined a Communist theoretician and asked him if he was in favor of Fascism. This, of course, drew an angry denial. He was then asked to define Fascism and did so with great feeling and precision.

[20] *Los Angeles Times,* July 31, 1955.

He declared that Hitler's Nazi regime was an excellent example of a Fascist government; so was Mussolini's Black Shirt regime in Italy. Pressed for details, this witness explained how under Fascist rule the will of the dictator is imposed on the people by force; how he controls all the machinery of government—transportation, communication, education, the military—and enforces his will by unleashing waves of secret police terror. This witness had unwittingly described the Fascist character of the Soviet regime with its one-party system controlled by an absolute dictator who also enforces his will through a secret police, controls the entire machinery of government, and sweeps his colleagues out of office whenever the mood strikes him. An example of this occurred in the Soviet Union recently when Malenkov, Kaganovich, Molotov and Shepilov were summarily removed from office by Khrushchev and swept into relative oblivion as traitors to the Communist Party, which is the only party in the Soviet Union and which actually wields the power through its Presidium which, in turn, is the creature of Khrushchev.

The inhuman tortures inflicted by the Soviet Secret Police are far more horrible than any ever employed by the Nazis; they covered a much longer period and affected more people by many millions. Those who have read Mr. David Dallin's authoritative studies of slave labor in the U. S. S. R., will know that the Nazi and Italian Fascists combined never even approached this massive forced labor program where human slaves were used like animals.

Dr. Mark Graubard, Associate Professor of Natural Science at the University of Minnesota, commented pointedly on this peculiar political astigmatism on the part of many intellectual leaders in the United States in an editorial which is worth quoting in this connection:

"Whatever happened to the American sense of proportion, not to mention the American conscience? At a time when millions of people in Europe and Asia live under a Communist terror, denied the elemental freedoms of action and thought which we take for granted, leading writers and intellectuals in the free United States spread abroad the falsehood that oppression and book-burning prevail in the United States, that terror stalks our universities, school boards, libraries, and even haunts the average citizen.

What a contrast to the situation in the U. S. A., when another totalitarian tyrant, Adolf Hitler, rose to power! Even before the Ayrian laws, the pogroms, and the incineration chambers darkened the German horizon, the reaction of the American public, its government and the college campus was prompt and unequivocal.

In the fall of 1933, as the Executive Secretary of the first anti-Nazi Student Congress in America, at Columbia University, I felt the pulse of this moral response. Our organization expressed the deep current of American sentiment that pervaded Rotary Clubs as deeply as labor unions, cultural societies as much as corner pubs. Opposition to Naziism in the United States was nation-

wide. In colleges committees were formed to aid refugees from
Nazi persecution; student newspapers protested the exclusion of
Jews from German universities, the burning of books and the race
laws. Some Americans even suggested intervention; others demanded a boycott of German goods.

Others, of course, during war or having some sympathy with
Hitler's supposed aims, denounced these protests as interven-
tionism, insisted that each nation had a right to act as it pleased,
and declared that the Roosevelt administration's anti-Nazi actions
were propaganda equaling that of the Nazis. But, regardless of
differences as to what this country should do about it, there was
little confusion about the evil of Naziism.

How different the scene today! For the past 10 years Communism has shouted to the world that America must be destroyed,
that America is the chief warmonger, the cause of world poverty
and mainspring of tyranny and oppression. Its first task was to
obliterate America's good name among the peoples of the world.
For this enterprise the Soviet propaganda machine has received
aid from the writers of hysterical books and articles deriding
America as a tyrant.

Soviet propaganda has encountered no opposition of the kind
that Nazi propaganda futile in the United States. There is hardly
a single campus committee to aid refugees from the Sovietized
universities in Europe and Asia; no Student Anti-Communist Con-
gresses; no Women's Leagues Against Concentration Camps. The
eloquent voices of our liberal leaders are raised more passionately
against alleged American misdeeds and tyranny than against the
darkness behind the Iron Curtain. One receives no telegrams urging ones signature under a Manifesto pledging the signers 'lives,
fortunes and sacred honor' to the downfall of the Red tyranny.
There are no placards reading 'Stop Khrushchev!' attached to
the front bumpers of motor cars. There were some silly aspects of
the anti-Nazi campaign in the late 1930's, but at any rate few of us
confused slavery with 'human engineering,' or tyranny with
progress.

Had American liberalism displayed the same moral vigor
against Communist fanaticism that it did against Hitlerism, the
world might be a safer place, and our moral leadership, established
by our stand against aggression in the 1930's and our unstinted
effort in World War II, would be unquestioned. We are now
paying dearly in taxes, confusion and fear for maintaining a
double standard of political morality." [21]

Despite these facts there are still far too many educators who, for
some obscure reason, stubbornly cling to the notion that somehow the
Nazis were foul and evil and the Communists much nicer; that whereas

---

[21] "Where Are Yesterday's Foes of Dictatorship?" by Dr. Mark Graubard. Editorial,
  Saturday Evening Post, July 2, 1955, p. 10.

every intellectual had a solemn duty to oppose Naziism and Fascism a la Mussolini with all the strength he could muster, it was somehow unfashionable to oppose Fascism of the Red variety. This attitude no doubt stemmed from several causes and chief among them was the fact that during the era of the Spanish Revolution and thereafter until the close of World War II, thousands of American educators, writers, artists, actors, musicians and liberals flocked in droves to join the Communist front organizations of that era; that many of them actually became members of the Communist Party in the deluded idea that they were striking a blow for humanity on a world-wide basis. After World War II, when it became apparent that the Communists had been using us for their own hypocritical purposes during the time they were collaborating with us against a common enemy, and with their enslavement of the six Balkan nations behind the Iron Curtain, their acceleration of Communist Party activity in the United States and their espionage activities that were exposed throughout the world, these American intellectuals became disillusioned. They were faced with the necessity of shrouding their Communist Party front affiliations and their Communist Party membership in the deepest secrecy, and it was therefore quite easy for them to adopt the idea that Communism was not so bad. Then, too, we were engaged against the Italian and German Fascists in a common cause with the Red Army, and consequently many Americans adopted the idea that while Italian and German Fascism were evil, Russian Fascism was relatively innocuous.

Whatever the basic causes for this phenomenon among the American intelligentsia, it constitutes a formidable obstacle to the effective protection of colleges and universities against subversive infiltration by members of the Communist Party, or individuals under Communist discipline. People who have been banded together in Communist Party activities, acting in a tight conspiratorial group, or engaged in a common cause through front organizations, are inclined to protect one another after leaving this type of activity. Thus in a university the ultra-liberal Left composed of individuals who have been party members or active in front organizations find it expedient to protect one another against exposure, thereby forming a somewhat antagonistic clique against their more conservative colleagues. A university professor, Morton Cronin, who was associate professor of English at Los Angeles City College, has recently declared that the outwardly serene collegiate air frequently serves as a veneer under which there exists an academic jungle where the competition is indeed savage and where each department solidly establishes its own moral, sociological, political and academic standards which it nurtures and perpetuates by inflicting quick academic penalities on anyone who violates them. He tells us that ambitious young graduate students are being steeped in the liberal tradition, and continues by declaring that:

"The world of academic liberals, in short, is saturated with careerism. There is a kind of liberal who cannot conceive a greater tragedy than to lose his job or fail a promotion. When he feels, as he occasionally does when someone is sacked because of his politics, that America is no better than Russia, he is being quite sincere. For him nothing could be worse than to impede a man's advancement in the world. But this sympathy does not extend to conservatives—businessmen, professional men, and publishers, for instance, whose views conflict with his. He will merrily cheer a boycott among their customers, clients and subscribers. And, what is more to the point, his sympathy does not extend to his conservative or independent colleague who finds himself unpopular because of his departures from liberal doctrine. . . ."

"Liberals," continues Professor Cronin, "may err at times, but are quite incapable of committing a real sin. * * * This is why so many liberals who have flirted with Communism now feel, even in the face of genuine disillusionment, no actual guilt. They feel, in fact, that their mistake was one that any decent person should have made.

"The morally complacent, since they feel that they are never *really* wrong, easily become morally authoritarian. * * * " 22

We have observed this antagonism of the extreme liberal members of college faculties toward even the mildest of their conservative colleagues and we have discussed this phenomenon with responsible faculty members at several large universities. In many instances we have found honest liberals who would be indignant if accused of conducting their academic researches in a biased and unscholarly manner; yet their prejudices run so deep that they will stubbornly proclaim the innocence of Hiss and Oppenheimer without even reading the transcripts and the official reports in these cases—documents easily procured from the United States Printing Office, Division of Public Documents, Washington 25, D. C.

During the last war these same liberals would have been aghast if members of the German-American Bund had been allowed to teach political science—or law. And the Bund was only a front organization. But if members of the American-Russian Institute or the California Labor School or the Jefferson School of Social Science wanted to teach —then, by some peculiar process of the liberal-academic mind, it became quite proper. The Nazis and the Bund were subversive; the Communists and their fronts and their training schools are also subversive, this could not be denied—but it was wrong for the former to teach but quite all right to open the halls of ivy to the latter.

While on this topic we should at least make some passing reference to what seems to us an example of how the normal precision and objectiveness of true scholarship may be warped by prejudice. Several years ago a book was financed by one of the large tax-exempt foundations as a part of some studies in civil liberties. This particular book,

---

22 Abstracted from *The Individualist,* Vol. 3, No. 1, Intercollegiate Society of Individualists; see *National Review,* Dec. 20, 1958, p. 392.

The Tenney Committee, was written by Edward L. Barrett, Jr., Professor of Law at the University of California in Berkeley. We wish to make it clear that we cast no aspersions on Professor Barrett's loyalty, but we are convinced that he was yet another sincere liberal whose lack of practical experience in the amorality of Communism led him to act as an innocent victim of a smear job.

While Professor Barrett wrote this book, there is no question about the fact that the entire study, including the attack on the committee, was directed by Professor Walter Gelhorn, a faculty member on the staff of the largest Communist indoctrination center in the United States: The Jefferson School of Social Science.

Anyone certainly has the right to criticize the committee or any agency of government or any public official and many have availed themselves of the privilege. Suppose Professor Gelhorn had been teaching at a school for the training of kleagles of the Ku Klux Klan, or in an academy operated by Gerald L. K. Smith, or in a school for the perpetuation of Naziism. We are convinced that the reaction against the selection of a man with such a background would have provoked an immediate, loud and insistent objection from the highly alert and articulate Left. But the fact that a professor in a Communist school was acting as the editor-in-chief of a study of a committee investigating Communism provoked no ripple on the academic waters. The Legislature has taken the position, based on pertinent information, that no person under the discipline of the Communist Party should be afforded the privilege of teaching in the schools of this state. This attitude was expressed in legislation that provided boards of education with the necessary authority to fire teachers who sought refuge by invoking the Fifth Amendment when questioned about subversive affiliations and activities, or who defied the board of education by refusing to discuss these matters or revealing their membership in the Communist Party.[23]

This legislation has been used with success by the Los Angeles City Board of Education, and its constitutionality has been uniformly upheld in a series of suits instituted and vigorously prosecuted by several teachers. The law does not, however, reach the Communist teacher concerning whom there is no available evidence of affiliation with the party since September 10, 1948, which is the period specifically covered by the act. Formal membership in the party has always been difficult to prove, and since no cards or books have been issued to members since 1947, the period covered by the act coincides with the period of extreme caution by Communists to conceal the identity of members. The persistent investigations, exposures, prosecutions and disruption of leadership mentioned earlier have been largely responsible for this retreat to underground positions and the elaborate precautions set in operation by the party for its own protection. Thus, while many

---

[23] See Senate Bill No. 1367, Ch. 1632, Stat. 1953; an act to add Ch. 2 to Div. 7 of the Education Code, and to add Sec. 14130.5 to said code, and to amend Secs. 13521 and 13526 of said code, relating to School District employees.

members whose Communist activities precede 1948 have impressive and easily documented records, those who have become members since 1948 are much more difficult to expose.

Detecting Communist Teachers

While these undercover members can often be slipped into our schools, the supply is begining to run thin. And if a teacher or university professor teaches without trying to influence his colleagues or indoctrinate his students for any considerable length of time, he is not only useless to the party during that interval but his enthusiasm tends to wane because of this inactivity. We have learned from the testimony of hundreds of former Communists who spent many years in the party apparatus that their lives are completely dedicated to Communist work, and every waking hour is devoted to some sort of Communist activity. Operating at such a feverish pitch the average party activist has little time for critical analysis of the party, and his enthusiasm is kept aflame by constant association with his comrades in an endless series of front organization activity and secret party meetings. The instant an undercover teacher is permitted to become active he must do so by spreading the party line as subtly as possible to avoid detection and exposure; he must make contact with his colleagues and urge them to attend at least a few meetings of organizations that espouse the Communist party line, and he must carry on these activities constantly, reporting the results thereof for evaluation by his party superiors. This is a very difficult thing to do, and the job is becoming more difficult in direct proportion to the degree of exposure and education of the public at large, and school administrators in particular, in the techniques and methods employed by just this type of Communist.

Issuance of a Communist book or card, embossed with the hammer and sickle and containing little spaces for the pasting of dues stamps, is, after all, merely a symbol of membership, a matter of bookkeeping. The real and only infallible test to be applied is to determine by an individual's activities and affiliations over a long period of time whether or not he is under Communist Party discipline and performing his Communist duties in accordance with the current party line. This is not a very difficult matter to determine, because the undercover Communist is always on the horns of a dilemma: if he lies dormant thereby guaranteeing that he will not be exposed and rendered useless to the movement, he is without value to the party; if he is activated and carries on his Communist duties according to plan, he invariably risks exposure and is ultimately rendered useless. Consequently, the most valuable weapon that can possibly exist to combat Communist infiltration—not only in our school system but throughout the entire fabric of our government and our way of life—lies in a complete familiarity with the nature of the Communist movement, its history, its growth, its physical organization, its ideology, its discipline, the constantly changing international party line which is invariably echoed in this country, and the little tricks and artifices the Communists employ. Armed with this type of information the problem becomes greatly simplified, and so successful has been the dissemination of accurate information that the Communist Party, in 1952, was compelled to take a drastic step and to declare positively and clearly that it would attempt to bring about a change in the legal precedents established by the Supreme Court of the United States in order to give themselves time to gather their forces and renew their subversive efforts under more favorable legal circumstances. We will discuss that matter in detail in a later section dealing with Communist penetration of our legal system.

Can Communists Teach Objectively?

It has been emphasized many times by official agencies charged with the duty of investigating these matters, and by the testimony of many former Communist teachers, that no person can become steeped in Communist literature, subjected to the rigidity of Communist discipline, thoroughly imbued with the Communist ideology, and then step into a classroom and do objective teaching. Any layman who has the slightest knowledge about the practical aspects of the Communist movement knows that this is true. Bella V. Dodd, Ph. D., was formerly an undercover Communist member of the New York Teachers' Union, and for a time operated its legislative program. Dr. Dodd masqueraded for many years as a non-Communist liberal, stoutly denying her Communist affiliations and earnestly supporting the Communist cause until she became disillusioned, broke with the party and rendered her country an invaluable service by giving the benefit of her experiences to the Senate Judiciary Subcommittee on Internal Security. In testifying before that body she said, in part:

"All Communist teachers who read the literature of the Communist Party and of the Communist movement cannot help but slant their teaching in that direction. I was a teacher of economics, and of political science, and it was very easy for me to slant my teaching that way. As a matter of fact, I wasn't even conscious of slanting it. That was the way I was thinking, and that was the way I was teaching it, because I had become imbued with the whole philosophy and system of Communism. * * * Yes, Communism is a total philosophy. If you believe in it you live it, you breathe it, you teach it. * * * You take it with you seven days a week, 24 hours a day. * * * The students wouldn't recognize it as Communism; nobody else might recognize it as Communism. But there is no doubt in my mind that the Communist teacher teaches the Communist way." [24]

There are some teachers and educators who maintain that members of the Communist Party should have the same right to teach in our educational institutions as any other member of a legal organization

[24] Testimony of Bella V. Dodd, Ph.D., before Senate Internal Security Subcommittee, March 10, 1953, pp. 543, 544.

providing they are academically equipped to do so. This group urges that the only reason Communists should be fired is when they are caught indoctrinating students in the classroom with Communist ideology. We hasten to point out that in order to monitor every teacher and every professor in every class that might be used as a medium through which to indoctrinate students with Communist theories, each school would have to maintain a staff of investigators and informers of enormous size, and that such an activity is completely reprehensible and inimical to our American way of life. The operation of any such undercover organization of investigators would truly strike a serious blow at academic freedom and destroy the very processes we are endeavoring to preserve. Furthermore, in our opinion, it is quite unnecessary to resort to such tactics. We have been accused in the past of having used such a system on the campuses of California universities, and we have denied the charge with all the emphasis at our command. We still deny it and reaffirm that we have no intention of adopting any such system. At the same time, we assuredly have no intention of disclosing our confidential sources of information to the Communist Party or any of its supporters.

The Objective Teaching of Communism

It is a gratifying privilege to be able to report that in California during the last four years there has been a growing awareness among university students concerning the true nature of the Communist menace, and a far greater resistance to attempts at indoctrination. Reports from the major universities in the state, as well as from many of the state and junior colleges, indicate that as these institutions have been concentrating more on objective teaching about the origin, development and operation of the Communist Party and the world Communist movement, there has been a steady decline in Communist activities on the campuses. This is not to say that the danger is by any means over; we will point out at the conclusion of this article persuasive evidence that the menace is still very much with us, but it is definitely on the decline and we see no reason to anticipate that the decline will not continue. The expulsion of the Los Angeles Federation of Teachers from the American Federation of Labor, the exposure of the United Public Workers of America as a Communist front organization that was directing the activities of the Los Angeles Federation of Teachers in the southern part of the state, and the co-operation between educational administrators and this committee, have all contributed toward the common objective of preventing the infiltration of our educational system by members of subversive organizations.

In July, 1957, Assistant Secretary of State Francis O. Wilcox addressed the National Educational Association's Centennial Convention in Philadelphia, and declared it imperative that the cold, hard facts about Communism, both in theory and in practice, be taught in the schools and colleges throughout the country. He was followed by James B. Conant, former president of Harvard, who has declared on many occasions that no person under Communist discipline should be permitted to teach in an educational institution. Now that we have been jarred out of our complacency by the realization of the astounding progress the Soviet Union has been making in the scientific and educational fields, we have begun to re-examine our own educational system. The slowly mounting resistance to the blandishments of these subtle recruiting techniques in our educational institutions is apparently not confined to California. At Harvard a group of students recently got fed up with listening to the apostles of Marxism, and became particularly resentful when Dr. J. Robert Oppenheimer was welcomed as a featured speaker on the campus. Joining with influential alumni who had also become disgusted, they formed an organization called The Veritas Foundation and started a backfire. This move attracted such quick and widespread support from other universities that it is now national in scope with headquarters in New York City.[25]

At the University of North Carolina the student paper recently observed that: "The University used to be a political hotbed. It used to be a place where Communism ran rampant and radical organizations sprang from the ground. There are no such organizations currently present on the campus. * * *"[26]

Brooklyn College

Brooklyn College in New York is a good example of how students reject Communist attempts at indoctrination and recruiting once they are equipped with information that enables them to understand this subversive movement for what it really is. During the thirties, and until the middle forties, Brooklyn College had the reputation of being one of the most heavily infiltrated institutions in the nation. There was an exceedingly active branch of the Young Communist League at the college, and its members obtained solid control of the student newspaper, perpetuating each other in key positions on the editorial staff year after year and using the paper as an influential propaganda weapon. In a previous report we have described an identical technique that was used by the Communist group at U. C. L. A. At Brooklyn College there were the usual well-organized and rebellious demonstrations against constituted authority, there were picket lines and circulation of leaflets, recruiting was widespread, front organizations flourished, and, in short, there was the general and familiar pattern of activity that is characteristic of every institution where Communist infiltration is allowed to get out of control.

With the advent of a new president, Dr. Harry D. Gideonse, there came a stiffening of the administration's attitude toward this problem. Dr. Gideonse was not only aware of the real menace of Communism, he was also thoroughly familiar with its amorality, its tricks and its real objectives. Furthermore he displayed a remarkable sense of perspective

[25] The Veritas Foundation, P. O. Box 340, New York 5, New York.
[26] Excerpt from *The Tar Heel*, University of North Carolina; see National Review, Dec. 20, 1958, p. 392.

that was reflected in his determination to effect a transition of power from radical student leaders who were primarily concerned with perpetuating their political ideas, to student leaders who were interested in the college as a college and at the same time to preserve academic freedom in its true sense.

The student paper was emancipated from the grip of the radical clique; every outburst of party-line propaganda was countered by a calm and well-reasoned statement on the president's bulletin board; courses in Russian and on the history of the Communist movement were established, and the situation was gradually but firmly brought under control.

President Gideonse has, like Chancellor Raymond Allen at U. C. L. A., written some excellent articles on the problems of Communist infiltration. He, like Dr. Allen, has been to the Soviet Union, and he is admirably equipped to maintain constant vigilance against a resumption of subversive infiltration at Brooklyn College, and at the same time to preserve its academic and democratic integrity. There are still radical student groups at the college and they exist in complete freedom— but they are not subversive.

It has been charged that President Gideonse has throttled freedom of the press by wresting control of the paper away from the radicals and restoring it to the students at large so it can present a divergence of views instead of one ideology. There has also been some criticism of his alleged tendency to insist upon a conformity to the conservative point of view. But this sort of thought comes mostly from the extreme left and ignores the fact that in this college, with 85 percent of the students Jewish, 11 percent Catholic and 4 percent Protestant, the rejection of Communism has come from the students themselves. They show little evidence of being cowed or regimented by the administration; their emphasis is on getting an education instead of participating in radical politics.[27]

If one student is subjected to intensive recruiting pressure, succumbs through a lack of knowledge of Communism, and gets drawn into the vortex of the conspiracy to the point of no return, he can and usually does cause untold damage to our society. Take the case of Abram Flaxer.

According to an abundance of sworn testimony by many witnesses,[28] Flaxer was born in Lithuania on September 12, 1904, came to the United States in 1911, and obtained derivitive citizenship in 1917. After graduating from Boyce High School in Brooklyn, he entered New York City College where he was successfully indoctrinated with the Communist ideology. He did graduate work at Columbia where the indoctrination was accelerated and he became a party member. He used an alias, or party name, John Brant, and although having majored in science he devoted much of his time to the performance of party work in trade unions.

[27] See "Brooklyn College," by David Boroff, *Harpers,* Dec., 1958, p. 42.
[28] See: United Public Workers of America, report of Senate Internal Subcommittee, 1952.

In 1936, Flaxer became President of the United Public Workers of America, a union that was expelled from the C. I. O. 14 years later because, as the parent organization put it: "* * * The policies and activities of the UPW are consistently directed toward the achievement of the program and purposes of the Communist Party rather than the objectives and policies set forth in the C. I. O. Constitution."

This Communist-dominated union was comprised of members who were employed by the munipical, state and federal governments and who occupied many highly sensitive positions. By 1952, the United Public Workers of America had absorbed the State, County and Municipal Workers of America and its membership totaled 35,000 persons. There was one postoffice local in Los Angeles.

In previous reports we have documented many instances where graduates of the state university and other California educational institutions have become indoctrinated while attending school and then went on to occupy extremely high and influential positions in the Communist apparatus of this country. We wish to make it crystal clear, and cannot overemphasize the fact, that while there has been an apparent waning of Communist activities in the California universities and colleges, and that this seems to be reflected in other institutions throughout the country, the danger is still with us. There has been a growing resistance on the part of students that comes with the possession of facts concerning the real nature and practices of Communism. But we must also bear in mind that the Communist Party is now working underground; that it has adopted the Khrushchev directive of working through liberal non-Communist organizations instead of through its own front groups, and that Communist activity is much harder to detect than it was during the period when the party was working in the open.

Reverting once more to Brooklyn College, since we have selected this as formerly one of the heaviest-infiltrated institutions in the country, we find the following faculty members who invoked the Fifth Amendment regarding their Communist Party membership, or admitted such membership, when questioned by the United States Senate Internal Security Subcommittee.[29]

They were Joseph Bressler, Assistant Professor of Health and Education, who invoked the Fifth Amendment on February 10, 1953; Frederic Ewen, Assistant Professor of Literature, who followed the same procedure on September 24, 1952; Irving Goldman, instructor in Anthropology, who admitted having been a member of the Communist Party until 1942, in a session of the subcommittee held on April 1, 1953; Elton Gustafson, instructor in health and education, who invoked the Fifth Amendment on past and present membership in the Communist Party on February 24, 1953; Eugene Jackson, instructor of German and former Chairman of the Foreign Language Department of the New York City Schools, who invoked the Fifth Amendment on September 23, 1952; Alex Benjamin Novikoff, part-time instructor in Biology who invoked the Fifth Amendment on April 23, 1953; Melba Phillips, instructor in Mechanics and Physical Science, who invoked the Fifth Amendment on October 13, 1952; Sara Riedman, assistant instructor in Biology, who invoked the Fifth Amendment on October 13, 1952; Harry Slochower, Associate Professor of German, who invoked the Fifth Amendment on September 24, 1952; Bernhard J. Stern, instructor in Chemistry, who invoked the Fifth Amendment on September 24, 1952, and Murray Young, instructor in English, who invoked the Fifth Amendment on February 24, 1953.

It is interesting to note the results of the series of hearings whereby the Internal Security Subcommittee investigated infiltration of the educational process of the country by the Communist Party. In the preface to the report heretofore referred to, the subcommittee said:

"The Internal Security Subcommittee, in the second year of its inquiry into Communist penetration of the educational system, held hearings in Washington, New York, Boston, and Chicago. The subcommittee was continuing under Chairman William E. Jenner (R., Ind.) the inquiry into Communist penetration into the educational process begun in 1952 under the chairmanship of Senator Pat McCarran (D., Nev.).

Altogether it heard more than a hundred witnesses in the field of education in public session and many more in executive session. Of this number 82 educators, about whom the subcommittee had evidence of Communist Party membership, refused to answer questions about their Communist affiliations, invoking instead their constitutional privilege against self-incrimination. Three others admitted Communist Party membership, but defied the committee in refusing to supply further details. Twenty were responsive witnesses.

Of the 82, 40 were faculty members or employees of 16 different universities. The others were teachers in secondary school or persons who held other positions in the educational system.

The subcommittee received impressive evidence from former Communist organizers that the Soviet organization was continuously engaged in a plan to penetrate our educational institutions at every possible point, thus posing a serious threat to our national security. The Communist agents who spun the very real web of conspiracy and intrigue within the framework of the United States Government departments, in almost all cases, were cradled in our distinguished universities and colleges. The subcommittee observed that the universities and colleges are, understandably, more and more participating in government, creating policy and shaping our national destiny and that the expressions and sentiments of educators are more and more flowing into the main stream of our national culture.

The subcommittee's function in the educational field is to examine the workings of the Communist apparatus and to determine whether it is necessary to have additional legislation against new and undefined crime. The subcommittee has no authority or power to prosecute for criminal action. That is the function of the prosecuting arm of the executive branch of the government. It is the function of the legislative branch of the government to go forward and determine whether or not new laws are necessary or old laws are outmoded. For these reasons, congressional committees must operate in an area where actions dangerous or undesirable to the public welfare are not yet defined in the law as crimes. This distinction was the determining factor in setting up our standards and procedures.

At the beginning of this year, Senator Jenner issued for the subcommittee a statement of policy in which he said: 'If a totalitarian organization such as the evidence shows to exist in our nation's schools is allowed to flourish in our institutions of learning, unexposed and unchecked, not only will our youth be infused with seeds of their own and the nation's destruction, but academic freedom, the right to free inquiry, the right to dissent, the development of our culture, and the right to express free ideas and free thoughts will be choked and stifled.

* * * Our purpose is to protect and safeguard academic freedom. Academic freedom is under attack by a monstrous growth no individual or community of scholars can fight alone. Traitors cannot operate in the free market if armed highwaymen constantly harass them from secret hideouts on the public roads. The free market of ideas cannot function if hidden conspirators are waiting at every vantage point to break and destroy the loyal people who are going quietly about the business of teaching our youth to the best of their ability.

Our committee is not concerned about telling the leaders of our schools and colleges what to teach, or how to teach. It is concerned with showing them where this alien conspiracy is hidden, that it is fully armed with every weapon, waiting to attack at every vantage point. It is concerned with helping our academic leaders to meet the threat. There can be no academic freedom until this Soviet conspiracy hidden in our schools and colleges is exposed to the light, and the rule of Moscow over its adherence in the educational world is broken.' " [30]

So far as the situation in California is concerned, the committee need only remind interested readers that a few years ago we reported the case of a young student who received his first Marxian indoctrination while attending high school in Southern California, then went to Stanford University where he was recruited into the Communist Party and

[30] Subversive Influence in the Educational Process, Senate Internal Security Subcommittee, op. cit., pp. 1 and 2.

developed for high-level Communist work abroad. Finally realizing the inherent danger of this type of work in the Communist apparatus and resolving to break away from the party, this young man left Stanford against the wishes of his Communist superiors and started his studies at U. C. L. A. His dead body was found in the basement of a student dormitory near the campus shortly after he had attended a Communist Party function in downtown Los Angeles with four students who were also members of the apparatus. According to expert witnesses, including the chief autopsy surgeon of the Los Angeles County Coroner's Office, this young man was murdered in order to prevent him from disclosing what he had learned about high-level operations of the party abroad and on the Pacific Coast. The committee still has an abundance of documentary proof, including the death threat, that was received by this young man from his Communist superiors.

In 1956, there was a similar instance at U. C. L. A. where a graduate student was found dead in his apartment, and again expert testimony established the fact of his murder and the committee retains in its possession records of his attendance at Communist functions and meetings with important Communist functionaries that amply demonstrates a motive to keep him from making more disclosures. This latter young man was not a member of the Communist Party, and had not been submitted to its discipline so far as we know.

There is not the slightest doubt about Communist infiltration of California institutions of higher learning. The Communist Party would obviously be idiotic to suddenly neglect this abundant field for recruiting and indoctrination, and for the development of reliable members who can keep the underground apparatus of the party informed about current strategic defense researches that are being carried on in our universities.

When this committee undertook to make some inquiries about subversive infiltration at the University of California in 1952, there was a storm of faculty protest. Three years later the Fund for the Republic undertook a completely unofficial and gratuitous investigation in the same identical field. In the first instance the committee and the president of the university, then Dr. Robert Gordon Sproul, were made the objects of a tirade of abuse, innuendo, unsupported accusations and attacks from all quarters—including the leftwing element in some of the Bay area newspapers—simply because the State University and the State Legislature presumed to co-operate for the purpose of determining the extent of subversive infiltration of the institution and to take such measures as might be deemed necessary to combat it. When the Fund for the Republic set up shop in April, 1955, for the purpose of making a detailed study of civil liberties, loyalty and subversion in connection with the university, there was not a whisper of protest. Even when representatives of the Fund for the Republic circulated a detailed and loaded questionnaire among the faculty members there were no eruptions from the faculty about this nosiness, no expressions of indignation from the Academic Senate because the Fund for the

Republic presumed to pry into university affairs, there was no displeasure because the academic freedom of the institution was being damaged. The American Civil Liberties Union looked on with tacit approval, and there was no objection from the Regents of the university at this unofficial snooping expedition. The Fund for the Republic established a base of operation within walking distance of the university campus and happily set about quizzing everybody it could find, and actually making a written survey which would indicate to whomever might be interested the division between the pro-Communist, ultra-liberals, freewheeling Socialists, and fellow travelers on the one hand, and the usually inarticulate, conservative faculty members on the other. Many of the questions propounded in this Fund for the Republic survey are of great significance.

If we had undertaken to make this survey in writing there would have been a truly earth-shaking revulsion. Why? Why this supine submission by faculty and acquiescence by administration to this undertaking by an unofficial, purely gratuitous, self-appointed group, and such violent resistance when, without going to anything like these extremes, the Legislature sought to tender its services in a co-operative effort to stem the tide of subversive infiltration? The highly vocal spokesmen for the "liberal" clique are quick to protest about the invasion of academic freedom, but they apparently have one standard for those who seek to protect the state against subversion in the performance of official duties, and another standard for the same kind of a survey in greater detail by written questionnaire by an unofficial organization like the Fund for the Republic. We consider this questionnaire of such importance that we set it forth herewith, all italics being emphasis added by the committee.

Faculty Questionnaire, Fund for the Republic Study, April, 1955

Q. 1-a. Is it your impression that there is greater concern these days than six or seven years ago on the part of the public and groups outside the college over teachers' political opinions and what political matters are taught in the classroom, or not?
Greater concern_____; not greater concern_____; don't know_____.

b. In general, do you feel this greater concern has caused any harmful effects on the climate of freedom in the country, or do you think this charge of harmful effects has been overdone?
Caused harmful effects_____; charge overdone_____; not sure_____.

c. In what ways does this greater concern cause harmful effects? Any others?

d. Can you tell me any advantage in this greater concern on the part of the public? Any others?

e. Now, while there may be disagreement over the seriousness of the effect of this greater concern, let's talk for a moment about the areas that some people say might be affected in a harmful way. Here is a list of such areas. (Hand respondent card.) If you had to make a choice, can you tell me the one area on the list where you think the most harmful effects might be felt?

It impairs the intellectual role a college should play in a democracy_____; It discourages constructive public discussion of important issues_____; it degrades the academic profession_____; it prepares the ground for totalitarianism _____; it really has no serious effects_____.

Q. 2-a. In the past few years have you felt that your own academic freedom has been threatened in any way or not?

Threatened_____; not threatened_____; don't know _____.

b. In what way or ways do you feel your academic freedom has been threatened?

Q. 3-a. Do you feel there is a greater threat to intellectual activity in America than there was a generation ago, less of a threat, or don't you see any difference?

Greater threat_____; less of a threat_____; no difference _____; don't know_____.

b. What is that greater threat? Anything else?

Q. 4. There has been a good deal of discussion recently about whether or not the proposed admission of Red China to the U. N. is a proper subject for intercollegiate debate.

a. How do you feel about it_____; do you approve or disapprove of intercollegiate debates on the admission of Red China to the U. N.?

Approve_____; disapprove_____; don't know_____.

b. Suppose you were a faculty adviser to the debating team right here and the president told you he wouldn't allow the team to debate the admission of Red China issue, would you protest vigorously to him, or just say you disagreed and leave it at that, or would you accept his order and not say anything?

Protest vigorously_____; just say disagree and leave it _____; don't know_____; comments:

c. Suppose the president of this college (university) said that he wanted the team to debate the admission of Red China issue, would you do anything about it?

Yes_____; no_____; don't know_____.

4. What would you do? Anything else?

Q. 5-a. Suppose you were faculty adviser to a student organization here on this campus that proposed inviting Owen Lattimore, Far Eastern expert (now under indictment in Washington), to speak at a public meeting here. Do you think Lattimore ought to be allowed to speak here or not?

Out to be allowed_____; ought not to be allowed_____; don't know_____.

d. Suppose the president did ban Lattimore from speaking and the students who invited him asked you to join with them in protesting the ban. Would you protest the ban vigorously, or just say you disagree and leave it at that, or would you accept his ban and not say anything?

Protest vigorously_____; just say disagree and leave it _____; not say anything_____; don't know_____.

c. Suppose the president of this college (university) said that he would not interfere with the invitation to Lattimore, would you do anything to try to prevent his appearance on this campus?

Yes_____; no_____; don't know_____.

d. What would you do? Anything else?

Q. 6. Here is a list of things *that some people say have happened to social science faculty members.* I wish you would run down the list and then tell me for each whether or not this has happened to you or crossed your mind here at _____ (name of college/university). (Hand respondent list.)

1. Have some colleages here on the campus ever given you advice on how to avoid getting into political trouble at this college?

Yes_____; no_____; don't know_____.

2. Do you find yourself being more careful now and then not to bring up certain political topics with your colleagues in order not to embarrass them?

Yes_____; no_____; don't know_____.

3. Have you noticed more of a tendency lately in social gatherings on the campus to avoid controversial political topics?

Yes_____; no_____; don't know_____.

4. Do you find in your recommendations of reference materials to students that you are more careful today not to recommend something that might be later criticized for being too controversial?

Yes_____; no_____; don't know_____.

5. Have you ever wanted to join an organization, and despite the possibility of personal criticism for joining it, you went ahead and became a member anyway?

Yes_____; no_____; don't know_____.

6. Do you find in your conversations with your fellow faculty members that there is lots more talk these days about teacher firings than other political security problems?

Yes_____; no_____; don't know_____.

7. Do you feel more inclined these days to advise the student political group not to take extreme positions for their own well-being?

Yes_____; no_____; don't know_____.

8. Have you ever wondered that some political opinion you've expressed might affect your job security or promotion at this college?

Yes_____; no_____; don't know_____.

9. *Have you ever thought about the possibility that the administration of the college has a political file or dossier on every faculty member, including yourself?*

Yes_____; no_____; don't know_____.

10. Do you find that you are more hesitant today to sponsor a student political group that advocates unpopular ideas?

Yes_____; no_____; don't know_____.

11. Do you ever find yourself wondering if because of your politics or something political you said or did that you might be a subject of gossip in the community?

Yes_____; no_____; don't know_____.

12. *If a student had told you about some political indiscretion in his youth, but now you were convinced of his loyalty, and if the FBI came to you to check on that student, would you report this incident to the FBI?*

Yes_____; no_____; don't know_____.

13. If you were to hire a teaching assistant, would you wonder if his political background might possibly be embarrassing to you?

Yes_____; no_____; don't know_____.

14. If you were considering a move to another college, have you wondered if anyone at that college would ask anyone at your present college about your political background and political biases you might have in your teaching?

Yes_____; no_____; don't know_____.

15. Have you toned down anything you have written lately because you were worried that it might cause too much controversy?

Yes_____; no_____; don't know_____.

16. Have you worried about the possibility that some student might inadvertently pass on a warped version of what you have said and lead to false ideas about your political views?

Yes_____; no_____; don't know_____.

17. When you have private talks outside of the classroom with a student whose views are unpopular do you try to help him to conform to the prevailing views on the campus?

Yes_____; no_____; don't know_____.

18. Have you ever wondered if there was something political you said or did that would cause you to become unpopular with any group of alumni?

Yes_____; no_____; don't know_____.

19. Have you occasionally refrained from expressing an opinion or participating in some activity in order not to embarrass the trustees of the college administration?

Yes_____; no_____; don't know_____.

20. Have you recently wanted to express publicly a political point of view on something, and despite your worry that you might be criticized for saying what you did, you said it just the same?

Yes_____; no_____; don't know_____.

21. Do you occasionally go out of your way to make statements or tell anecdotes in order to bring home the point directly or indirectly that you have no extreme leftist or rightist leanings?

Yes_____; no_____; don't know_____.

Q. 7-a. Have you signed any loyalty oath here at this college in which you pledged to disavow all subversive activities and ideologies?

Yes_____; no_____; don't know_____.

b. Did you welcome the chance to sign the oath, or did you feel some reluctance about signing it, or didn't you have any strong feelings one way or the other?

Welcomed the chance_____; reluctant about it_____; no feelings either way_____.

c. Why did you sign it—because you felt your job was at stake or that it wasn't worth making an issue over this, or what?

Job at stake_____; not worth making issue over_____; other_____.

d. Suppose you were asked to sign an oath in which you pledged to disavow all subversive activity and ideologies, would you refuse, sign it with some reluctance, or welcome the opportunity?

Refuse_____; sign with reluctance_____; welcome opportunity_____; don't know_____.

e. What's the main reason you feel this way? Any other reasons?

f. Why would you sign it—because you would feel that your job was at stake or that it wasn't worth making an issue over this, or what?

Job at stake_____; not worth making issue over_____; other_____.

Q. 8-a. Have you ever worked on a project or received a government grant or worked for the government at a job in which security clearance from the government was necessary?

Yes_____; no _____; don't know_____.

b. Have you ever been turned down for a government job or for work on a government project on which you suspect might have been *political* grounds, or hasn't this happened to you?

Have been turned down_____; hasn't happened_____; don't know_____.

Q. 9-a. Can you tell me which periodicals dealing with politics or public affairs you generally read—(here we don't mean technical journals)? Any others?

b. I wonder if you would tell me what political groups or organizations interested in public affairs you belong to or make contributions to? Any others?

Q. 10-a. Do you usually express your own political views on the subjects you teach, or do you usually try to avoid expressing your point of view?

Usually express own views_____; avoid expressing own views_____; don't know_____.

b. After expressing your own point of view, have you ever wondered afterward if you should have said it or not?

Wondered_____; never wondered_____; don't know_____.

c. Can you tell me more about it?

Q. 11-a. *Have you ever felt your point of view on a political subject was reported unfavorably to higher authorities or hasn't this happened to you?*

Yes_____; no_____; don't know_____.

b. Can you tell me more about it? Anything else?

c. *Have you ever felt that you were being watched in a classroom?*

Yes_____; no_____; don't know_____.

d. Can you tell me more about it? Anything else?

Q. 12-a. Leaving aside Communist groups, are there any groups that teachers like you might belong to that you feel are likely to be attacked as being subversive? Any others?

b. Again, leaving aside Communist publications, which publications that teachers like yourself might receive do you feel are likely to be attacked as being subversive? Any others?

Q. 13-A. Have you ever been a member of a political group which advocated a program or a cause which has been unpopular or controversial, or haven't you been a member of any such group?

Been a member_____; never been a member_____; don't know_____.

b. Has anyone ever criticized you for belonging to such a group or not?

Yes_____; no_____; don't know_____.

c. Can you tell me more about that criticism? Anything else?

d. Do you think your having belonged to this political group adversely affected your academic career, or don't you think it had any bearing on it?

Adversely affected_____; no bearing_____; don't know _____.

e. Even though nothing has happened so far, are you very worried that this past association might some day have an effect on your academic career, only a little worried, or aren't you concerned about it?

Very worried_____; a little worried_____; not concerned _____; don't know_____.

Q. 14-a. If someone accused you of Leftist leanings, would you expect most, some, only a few, or hardly any of your colleagues to rally to your support?

Most_____; some_____; only a few_____; hardly any _____; don't know_____.

b. Now what about the administration of the college—do you think they would support you wholeheartedly, with reservations, or hardly at all?

Wholeheartedly_____; with reservations_____; hardly at all_____; don't know_____.

Q. 15. Some claim there hardly exists an area in the social sciences which does not lend itself to value judgment—that is, subject to difference of opinion.

a. Now, in general, for the courses you teach, which emphasis would you lean to: (hand respondent card)

(1) Such controversial matters should be discussed frequently in undergraduate teaching because of the educational value of such discussion_____.

(2) One should answer such questions honestly when they come up but not seek out such discussions_____.

(3) In times like these it is better to avoid the discussion of such controversial issues as much as possible.

COMMENTS

b. Have you always generally held this point of view or have you come to feel this way in the past few years?

Always held this view_____; come to feel this way in the past few years_____; not sure_____.

Q. 16. In teaching subjects which might require questioning of traditional values, which of these two approaches do you personally
feel is the better educational policy for teachers to follow:
(1) After proper discussion, to argue in a measured way
for his own point of view_____; or,
(2) To give all sides of the question impartially without
revealing his own views_____.
Hard to decide_____.

Q. 17. If you *had* to make a choice, in general, which of these two
approaches do you think ought to be more emphasized more
in teaching the social sciences to students in their first two
years of undergraduate studies?
(1) To give the students a basic grounding of facts on the
subject_____; or
(2) To get the students thinking about the problem areas
in the subject_____.
Hard to decide_____.

Q. 18. (Hand respondent card) (Don't read question)
In an engineering school education, it is said to be important for
students to understand the prevailing state of the mechanical
arts. In addition, their education should prepare them to make
their *own* original contributions and to accelerate new developments.

Some say this is directly comparable to the *intellectual* training of students in the social sciences. It is argued that these
students should be prepared to make their own original contributions to help society to better meet the needs of its people.

How important do you see this element of creative preparation
in the teaching of the social sciences to undergraduates: An
urgent part of undergraduate teaching, or a quite important
part of undergraduate teaching, or a minor part of undergraduate teaching, or not the proper function of undergraduate
teaching, or you have honestly not given it much thought?
Urgent need of undergraduate teaching_____, or quite
important part of undergraduate teaching_____, or
minor part of undergraduate teaching_____, or not proper
function of undergraduate teaching_____, or
honestly have never given it much thought_____, or don't
know_____.

Q. 19. Do you feel your philosophy on how to teach is pretty typical
of that of most of your colleagues on the social science faculty
here, or do you feel your philosophy is slightly different or very
much different from that of your colleagues?
Pretty typical_____; slightly different_____; very much
different_____; don't know_____.

Q. 20-a. How closely do you follow civil liberties problems and issues in the news—as much as any other news, more than most other news, or not as much as other news?

As much as any other news_____; more than most other news_____; not as much as other news_____; don't know _____.

b. Can you tell me which specific cases, if any, came to your mind when I asked you this last question? Any others?

c. Apart from any cases here in this college, what civil liberties or academic freedom cases, if any, have occurred around here in this area even though they may not have been in the national news? Any others? Tell me which specific cases, if any, came to your mind when I asked you this last question? Any others?

d. Do you find yourself discussing civil liberties issues and problems with your friends, colleagues, or family members fairly often, just occasionally, or hardly ever?

Fairly often_____; just occasionally_____; hardly ever _____; don't know_____.

Q. 21. Compared to six or seven years ago, is it your impression that individual students are less willing to express unpopular political views (in the classroom, etc.), more willing, or hasn't there been much change?

(a) In the classroom less_____; more_____; no change _____; don't know_____.

(b) In private talks with faculty members outside the classroom, less_____; more_____; no change_____; don't know_____.

Q. 22. Compared to six or seven years ago, is it your impression that students seem to be less willing to form and to join student political organizations advocating what might be unpopular political beliefs, are they more willing, or would you say there has been no appreciable change?

Less willing_____; more willing_____; no change_____; don't know_____; no such groups here_____.

Q. 23. In your judgment, what are the things that could make a member of the social science faculty here controversial? Anything else?

Q. 24. Is it your impression that members of the social science faculty here are less willing (to express unpopular political views, etc.) than they were six or seven years ago, more willing, or hasn't there been much change?

(a) To express unpopular political views in the classroom: less willing_____; more willing_____; not much change _____; don't know_____.

(b) To express unpopular political views publicly in the community: less willing_____; more willing_____; not much change_____; don't know_____.

(c) To express unpopular political views privately among friends: less willing_____; more willing_____; not much change_____; don't know_____.

(d) To serve as faculty advisers to student political groups that might advocate unpopular causes: less willing_____; more willing_____; not much change_____; don't know _____.

Q. 25-a. Do you have the impression that compared to six or seven years ago, some members of the faculty here are more worried about possible attacks and accusations on their political beliefs and activities, less worried, or don't you think there has been much change?

More worried_____; less worried_____; not much change _____; have become bolder_____; don't know_____.

b. From what sources do they think the attacks might come? Anywhere else?

Q. 26-a. *Now I would like to ask you about the research your colleagues do, the papers they publish, or the books they write, and the speeches they make.* Any or all of these; do you feel that some of your social science colleagues here have avoided subjects that might have political repercussions more than they might have had six or seven years ago, less than they might have had then, or don't you think there has been much change?

Avoid subjects more_____; avoid subjects less_____; no change_____; don't know_____.

b. Without naming names of individuals, can you give me some specific illustrations of the sort of thing they have done in these cases? Anything else?

Q. 27. Do you feel that in the selection of reference materials they recommend to students, your social science colleagues here have become more careful today, as compared to six or seven years ago, or less careful to keep out material that might prove too controversial, or don't you think this has generally happened?

More careful_____; less careful_____; have become bolder _____; don't know_____.

Q. 28-a. Have there been any cases here in this college where you feel that academic freedom of any member of the faculty has been threatened?

Yes_____; no_____; don't know_____.

b. Can you tell me about it? (Them?) Any others?

c. What effects did the incident(s) have on the rest of the faculty here? Anything else?

Q. 29-a. *Has any group or person accused anyone on this faculty here of being subversive or of engaging in any un-American activities in the past few years?*

    Yes_____; no_____; don't know_____.

b. Can you tell me about it? (Them?) Anything else?

c. What did you think of the whole affair(s)?

d. Do you feel the administration handled the incident in a way which protected the reputation of the college (university, etc.) or not?

    Protected the reputation of the university with the public at large: yes_____; no_____; don't know_____.

    Protected the rights of the faculty: yes_____; no_____; don't know_____.

    Protected the educational standards of the college (university): yes_____; no_____; don't know_____.

Q. 30. If you had to make a choice, in a case in which a member of the faculty is accused of being subversive or engaging in un-American activities, which do you think it *most* important for the college (university) administration to protect—the reputation of the college (university) or the rights of the faculty members?

    Reputation of college (university)_____; rights of faculty member_____; depends_____; don't know_____.

Q. 31-a. *Thinking back over the last few years, do you know of any cases of teachers here who probably would have been added to the staff if they hadn't had controversial political views, or don't you know of any such cases?*

    Know of such a case_____; don't know of any case_____.

b. *Do you know of anyone who is no longer teaching here as a result of his political views, or don't you know of any such cases?*

    Don't know of such a case here_____; don't know of any _____.

c. Do you think it is possible at this college (university) that a man with slightly greater merit who was *unconventional* could be passed over for a permanent appointment in favor of a man with somewhat less merit who was *conventional*, or don't you think that could happen here?

    Could happen here_____; could not happen here_____; don't know_____.

d. Can you tell me about any cases here such as this—again without mentioning names? Any others?

Q. 32. Compared to what you know about other academic institutions, would you say that working conditions here (teaching load, salaries, and so on) are: unusually good; good, but could be improved; fair; or not good, but could be worse; or unusually bad?

> Unusually good_____; good, but could be improved_____; fair_____; not good, but could be worse_____; unusually bad_____; no opinion_____.

Q. 33-a. Compared to what you know about other academic institutions, by and large, would you say that relations among faculty members here are: unusually good; good, but could be improved; fair; are not good, but could be worse; or unusually bad?

> Unusually good_____; good, but could be improved_____; fair_____; not good, but could be worse_____; unusually bad_____; no opinion_____.

b. Compared to what you know about other academic institutions, by and large, would you say that relations between the faculty and administration of this college (university) are: Unusually good; good, but could be improved; fair; are not good, but could be worse; or unusually bad?

> Unusually good_____; good, but could be improved_____; fair_____; not good, but could be worse_____; unusually bad_____; no opinion_____.

Q. 34-a. Has the faculty and the administration discussed the questions of academic freedom in joint meetings within the last year ar not?

> Yes_____; no_____; don't know_____.

b. Do you feel the administration of the college has taken a clear stand on matters of academic freedom or not?

> Yes_____; no_____; don't know_____.

c. How would you describe the administration's stand on matters of academic freedom? Anything else?

Q. 35-a. Of course it is possible to have events that stir up strong feelings on the local or state as well as the national level. Which would you say you have had more of around here—local, state, or national controversies?

> Local_____; state_____; national_____; don't know_____.

b. Can you tell me about any local events that have created strong pro and con feelings here in the past few years?

Q. 36. Is it your impression that the administration of this college (university) is under more pressure to avoid controversy from (trustees, etc.) than it was six or seven years ago, less pressure, or that there hasn't been much change?

> (a) Trustees: more_____; less_____; not much change _____; don't know_____.
>
> (b) Alumni: more_____; less_____; not much change _____; don't know_____.

(c) The community right here: more_____; less_____;
not much change_____; don't know_____.
(d) The Legislature or local politicians: more_____;
less_____; not much change_____; don't know_____.

Q. 37. If you had to choose one, who would you say has the most powerful voice here on this campus in determining the degree of academic freedom that exists here—the trustees, the president, the dean, the heads of departments, the faculty, the students, or who?

Trustees_____; president_____; dean_____; heads of departments_____; faculty_____; students_____; all _____; none_____; other_____; don't know_____.

Q. 38. Now, I should like to ask you some questions about a man who admits he is a Communist.
(a) Suppose he is working at a defense plant.
Should he be fired, or not?
Yes_____; no_____; don't know_____.
(b) Suppose he is a clerk in a store.
Should he be fired, or not?
Yes_____; no_____; don't know_____.
(c) Suppose he is teaching in a college.
Should he be fired, or not?
Yes_____; no_____; don't know_____.

Q. 39. Now I would like you to think of another person. (Hand respondent card.) A man whose loyalty has been questioned before a Congressional committee, but swears under oath he has never been a Communist.
(a) Suppose he has been working in a defense plant.
Should he be fired, or not?
Yes_____; no_____; don't know_____.
(b) Suppose he is a clerk in a store. Should be be fired or not?
Yes_____; no_____; don't know_____.
(c) Suppose he is teaching in a college or university.
Should he be fired or not?
Yes_____; no_____; don't know_____.

Q. 40. *How great a danger do you feel that American Communists are to this country at the present time—a very great danger, a great danger, some danger, or no danger?*
A very great danger_____; a great danger_____; some danger_____; hardly any danger_____; no danger_____; don't know_____.

Q. 41. If there are students who want to join it, do you think that a (Young Democratic Club, etc.) ought to be allowed on this campus or not?

> Young Democratic Club: allowed_____; not allowed_____; depends_____; don't know_____.
> Young Republican Club: allowed_____; not allowed_____; depends_____; don't know.
> Students for Democratic Action: allowed_____; not allowed_____; depends_____; don't know_____.
> Young Socialist League: allowed_____; not allowed_____; depends_____; don't know_____.
> *Young Communist League:* allowed_____; not allowed _____; depends_____; don't know_____.

Q. 42. *In general, how do you feel about a social science teacher who is an admitted Communist? Do you or don't you feel that he is not very different from any other teacher with unorthodox views, etc?*

> (a) He is not very different from any other teachers with unorthodox views: Yes_____; no_____; don't know_____.
> (b) He is troublesome mainly as a source of embarrassment to the college: Yes_____; no_____; don't know_____.
> (c) He is not fit to be a teacher: Yes_____; no_____; don't know_____.
> (d) He is a dangerous person to have students exposed to: Yes_____; no_____; don't know_____.

Q. 43. Do you think there is a definite advantage in having a teacher with radical or nonconformist views on the social science faculty here, or do you think *that is a luxury at best,* which this faculty cannot afford?

> Definite advantage_____; luxury cannot afford_____; cannot decide_____.

Q. 44. On political matters, do you feel that you are more liberal or more conservative than most of the trustees here at this college, etc.?

> (a) Most of the trustees here at this college: more liberal _____; more conservative_____; same_____; don't know _____.
> (b) Most of the administration here: more liberal_____; more conservative_____; same_____; don't know_____.
> (c) Most of the faculty here: more liberal_____; more conservative_____; same_____.
> (d) Most of the alumni of this college: more liberal _____; more conservative_____; same_____; don't know_____.
> (e) Most people in the community in which the college is located: more liberal_____; more conservative_____; same _____; don't know_____.

(f) (If "more liberal" or "more conservative" in a, b, c, d, or e above) Have you felt some pressures—direct or indirect—to conform to the prevailing political pattern or haven't you felt any of these pressures?

Have felt_____; have not felt_____; don't know _____.

(g) How have these pressures shown themselves? In any other ways?

Q. 45. Here is a list of four occupations (hand respondent card).

A. Now suppose a typical businessman were to rank these four occupations by the prestige he holds for each—in what order do you think he would rank each?

B. How do you think a typical Congressman would rank them?

C. Finally, how do you think the typical trustee of your college (university) would rank them? (Note: rank from 1-4 for each category.)

Manager of a branch bank:
(a) Businessman_____; (b) congressman_____; (c) trustee_____.

Account executive of an advertising agency:
(a) Businessman_____; (b) congressman_____; (c) trustee_____.

Lawyer:
(a) Businessman_____; (b) congressman_____; (c) trustee_____.

A college professor:
(a) Businessman_____; (b) congressman_____; (c) trustee_____.

Don't know_____.

FACTUAL DATA

1. How long have you been teaching in colleges or universities?
Less than five years_____; 5 up to 10 years_____; 10 up to 20 years_____; 20 up to 30 years_____; 30 years or more_____.

2. How long have you been teaching at *this* college or university?
Less than five years_____; 5 up to 10 years_____; 10 up to 20 years_____; 20 up to 30 years_____; 30 years or more _____.

3-a. Do you have a permanent or rotating chairman of your department?
Permanent chairman_____; rotating chairman_____.

b. Are you now or have you been a department head here?
Yes_____; no_____; don't know_____. [Sic.]

c. (Do you) (Does your department chairman) (department head) have a considerable amount of latitude and authority in making policy decisions or would you say (you) (he) (are) is essentially concerned with administrative details?

Considerable amount of latitude and authority_____; essentially concerned with administrative details_____; don't know_____.

4. Can you tell me what degrees you hold?

B.A._____; B.S._____; M.A._____; M.S._____; Ph.D._____; other_____; don't know_____. [Sic.]

5-a. What department are you in?

Economics_____; History_____; Government_____; Anthropology_____; International Relations_____; Sociology_____; Geography_____; Social Science_____; Social Studies_____; Political Science_____.

b. What courses do you now teach?

c. Do you get a great deal of opportunity in the courses you teach to discuss controversial issues, only little opportunity, or hardly any at all?

Great deal of opportunity_____; only little opportunity_____; hardly any at all_____; don't know_____. [Sic.]

6. Will you tell me what ranking you hold—instructor, lecturer, assistant professor, associate professor, or full professor?

Instructor_____; lecturer_____; assistant professor_____; associate professor_____; full professor_____; don't know_____. [Sic.]

7. Do you have a permanent appointment here on this faculty or not?

Yes_____; no_____; don't know_____. [Sic.]

8. Have you ever hired any teaching assistants?

Yes_____; no_____; don't know_____. [Sic.]

9-a. Have you written a dissertation?

Yes_____; no_____.

b. Has it been published in full or in part?

In full_____; in part_____; not been published_____.

c. Have you published any (other) papers?

Yes_____; no_____.

d. How many?

Two or less_____; two or more_____.

e. Have you published any (other) books?

Yes_____; no_____.

10-a. Can you tell me any academic honors which have been bestowed on you?

b. Have you served on any college or university committees?

Yes_____; no_____.

c. Have you held office in any professional or academic societies?

Yes_____; no_____.

d. Have you delivered any papers at the meetings of any professional or academic societies?

None_____; one or more_____; three or more_____.

11. Have you ever applied for a Fullbright Lecturer or Scholar Award?

Yes_____; no_____; don't know_____. [Sic.]

12. Have you served as a consultant to industry or any other organizations excluding the Federal Government?

Yes_____; no_____; don't know_____. [Sic.]

13-a. Is you salary today higher than it was five years ago?

Yes_____; no_____.

b. By what percent has it gone up?

Less than 5 percent_____; less than 10 percent_____; 10-20 percent_____; 20-30 percent_____; 30 percent or more _____; don't know_____. [Sic.]

c. Do you have any outside source of income besides your salary?

Yes_____; no_____.

14. Are you a member of the American Association of University Professors?

Yes_____; no_____.

15-a. Are you married, single, widowed, or divorced?

Married_____; single_____; widowed_____; divorced _____.

b. Do you have any children?

yes_____; no_____

c. How many?

1_____; 2_____; 3_____; 4_____; 5_____; 6 or more _____.

16. Have you (your husband) ever served in any branch of the Armed Forces?

yes_____; no_____

17. Sex?

Male_____; female_____.

18. What is your age?

20-30_____; 31-40_____; 41-50_____; 51-60_____; 61 or older_____.

19. Race:

White_____; Negro_____.

20. Do you mind telling me where your grandparents were born?

United States_____; Canada_____; Great Britain_____ (England, Scotland, Wales)_____; Ireland_____; Germany_____; Scandinavia (Norway, Sweden, Denmark)

_____; Italy_____; other Western Europe (Netherlands, Belgium, France, Switzerland, Spain, Portugal)_____; Poland_____; other Eastern Europe (Austria, Hungary, Czechoslovakia, Rumania, Bulgaria, Greece, Yugoslavia, Albania, Russia, Finland, Latvia, Lithuania, Estonia) _____; all other_____; don't know_____.

21. Can you tell me your father's occupation?
22. Do you mind telling me your religious preference?
   Protestant_____; Catholic_____; Jewish_____; other _____; none_____; don't know_____.
23. *How many times in the past year, if at all, has a representative from the F. B. I. talked with you—for any purpose?*
   None_____; one or two_____; three or more_____.
24. Are the people you see the most of socially mainly from your department, from the faculty generally, or from the community?
   Own department_____; faculty generally_____; community_____; don't know_____. [Sic.]
25. Would you classify yourself politically as a Republican, Democrat, Independent, or what?
   Republican_____; Democrat_____; Independent_____; other_____; don't know_____.
26. Would you mind telling me whom you voted for in 1952 for president?
   Eisenhower_____; Stevenson_____; Other_____; did not vote_____; don't remember_____.
27. Do you mind telling me whom you voted for in 1948 for president?
   Dewey_____; Truman_____; Wallace_____; Thurmond _____; other_____; did not vote_____; don't remember_____.

What was accomplished by this survey? An examination of the key questions discloses its main objectives. It starts by inquiring about the increasing public concern over teaching political opinions, the sort of political matters being taught, and whether this concern has caused any damage to academic freedom. This general topic is pursued, asking for more and more detail, until the respondent is asked if it ever occurred to him the university might be keeping ''a political file or dossier on every faculty member, including yourself.'' (Questionnaire, page 4.) It would seem obvious that if such data were maintained on every faculty member, it would necessarily include the member being interviewed, and we wonder what is meant by ''a *political* file or dossier.'' Does it mean that the administration wants to know how many Democrats and Republicans it employs? If so, the county recorder's office would provide this information to the Fund for the Republic without necessitating the repetition of the question to every person interviewed. And if it refers to some sort of *subversive* political organization, and compendia of this type of information maintained by the administration, it would appear that the question should state this fact plainly and without quibbling. As it stands, this particular question is intriguingly ambiguous.

Another inquiry in the general category asks whether, if the respondent had been given information by a student about "a *political* indiscretion in his youth," and thereafter the F. B. I., in the performance of its duty to protect the government against subversion, asked the respondent about the student, would he frankly assist the F. B. I. by reporting the incident, or would he refuse to do so if, *in his own opinion*, the student was now loyal? (Questionnaire, page 5.) The wording of this question plainly indicates that the word "political" here refers to a subversive affiliation since it is related to the fact that the respondent may now be convinced of his student's loyalty.

At this point it is perceived that the Fund for the Republic is itself keeping a rather elaborate "file or dossier" on every faculty member it questions. And this particular inquiry should provide a list of those who would refuse to disclose loyalty information about students when requested to do so by the F. B. I. It collects information about whether respondent believes he was fired or rejected from a government position for "political grounds," and solicitously adds, "or hasn't this happened to you?" (Questionnaire, page 7.)

The faculty members are then asked for a list of the periodicals they read dealing with politics or public affairs; the political organizations to which they belong or to which they contribute; and, "have you ever felt your point of view on a political subject was reported unfavorably to higher authorities?" To which is once more appended the commiserating inquiry, "or hasn't this happened to you?" (Questionnaire, page 8); and then the respondent is asked if he ever felt he was being *watched* in the classroom, but this question doesn't specify who might be doing this teacher-watching: student spies, administration spies, or government spies.

The first part of the questionnaire—there are three parts—concludes with two questions that, for the first time, specifically mention Communism and ask whether the respondent is aware of any groups or publications "other than Communist," that might be attacked as being subversive. (Questionnaire, page 9.)

Section 2 commences with questions that are obviously designed to draw out the attitudes of faculty members who once belonged to "a political group that advocated a program or a cause which has been unpopular or controversial." The questioner wants to know whether the respondent has "been a member, never been a member, don't know." (It is difficult to imagine how anyone fit to teach could be a member of such an organization and not know it). Then the respondent is asked if he has been criticized because of this affiliation, if such membership has jeopardized his academic career, and even if nothing has happened yet—does he *worry* that this past association might one day injure his career; whether, if accused of "leftist leanings," most, some, only a few, or hardly any colleagues or the administration would rally to his support.

After thus exploring the respondent's attitude toward the teaching of controversial subjects, the questions shift to a revelation of his attitude about civil liberties, seeking information about whether he is interested in these matters as much, more, or not as much as other news; whether he will describe "cases around here in this area" other than at the college; how often he discusses civil liberty issues with others; if students have become more unwilling to express unpopular political views in class during the past six or seven years, or to join groups advocating such ideas.

In discussing faculty attitudes with the respondent he is asked whether social science teachers are less willing to express "unpopular political views" than they were six or seven years ago—in the classroom, in the community and among friends, and to act as faculty advisors to "student political organizations advocating unpopular causes."

Continuing to explore general faculty attitudes, the questions now move to a wider field, utilizing the respondent as a source of information about his colleagues. He is asked if they seem more worried about being assailed for their unorthodox political beliefs and activities than they were six or seven years ago, or "less worried, not much change, or have become bolder;" the respondent is asked about his colleagues' research, the books they write, the papers they publish—even the speeches they make and whether he believes any of this work has become restricted because of their dread of political repercussions; whether selection of reference material for use by students is likewise restricted for the same reason. He is asked to describe specific cases where the academic freedom of any of his colleagues has been threatened, and whether he knows of any person or group that has accused any faculty member of being subversive or engaging in un-American activities "in the past few years," and his opinion is solicited concerning how each case was handled by the university administration. The respondent is then asked whether he considers it most important to protect the reputation of the university or the faculty member. Nothing is ever mentioned about protecting the state, the students or the parents. The respondent is asked about persons who were not hired because of their "controversial political views," and is asked to describe all cases he knows of where persons were fired because of such views. Questions involving discrimination by the university administration are handled by inquiring whether a slightly inferior man might be promoted ahead of his more capable but "unconventional" colleague, and specific instances are requested.

Outside influences are considered when the respondent is asked if, within the past six or seven years, the university administration has been subject to more pressure from the regents, the alumni, the local community, the Legislature, or "local politicians."

The closing question in Part 2 inquires who is most influential in determining questions of academic freedom: the regents, the president, the deans, heads of departments, faculty, or students.

Section 3 commences by putting questions about the admitted Communist, the respondent being asked whether such a person should be fired from a defense plant, a store, a university. The same questions are then asked concerning a man who swears to a congressional committee that he has never been a Communist. Then comes a significant inquiry asking whether the respondent regards American Communists "a very great danger" to the country, "a great danger, some danger, hardly any, or no danger." Then whether any of these students organizations should be allowed on the campus: "Young Democratic Club, Young Republican Club, Students for Democratic Action, the Young Socialist League, Young Communist League."

This is followed by narrowing the scope of a previous question about whether an open Communist should be fired from the university; this one asking if such an admitted party member should be permitted to teach any of the *Social Sciences*. There are also some subquestions to further explore the respondent's attitude in this field: he is asked whether he regards the admitted Communist as virtually the same as any other teacher with unorthodox ideas—(a member of a world-wide Fascist movement to subvert the United States, we presume, would be a teacher with "unorthodox" ideas); or only as a source of embarrassment to the university; that he is not fit to be a teacher; that he is a dangerous person to place in contact with the students. Then comes another peculiarly-worded inquiry: "Do you think there is a definite advantage in having a teacher with radical or nonconformist views on the social science faculty here, or do you think *that is a luxury* at best, which this faculty cannot afford?" We believe the wording of this question is so obvious in purport that it requires no further comment.

The respondent is then requested to evaluate the degree of his own liberal attitude—whether he is more liberal or conservative than the regents, than most of the administration, most of the faculty, most of the alumni, most of the community where the university is located. And, unless he turns out to be on an even keel with all of these groups, he is asked if he hasn't felt some pressures nudging him toward conformity with them.

The rest of the questions in this third and last section of the questionnaire deal mainly with factual data such as family status, employment record, religion, race, social contacts, politics and voting record. But, sandwiched into these is this one: "*How many times in the past year, if at all, has a representative from the F. B. I. talked with you— for any purpose?*"

We have isolated many of these questions because they seem to us very significant; and we have discussed this project of the Fund for the Republic on the University of California campus because it emphasizes the point we made earlier. It is this: the ultra-liberal educators who profess to be so grimly determined to preserve academic integrity, have no compunction whatever about adopting one set of standards to apply to projects such as this launched by the Fund for the Republic, the American Civil Liberties Union, and other such groups, and an entirely different set of standards for the F. B. I., legislative committees, and other *official* groups that are endeavoring to carry out their duties to protect our institutions against destruction by the forces of subversion.

When, as we have pointed out, the simple arrangement whereby this committee agreed to co-operate with the university in an attempt to protect it against infiltration was announced, we were met with a blast of outraged protest from these ultra-liberals, enthusiastically abetted by the American Civil Liberties Union of Northern California, and the tactics that were employed were so unethical that some of the directors of the latter organization wrote it letters of indignation. The attack came to nothing, really; but it does demonstrate most forcibly the lengths to which this highly active group will go to prevent any attempt, however restrained and objective, to investigate subversion by any official agency. If representatives of the State Legislature had presumed to enter upon the campus of the state university with a 27-page questionnaire asking questions about the extent of subversive infiltration and influence in the university, there would have been an immediate expression of outrage and indignation and accusations that we were battering away at the institution's academic freedom.

But when the Fund for the Republic appeared three years after our co-operative arrangement with the university was announced and launched its survey, there was no resentment. The project was quietly accepted, resulted in interviews conducted with many faculty members along the lines heretofore set forth, and provided the Fund for the Republic, (or anyone else who might have access to its records), with a wealth of information that we will analyze below. We are aware that many faculty members at the university refused to answer any of these questions, did not in any way co-operate with the project, and resented the intrusion into their affairs and the taking of their time by this wholly gratuitous and unofficial project.

In the process of asking members of the faculty at the state university to give information about each other and about the administration, this questionnaire could provide the Fund for the Republic with information resulting from a winnowing through the faculty, separating conservatives from liberals, and breaking down the most liberal groups into degrees. It would thus be possible to isolate all faculty members who—to take the most "progressive" respondents—believe that they are justified in determining whether they should co-operate with the F. B. I. when asked about students' loyalty, or wheather they should deliberately withhold such information about the students' subversive past, thereby arrogating to themselves the right to substitute their own judgment as laymen for that of security experts. Having thus lumped together all faculty members who would go this far, the Fund for the

Republic could add all those who believe that American Communists are wholly innocuous; that Communist Party members should be allowed to teach young students and freely bombard them with Communist propaganda; that the university should avail itself of the "luxury" of hiring teachers with radical views and scattering them throughout the social science subjects; that the Young Communist League should be allowed to function on the campus with some liberal professors as its advisors.

This questionnaire makes no bones about boring into the situation so far as curricula are concerned and delving into teaching methods, research projects and attitudes of faculty members towards all of the security precautions taken by the administration. It does not hesitate to question the respondents about each other, but infers very pointedly that similar scrutiny and questions by *official* agencies in the course of their duties is reprehensible, and that the administration should maintain no files on the subversive background of its employees because this would worry the employees too much and possibly interfere with their academic freedom.

Professors Refuse to Co-operate with F. B. I.

Three years after this questionnaire was circulated by the Fund for the Republic, and the questions about the Federal Bureau of Investigation were adroitly planted, the Northern Section of the Academic Senate of the University of California announced that thenceforth the university professors at Berkeley would flatly refuse to co-operate with the Federal Bureau of Investigation *in all cases* where inquiries were made about the loyalty of students who were being considered for federal jobs. According to an article which appeared in an East Bay newspaper [31] the Northern Section of the University of California Academic Senate expressed the idea that freedom of discussion in the classroom would suffer if students realized their beliefs might affect their future employment by government or in private business. The Northern Section of the Academic Senate, which has jurisdiction over all faculty members at the Berkeley, Davis and San Francisco campuses of the university, adopted this gag rule on October 28, 1958. A part of its resolution reads as follows:

"This faculty asserts that freedom of discussion in the classroom and in academic consultation is fundamental to higher education. The essential freedom of the university can be seriously jeopardized if argument and expression of opinion are inhibited, particularly in those subjects which are held controversial in some quarters and in some moments of history.

Therefore, reports by a teacher concerning the beliefs, attitudes, activities, and the associations of a student regarding religion, politics, and public affairs in general, are not permissible

[31] *Oakland Tribune,* Oct. 29, 1958.

when the reports are based on information acquired by the teacher in the course of instruction or in the course of other student-teacher relations that involve the student's academic program.''

The article points out that this rule was originally proposed by a member of the Speech Department, Professor David Rynin, at a meeting of the Academic Senate on May 20, 1958, the matter thereafter being referred to its Committee on Academic Freedom. It is to be noted at this juncture that the authority to make such rulings had been delegated to the Academic Senate by the University's Board of Regents.

Not all of the professors were happy with the adoption of this refusal to co-operate with the United States Government in its effort to protect itself against internal subversion, since some of the 50 voting members opposed the proposal strenuously. Professor Warren H. Giedt, Associate Professor of Mechanical Engineering, declared that the measure would create a conflict of basic loyalties and that he would feel responsible to inform the government about a student whose classroom comments and activities indicated that he was a security risk.

> "As a citizen," declared Professor Giedt, "I have a responsibility to the government. If we adopt this Resolution do we not go contrary to our fundamental responsibility?"

Professor Andreas G. Papandreou, of the Department of Economics, declared that the enactment of such a measure would notify the government that if it wanted information about the loyalty of students it would have to seek it through other means. Professor Frank C. Newman, of the Law School, actually presented the resolution in his capacity as Chairman of the Academic Senate Committee on Academic Freedom. There was a 90-minute discussion, and in extolling the merits of the resolution, Newman stated:

> "If it were generally known by students that their political and religious freedom to disclose beliefs, to express attitudes, to recount activities, and to refer to associations did not protect them from loyalty response to loyalty-security inquiries, many students, in the classroom and in academic consultation, would apply rules of caution differing markedly from the rule of free inquiry that we now tend to take for granted.
>
> Many loyalty-security inquiries—whether they related to government employment, private employment, military service, or other affected occupations—call for evidence . . . that a university should not supply if it aspires to be a free university," the committee's report stated.
>
> "To preserve the essential freedom of the university, your committee submits that freedom of communication both in the classroom and in academic consultation must not be violated by the teacher."

Newman informed the Academic Senate that his committee will present proposals for administering the resolution, and declared that the situation would be eased *if university officials would get the word to investigators that a new principle has been adopted at the University of California under which a faculty member could not say whether a student is or is not a security risk. He would have to state that university rules forbid him from answering.*

Some of the most articulate and emphatic opponents of this measure were Marine Colonel James Wilbur and Professor Denzel R. Carr, Chairman of the Department of Oriental Languages. Col. Wilbur declared that "activities and associations of students that can be observed should be reported." Professor Carr pleaded with his associates to "have a little common sense to protect our society from Communism."

Who Runs the State University?

Thus we have the ultimate amplification of the Fund for the Republic questionnaire in an action by what we presume must be a somewhat liberal element in the faculty of the University of California at Berkeley. The northern section of the Academic Senate has now undertaken to establish regulations for the conduct of the university business with the representatives of the state and federal governments, and has informed the university administration that it should get the word to investigators that is has adopted a new principle at the state university.

What this situation actually amounts to is a defiant statement by employees of the State of California that they will flatly refuse to reveal their knowledge of subversive affiliations and activities on the part of their students to authorized official representatives of the federal and state governments who are specifically charged with the gathering of precisely that type of information. To suggest that this sort of defiant attitude on the part of a large segment of the faculty of the state university needs immediate attention on the part of the Legislature and the university administration seems to us the understatement of the year. The Board of Regents of the university has already adopted a token statement to the effect that it doesn't believe the university should be pro-Communist. This seems a peculiar way to implement this declaration of anti-Communism on the part of the university regents, in suffering its faculty to thwart the activities of the Federal Bureau of Investigation.

If these state employees are permitted to thus defy the agents of our government, perhaps the practice could be spread to all of the other state employees. There is no reason why university teachers should have any particular monopoly on this sort of defiance. Then if the other states and territories would adopt a similar attitude on the part of all of *their* employees, the Federal Bureau of Investigation could devote all of its time to catching bank robbers, kidnappers, fugitives, and the other criminals, and leave the matter of determining loyalty to the Fund for the Republic, The American Civil Liberties Union and the northern section of the Academic Senate of the University of California. If it would be wrong for *all* universities and schools throughout the United States to adopt such a defiant attiude, then certainly the measure is equally wrong for the faculty of the northern campuses of the state university.

Stalin once declared that it took many men to build a bridge but only one to blow it up. It also requires the combined efforts of many people to prepare a student for college and only one to ruin him after he gets there. As these young people are drawn deeper into the Communist movement they gradually but inevitably lose all their warm, precious human traits so carefully inculcated at home, and acquire in their place the typical hard, cynical, materialistic, atheistic qualities that characterize all indoctrinated party members. If the co-operative efforts of the educational institutions and this committee can prevent one student from being thus indoctrinated each year, then the effort is, in our view, more than justified for that reason alone.

There has never been any mass infiltration by Communists of any of our educational institutions in California. There has been, and we anticipate there will continue to be, a persistent Communist effort to penetrate these institutions for the purpose of developing leadership and replacing the fall-out of party members that we have already described.

During the period of the party's open activity in the United States its youth organization was simply known as the Young Communist League, but when there came a gradual awareness on the part of the public concerning the real nature of Communism this organization changed its name to the American Youth for Democracy, and in more recent years to the Labor Youth League. Dennis James, a former active member of this organization, described it in testimony before the House Committee on Un-American Activities and pointed out that since the entire party apparatus had gone underground the danger was much greater than it had been during the period of open activity.

The Labor Youth League, according to Mr. James, was used by the Communist Party to obtain signatures for the Stockholm Peace Petitions to discontinue atomic tests, and petitions asking for an immediate ceasefire during the Korean war; for the collection of food and clothing for strikers that were supported by the Communist Party, and for selection to attend indoctrination classes in the Communist School in New York—the Jefferson School of Social Science. It will be remembered that it was Professor Walter Gelhorn who taught at this institution and who was the editor-in-chief of a series which included a book attacking this committee several years ago. Mr. James declared that "* * * I know in 1952, when I disassociated myself from the Labor Youth League, I felt that the danger was serious because the activities were now underground and could not be detected as easily as in the past." [32]

---

[32] House Committee on Un-American Activities, Hearings, pp. 2828-2829.

It is very easy for educators and other laymen who have had no practical experience in the actual techniques of the Communist Party to say it is a simple thing for a man to be a Communist and also teach objectively. Complete refutation of this naive attitude is found in experiences of people who have been both teachers and Communists. Louis Budenz, exmember of the National Committee of the Communist Party, and formerly editor of its New York publication, the *Daily Worker,* has written a book called "The Techniques of Communism," and in a chapter entitled, "Invading Education," he has this to say:

"In the classroom, the Communist teacher or professor very rarely, if ever, teaches Marxism-Leninism openly. There are hundreds of indirect ways of reaching the same end. Books by Howard Fast,[33] the author who has refused to state whether or not he would fight against the Communists if drafted, are proposed as suggested or recommended readings. The works and statements of many other 'authorities' who invariably take a pro-Soviet position, such as Professor Frederick L. Schuman of Williams College, can be freely used. The Red instructor has many other 'non-Communist' sources to draw on—those leading figures in public life who always follow the Communist line and whom Stalin has designated as the 'reserves' the conspiracy should call upon. An entire syllabus which would inevitably lead a student to embrace Marxism-Leninism or to be sympathetic to the Communist line, can be drawn up without one notably or openly Stalinite reference in it.

Building on that foundation, the Communist teacher or professor notes the pupil or student most susceptible to pro-Red ideas. This student is cultivated privately, with a view to drawing him toward the conspiracy. In like manner, colleagues on the faculty who indicate sympathy for pro-Communist ideas are influenced by personal association to join the Communist Party. The influence of the teacher who is committed to Marxism-Leninism goes far beyond these contacts—into Parent-Teachers Associations (often working behind the scenes with Communists in those groups), in the preparation of books, the presentation of lectures, the voicing of opinions, the raising of finances for the conspiracy."[34]

Elsewhere in the same work, Mr. Budenz states:

"We must constantly remind ourselves, as Dr. Dodd and I agree, that two or three Communists on any faculty are normally enough to dominate the school or campus. They do not act alone, but have aid from the outside. They work under the directives of Communist functionaries who seek out ways to influence trustees of the college involved or members of the Board of Education. It is not unusual that certain men of wealth on a board of trustees gives protection

---

[33] Howard Fast, the author of Citizen Tom Paine and other party line publications, has recently broken from the Communist Party and has written a book, The Naked God, in which he exposes the stranglehold on writers who publish while members of the Communist Party.
[34] "The Techniques of Communism," by Louis F. Budenz. Henry Regnery Co., Chicago, 1954, p. 210.

to the subversives on the faculty, to the detriment of those who are genuinely patriotic; these trustees being influenced by the cries of academic freedom, by a gross ignorance of the Communist methods, by personal considerations, or by partisan interests.

Beyond all this, the Communists on the faculty have the loud support of specific organizations in the community which other concealed Communists infiltrate and control. Nor do the Reds hesitate to resort to whispering campaigns against the character of an opponent, which frequently terrorize non-Communist teachers or professors. This goes far beyond the outspoken cry of 'Mc-Carthyite'; it extends into sly and organized gossip, reflecting on the work, the morals, and the integrity under attack because of his patriotic position. Here, again, the gangster character of the Communist philosophy, carried on by nongangsters, serves as a potent weapon. When to all of this we add the ease with which the subversives can persuade the champions of progressive education to come to their aid, the formidable character of even a small number of Communists can be properly mentioned. It is in this manner that the Reds, working through the Teachers' Union (which received high praise in the report of the Party's Cultural Commission), were able to wield great influence in the elementary and high schools." *

In concluding this section of the report, your committee again wishes to point out that while the Communist infiltration of the state's school system has abated since 1952, the problem is an ever-present one. The co-operation that this committee has received from most of the large school systems and universities has been most encouraging, and the results of that co-operative effort have been met with even more success than we anticipated. Indeed, we may close this section on a note of pride by quoting two sources that have taken notice of the California system for preventing infiltration of educational institutions, one from the state of Ohio and the other from Washington, D. C.

In a document entitled "Procedural Analysis and Plan for Correcting an Involved Situation in a State University," by Dr. William E. Warner, Chairman of the Ohio Coalition of Patriotic Societies, this statement appears:

"Basic Plan of Correction. This will take time and while difficult to accomplish, must be based on a continuing analysis like that outlined above. Several States in addition to the Congress, operate or have had Un-American Activities Commissions, as please see the list in Appendix II of the Maryland (Ober Law) Report of January, 1949. *California has the best State program.*"

---

* The author is here referring to the infiltration of the Teachers' Union of New York, an organization which was party controlled, and in which Dr. Dodd was an influential officer.

From an official Washington source we find the following:

"The subcommittee makes the following recommendations:

"That educational authorities give consideration to the establishment of criteria and the initiation of procedures whereby schools, colleges and the universities can eliminate teachers who have demonstrated their unsuitability to teach, because of their collaboration with the Communist conspiracy.

That states and educational institutions give consideration to the program adopted by the State of California, and the several colleges and universities therein, which, recognizing that subversion in the educational process is a matter of public concern, has put into operation a program that provides for a reservoir of security information, the free exchange of security information between colleges and legislative committees, and means whereby the facilities and powers of state agencies are made of service to educational institutions.

That school authorities, colleges, and local Boards of education initiate positive programs under qualified experts in the field of combatting Communism, to teach both teachers and school pupils the nature of the Communist conspiracy that is attacking the whole structure of society." [35]

INFILTRATION OF LABOR

As a prelude to the Russian Revolution the seeds of revolt were first sprinkled among the workers in the oil fields of Baku, in the Putilov locomotive works, in factories, in shops; from one group to another the fervor of revolution ran like an electric current, gathering momentum as it went, galvanizing them into action. Dropping their tools, deserting their posts, they left their jobs by thousands and hundreds of thousands. From the factories and the fields poured the torrent of artists, farmers and peasants. Armed with crude weapons they manned the barricades, jammed the streets, and stormed the government buildings.

All vital work ceased. The life of the country was paralyzed. This great mass of humanity, having been regimented by centuries of oppression was now seething with a frenzy of relief and defiance as the heavy burden was finally lifted. Their contagion ultimately spread to segments of the Czar's armed forces that deserted and turned their weapons against their still-loyal superiors. By then the vital arteries of transportation and communication had been cut and the downfall of the government was inevitable.

This revolution of October, 1917, was no carefully planned, shrewdly devised occurrence. On the contrary, it was the result of disturbances that had been pointing towards such a climax for many years. The Russian masses had been inured to oppression but they never lost their natural desire for freedom and personal dignity. There had been many

---

[35] Subversive Influence in the Educational Process, Senate Judiciary Subcommittee on Internal Security, op. cit., p. 29.

other attempts at revolt, all quickly crushed by the swords and whips and guns of the Cossacks, and the even deadlier information gathered by the Czar's *Ochrana,* or secret police. Our most eminent authorities, Secretary Dulles and Dr. Julian Towster among them, have pointed out that man is governed not only by rules of his own devising, but by great immutable laws that he is powerless to rescind or amend, and that these basic natural laws cannot be violated with impunity. No group of people can be permanently ruled by terror, deprived of the attributes of human dignity, forced to toil like machines for the benefit of the State, and to exist in a melancholy atmosphere of ignorance and subjugation. These conditions may be imposed for a considerable time, but the longer they exist the stronger become their counter-forces, until eventually such a regime must either be relaxed or destroyed entirely. The masses of restive people approaching the revolutionary climax after years of oppression need only a tiny spark to set off the chain reaction. In 1917, the Bolshevik leaders provided that spark. *But the masses of organized Russian workers won the revolution.*

We cite this historical material to emphasize the importance world Communist leaders have always placed on the concentrated infiltration of organized labor as the first vital prerequisite to revolution. Lenin never lost sight of this cardinal principle, nor did Trotsky, nor Stalin, nor any of their successors including Khrushchev. In the European countries, in the Balkans, in China, in the Middle East and Latin America, in Africa, and certainly in our own country, this steady penetration of labor organizations has gone forward. The logic of the strategy is obvious, but will not apply as readily in a free and prosperous country. Hence, the infiltration continues and undercover Communists are moved into strategic positions to patiently wait for the development of a "revolutionary situation." A severe economic depression is a "revolutionary situation"; so is a widespread epidemic or any other misfortune that renders a nation particularly susceptible. Then the small, solidly entrenched party members, in their positions of authority, spring into action and the strikes are commenced; transportation, communication, food production, the utilities, all are paralyzed. And if the tiny sparks sets off the chain reaction, then the angry tide of revolution is unleashed.

This precise technique has been successfully employed in a number of countries now under Communist control, and one after another we see this creeping menace expanding itself. If the revolutionary situations do not come fast enough, then they are accelerated by Communist propaganda, by infiltration of government positions, by all of the complicated devices and techniques that the world Communist movement has brought to such a high degree of perfection and employed with such ingenuity. And while all of this activity is progressing, there is an equal if not greater degree of action in the murky realms of the underground where espionage and sabotage are taking place day by day; and despite the astounding apathy of the American people, the tragic documentation of this penetration of our most sensitive areas can be had for the asking by writing to the Government Printing Office in Washington, D. C., and requesting the reports of the House Committee on Un-American Activities and the Senate Judiciary Subcommittee on Internal Security dealing with these matters. It is not the business of this committee to investigate espionage, but occasionally in the performance of our specified duties we have run across such activities and have invariably submitted the information to the proper authorities for the appropriate action.

The Profintern

In March, 1919, the Communist International (Comintern) was established in Moscow. All foreign parties were affiliated to it as subordinate sections, bound by the conditions to which they were obliged to agree at the time of their affiliation. Comintern representatives, such as Gerhardt Eisler who functioned for several years in this country, were sent to all parts of the world for the purpose of making sure that the international Communist party line was meticulously obeyed and that the work was progressing according to plan. When the Comintern was exposed as the high board of strategy for a world Communist revolution, it was "dissolved," but like many Communist fronts and other party organizations, the change was one in name only and the operations of the far-flung Communist apparatus were continued as before.

No better example of the closely co-ordinated activity of infiltration, directed from the Soviet Union, can be found than that which occured in the Latin American countries. In Mexico the story is particularly fascinating, and once the Soviet base of operations had been established in Mexico City, it was only a matter of time before the tentacles were extended into South America and the trade union organizations of the South American countries were heavily infiltrated.

The Comintern even had an entire division, which was called the "Profintern," devoted to nothing but the handling of this infiltration of trade unions in the various non-Communist countries throughout the world. It had its own organizational structure with the authority coming from the apex of the triangle down toward the base, as is the custom in all Communist organizations. We shall briefly trace its history in the United States as a prerequisite to obtaining the necessary perspective for understanding the present Communist infiltration of trade union organizations in our own state.

The Profintern fared better in Europe and Latin America than in Great Britain and the United States, but efforts were redoubled in these latter countries. The Russians believed that the strategy used so successfully in their own country would be infallible elsewhere. But there were no Cossacks, no Czarists secret police, no rule by terror and no mass oppression of workers in England and America. So when the Communists in this country were bluntly ordered to take over the American Federation of Labor and actually tried to do so, the result was only to arouse the wrath of union leadership. There were very few American "peasants" to stir up, but Moscow ordered the party in this country to start stirring, nevertheless. These early failures would seem funny, but by 1935 the situation had been shrewdly analyzed. During the twenties the Russian revolutionary leaders were provincial and had little contact with—and virtually no understanding of—the outside world. This was quickly remedied, and when the delegates from the Communist Parties of the world assembled in Moscow to attend the Seventh World Congress of the Communist International, that organization was prepared to change its tactics to suit the situations in the various foreign countries. The Comintern Secretary, Georgi Dimitroff, read a long speech which described the new strategy to be used in inaugurating the United Front movement throughout the world, and the Trojan Horse tactic of heavily infiltrating non-Communist organizations, principally labor unions, with secret Communist Party members.

This was the beginning of the United Front. It was, as we have said, signalized by almost feverish party activity in the United States. Hundreds of front organizations sprang into existence to spread the party line, to disseminate Marxian propaganda, to create a corps of fellow travelers and to provide a medium through which new recruits could be added to the party membership. William Z. Foster, now the chairman of the Communist Party of the United States, has always led the fight to infiltrate American trade unions. He was the head of the Trade Union Unity League through which an attempt was made to carry out Moscow's orders for the taking over of the American Federation of Labor. Foster had been a Socialist, a member of the International Workers of the World, a labor organizer, a fomentor of strikes and riots, and has been a member of the Communist Party since the twenties. His Trade Union League (then known as the Trade Union Educational League) issued a statement of its program and principles in February, 1922, removing any lingering doubt about its political complexion, its adherence to the Profintern and its purposes so far as American labor was concerned. It read, in part, as follows:

"The Trade Union Educational League proposes to develop the trade unions from their present antiquated and stagnant condition into modern, powerful labor organizations, capable of waging successful warfare against capital. To this end it is working to revamp and to remodel from top to bottom their theories, tactics, structure and leadership. * * * *The league aggressively favors organization by industry instead of by craft.* Although the craft form of union served a useful purpose in the early days of capitalism, it is now entirely out of date. In the face of the great consolidations of the employers the workers must also close their ranks or be crushed. The multitude of craft unions must be amalgamated into a series of industrial unions—one each for the metal trades, railroad trades, clothing trades, building trades, etc.—even as they have been in other countries. The league also aims to put the workers of America in contact with the fighting trade unionists of the rest of the world. It is flatly opposed to our present pitiful policy of isolation, and it advocates affiliation to the militant international trade union movement, known as the Red International of Labor Unions. The league is campaigning against the reactionaries, incompetents, and crooks who occupy strategic positions in many of our organizations. It is striking to replace them with militants, with men and women unionists who look upon the labor movement not as a means for making an easy living, but as an instrument for the achievement of working class emancipation. In other words, the league is working in every direction necessary to put life and spirit and power into the trade union movement." (Committee's emphasis.)[36]

It was easy to see why Foster and his comrades were in favor of industrial organization. It was far easier to plant a small nucleus of concealed Communists in positions of control in a mass labor organization and thereby dominate its policies and conformance to the Communist party line than it was to infiltrate dozens of small trade unions and accomplish the same purpose in each. The Communist Party has never had sufficient members to waste their talents, and it has therefore invariably followed the strategy of patiently working its most talented members into positions of control where, in government, in education, in the entertainment world, in the creative arts, and in the trade unions, it can use a relatively tiny membership to control much larger non-Communist organizations.

This same technique has been employed in the Soviet domination of every Iron Curtain country, first the infiltration and softening up process, then the propaganda and conditioning of the masses, and then the sudden eruption of the party into open activity with its own trusted members running the vital processes of the government: education, communications, transportation, production of food stuff, the armed forces and the secret police. In the United States, as we shall see, this pattern has been followed religiously by the American Communists with remarkable zest in their relentless effort to be in a position to exercise the necessary strength when the revolutionary situation develops.

Revolutionary Situations

There was such a revolutionary situation that developed in the thirties, when a widespread depression swept the country and forced hundreds of thousands of unemployed on the relief roles. Immediately there was a surge of increased Communist activity. In San Francisco we saw it in the bloody general strike of 1934, and we continued to experience its influences with the operation of the State, County and Municipal Workers of America and the Workers Alliance collaborating with Labor's Non-partisan League to secure political control of the State in the general elections, and in the amazingly successful infiltration of many of our trade unions during the late thirties and early forties.

[36] American Trade Unionism, Principles and Organizations, Strategy and Tactics, by William Z. Foster, International Publishers, New York, 1947, p. 80, 81.

We need only cite, once, again (but we believe this cannot be hammered home with sufficient emphasis), the complete proof of great trade unions being forced to obey the international party line when the situation required such a change for the benefit of the Soviet Union. The non-aggression pact between the Soviet Union and Hitler was consummated in August of 1939. From that time until June 22, 1941, there was a spirit of friendliness and co-operation between the Germans and the Russians. Suddenly, with the signing of that pact, American labor unions that had been infiltrated by the Communists began to hamper the American defense effort. An epidemic of strikes spread across the country, and it is to be carefully noted that they were principally launched by the most strategic unions, those that had to do with the maritime industry, the production of critical ores and metals, the transportation of critical goods, the conduct of secret research projects along scientific lines, mass communications, and production of food stuffs. The party line was to keep America out of the war, to campaign against universal military service and draft, and to spread the Communist party slogan, "The Yanks Are Not Coming!"

Then on June 22, 1941, the German armies rolled across the borders of the Soviet Union. The nonaggression pact was violated, Russia was drawn into the conflict, and overnight the party line of the American Communists reversed itself. Now the slogan was for the immediate opening of a second front and an all-out effort on the part of the unions to produce the sinews of war in this country for the benefit of the Soviet Union. Immediately there was a significant serenity on the labor front. There were no more strikes such as the bloody affair at North American Aviation Company at Inglewood, which actually was being masterminded by the Communist Party from a strategic vantage point in Alameda County.

Let those who now naively contend that there is no more danger from the Communists in this country consider carefully the enormous influence the American Communists wielded in completely changing the attitude of these significant trade unions overnight when the exigencies of the Soviet Union demanded such a change. The power to summarily turn off a widespread epidemic of strikes that was beginning to paralyze the defense effort of the nation is certainly an indication that in the early forties the Communists of this country had made astounding progress in their infiltration of labor.

According to Foster, the Communist Party, the Young Communist League, and the Trade Union Unity League collaborated with a great many other Communist-dominated organizations for the purpose of staging unemployment demonstrations, strikes, hunger marches and pressure groups during the depression of the 1930's. Fifteen hundred delegates attended the national unemployed convention in Chicago during the summer of 1930; 400,000 demonstrated at the National Unemployment Insurance Day on February 25, 1931; 500,000 workers staged another demonstration in February, 1932, and in December, 1931, 1,800 delegates participated in a national hunger march to Washington, D. C., which was followed by a second demonstration of the same character on December 6, 1932, with 3,000 delegates in Washington and an estimated one million participants in various cities.[37]

"The strikes of 1934 to 1936," declared Foster, "took on the most acute political character of any in the history of the United States. Against the violent opposition of the A.F. of L. leaders, the political mass strike, long a cardinal point in the Communist Party's agitation, became an established weapon of the American working class. The workers fought with splendid heroism and solidarity in the face of the Government, tricky union leaders, and an unprecedented use of troops, police, gunmen, and vigilantes among them."[38]

It is a peculiar coincidence, and one that played into the hands of Communist organizers, that at the same the Seventh Congress of the Comintern was convened in the Soviet Union in 1935, the C.I.O. was launched in the United States. Here was just the type of industrial organization that William Foster had longed for. John L. Lewis, long noted for his vitriolic and forthright attacks against all things Communist, was now surrounded by concealed party members who flocked into the newly organized industrial movement by the hundreds. Fanning out through the top echelons of the organization shortly after its creation, these undercover party members dug themselves in tightly at the command posts and within a few years managed to so concentrate their influence that they forced John Lewis out of the organization he had created and took it over, lock, stock and barrel. All of the A.F. of L. unions that had been successfully infiltrated left that organization and aligned themselves with the C.I.O. The American Newspaper Guild not only affiliated but was to provide a member who, after working for a time on a Los Angeles newspaper, was elevated to command the entire C.I.O. organization on the Pacific Coast. By July, 1941, the C.I.O. Union membership stood at 4,000,000, was solidly entrenched in activities closely linked with our national security, and was actually more important to the vital interest of this country than the A.F. of L. from which it was spawned.

Following is a partial list of the unions that suffered particularly from Communist infection. We should note carefully how this handful of Communist organizers was able to get a stranglehold on segments of labor essential for the very preservation of our country through the techniques that were tried out in the Russian revolution of 1917, perfected by trial and error in the United States, and brought to a high degree of perfection following the Seventh Congress of the Comintern in 1935, and the penetration of the C.I.O. They were: National Maritime Union; Transport Workers Union; Aircraft and Machinists Division of the United Automobile Workers; Die-Casters Association; American Communications Association; International Longshoremen

---

[37] American Trade Unionism, op. cit., p. 192.
[38] American Trade Unionism, op. cit., p. 197.

and Warehousemens Union; International Woodworkers Union; American Newspaper Guild; United Electrical, Radio and Machinists Union; Farm Equipment Organizing Committee; State, County and Municipal Workers Union; United Tannery Workers Union; Packinghouse Workers Organizing Committee; Mine, Mill and Smelter Workers Union; United Office and Professional Workers Union; Book and Magazine Guild; Quarry Workers Union; Fishermens Union; Furniture Workers Union; sections of the United Federal Workers of America; Fur Workers Union; sections of the Aluminum Workers; Federation of Architects, Chemists, Engineers and Technicians; Artists Union; United Shoe Workers Union; Retail and Wholesale Workers, Local 65; Inland Boatmens Union; Marine Cooks and Stewards Union; United Cannery Agricultural, Packing and Allied Workers of America; C.I.O. Industrial Councils of Greater New York, Queens, Chicago, Cleveland, Milwaukee, Seattle, Portland, San Francisco, Los Angeles, Bridgeport, Baltimore, etc.; also, State Industrial Councils (C.I.O.) of Connecticut, California, Wisconsin, Texas, Washington; Alabama Farmers Union; Local 5 of Teachers Union, A.F. of L. (expelled); Local 537 College Teachers Union, A.F. of L. (expelled); A.F. of L. Painters District Council No. 9, New York; Workers Alliance; Gas & Chemical Workers Union.[39]

World Federation of Trade Unions

In February, 1945, representatives of 60,000,000 trade union members gathered in London and formed the World Federation of Trade Unions. During the latter part of the year an implementing meeting was held in Paris and an organization was set up comprising a president, a general secretary and three assistant general secretaries who presided over an elaborate hierarchy of subordinate organizations and departments. Permanent headquarters was established in Paris, and the movement got off to an enthusiastic start, supported mainly by the Soviet Union and its satellites. The C. I. O. was originally a member of the movement, but later withdraw and charged that the organization was Communist dominated from its inception. This was not difficult to detect, and as time went on evidence of complete Communist domination was overwhelming. The American Federation of Labor denounced the organization from its inception and representatives of the C. I. O., after attending a few meetings, arrived at the same conclusion.

The World Federation of Trade Unions operates through five bureaus. Bureau No. 1 comprises the countries of North and South America, Spain and Portugal; Bureau No. 2, the territories of Africa and the Mediterranean (Greece, Turkey, Syria, Lebanon, Palestine, Israel, Egypt and Cyprus); Bureau No. 3, the countries of Western Europe and the Scandinavian countries (including Iceland, Germany,

---

[39] The Red Decade; the Stalinist Penetration of America, by Eugene Lyons, the Bobbs-Merrill Co., New York, 1941, pp. 229, 230.

Austria, Switzerland and Italy); Bureau No. 4, the countries of the Middle East, Asia and Austro-Asian; Bureau No. 5, the Soviet Union, Czechoslovakia, Hungary, Yugoslavia, Albania, Rumania and Bulgaria. This form of organization, together with the activities of the W. F. T. U., corresponds roughly with the organizational structure and activities of the Red International of Trade Unions that operated as a subdivision of the Comintern. Close organizational and disciplinary ties are maintained with all left-wing unions throughout the world, and the effect of W. F. T. U. influence is particularly powerful in Mexico and the Latin American countries.

In earlier reports we have occasionally referred to Vicente Lombardo Toledano as the pro-Communist leader of the Mexican Federation of Workers. When Vice-President Nixon visited several South American countries a year ago he was insulted and harassed by organized demonstrations that reflected the assiduous infiltration and planning that was carried on in these countries through the joint efforts of the second Soviet Ambassador to the United States and Vicente Lombardo Toledano. Since 1945, the World Federation of Trade Unions has played a major part in this massive attempt to dominate the trade unions of the Latin American countries, and we believe that a description of the parts played in this operation by the Soviet Union, Vicente Lombardo Toledano of Mexico, and the World Federation of Trade Unions will not be amiss here since it points up the carefully synchronized collaboration that is always evident between Communist dominated elements.

Constantin Oumansky was the second Soviet Ambassador to the United States. He had been trained in the Red Army, was a specialist in intelligence operations, and had exhibited a peculiar flair for languages—being conversant with several, including Spanish. When it was announced that he would be transferred from his position as Ambassador in Washington and take a position as Ambassador to Mexico, most laymen considered it a demotion. As a matter of fact, it was quite the opposite since Oumansky was being groomed for a far more important assignment. When he arrived at Mexico City with his inordinately large staff, he made his initial speech to the assembled representatives of the Latin American countries and the rest of the diplomatic corps, and apologized to the Mexican people for his inability to address them in their native tongue. He said that he had been studying Spanish, and that on the next occasion he would address them in their own language, although somewhat imperfectly.

After the lapse of an appropriate period of time, Mr. Oumansky did deliver his second diplomatic address in somewhat halting Spanish, and received the undying admiration of the entire Latin American corps, not only because of his obvious ability in learning so much about their language in such a short space of time, but even more because he—unlike most of the other foreign diplomats—had taken the time and trouble to pay this gracious courtesy. From that time on Oumansky had very little difficulty in getting anything that he wanted within reason. Vicente Lombardo Toledano was a constant visitor to the Soviet Embassy, and he and Oumansky launched an organization known as the Confederation of Latin American Workers, patterned after the Federation of Mexican Workers. Units of this new organization were planted throughout the South American countries, and so successful was their penetration of mass trade union organizations throughout South America that both Toledano and Oumansky were called upon to make many trips for the purpose of addressing them and lending leadership and direction to their activities. One morning Oumansky was scheduled to leave the Mexico City Airport and fly to one of these conferences. As his plane circled to gain altitude above the city there was a violent explosion and it literally flew to pieces when it was about 400 feet from the ground. Everyone in the plane was killed. The origin and nature of the explosion were never determined.

Since the death of Oumansky the ostensible leader of the Confederation of Latin American Workers has been Mr. Toledano, who is also a Vice-President of the World Federation of Trade Unions. His Confederation of Mexican Workers sponsored the constitution of the Latin American organization in 1938 and has been the "determinate influence in the development of the Latin American labor movement." [40]

When some of the Communist dominated C. I. O. unions were investigated by the parent organization during the years extending from 1948 through 1950, and were expelled after extensive proceedings, they immediately affiliated themselves with the World Federation of Trade Unions. Those union organizations that were dealing in maritime activities were particularly eager to make this affiliation, and chief among them was the Marine Cooks & Stewards Union, which recently went out of business and reopened its activities again under non-Communist leadership. We have already referred to its former President, Hugh Bryson, as having been the statewide director for the Independent Progressive Party's political campaign in 1948, and who was thereafter convicted in a federal court for having sworn falsely concerning his collaboration with the Communist Party in this state. The Commission on Government Security, in its report issued in 1957, had this to say about the Marine Cooks & Stewards Union:

> "The Marine Cooks & Stewards Union in its own right today represents between three thousand and four thousand seamen serving in the mess halls, galleys, and dining rooms aboard vessels plying between the Pacific Coast and the Far East. The union, in addition to this source of strength and support, also has very close attachments and support from the International Longshoremen and Warehousemen's Union headed by Harry Bridges. In a recent issue of the union newspaper, when the leadership felt that threats were being

[40] Report of Activity of the World Federation of Trade Unions, 15 October, 1945-30 April, 1949. Presented to the Second World Trade Union Congress at Milan, 29 June-10 July, 1949, p. 91. 3 Rue des Cloys, Paris, XVIII.

made about the way it operated its hiring hall, President Bryson
called upon the owners and the government to take heed of the
fact that not only did they face the Marine Cooks & Stewards
Union members, but also the possible strike sanction of the Longshoremen of the West Coast, and, in addition, the possible strike
sanction of Longshoremen in South Africa, Australia, and other
countries where other Longshoremen's Unions are closely associated
with the World Federation of Trade Unions.'' [41]

Thus it will be seen that some of the unions formerly in the C. I. O.,
and expelled from that organization because they were found to be
Communist dominated, have since affiliated with the World Federation
of Trade Unions; and instead of securing a strike influence within
the relatively limited sphere of their former activity, they can now
be instrumental in launching strike activities throughout the entire
world.

Four years after the London meeting that created the World Federation of Trade Unions, another important international trade organization was established at a meeting in that city. Delegates came from
Africa, Asia, Europe, North and South America and the Carribean,
the only stipulation being that the workers in the countries represented
should be free to organize in unions of their own choice, and in some
instances in countries where freedom had been ground almost to ex-
tinction by the dictatorial nature of their governments. During the four
years that elapsed since the formation of the World Federation of Trade
Union and the 1949 meeting in London that we are now discussing,
a great many of the original members of the W. F. T. U. had become
convinced that the organization was simply another creature of the
world Communist movement and resigned in order to affiliate with the
International Confederation of Free Trade Unions. The latter organization is predominantly anti-Communist, is affiliated in a consultative
capacity with the United Nations and various regional economic commissions for Europe, Asia and Latin America, together with the International Labor Organization at UNESCO. Permanent representatives
are maintained at New York, Paris and Geneva, and the former President of the World Federation of Trade Unions, Mr. A. Deakin, of Great
Britain, is now serving as a vice-president of the International Confederation of Free Trade Unions. Those from North America who are
listed as members of the executive board are: G. Meany, W. P. Reuther,
D. MacDonald, C. Jodoin, J. L. Lewis, M. Woll, J. Potofsky, C. H.
Millard, P. R. Bengough, P. Kennedy, I. Brown, M. Ross, F. W. Dow-
ling, G. J. Cushing and J. Owens.

Permanent headquarters is located in Brussels manned by a staff of
about 70 persons, branch offices being maintained in Paris, Geneva,
New York, Brussels, Mexico and Calcutta. Trade union organizations
affiliated directly to the I. C. F. T. U. are to be found in: Austria, Belgium, the Basque Country (in exile), Cypress, Denmark, France, Ger-

⁴¹ Report of the Commission on Government Security. Public Law 304, Eighty-fourth
Congress, as amended, June, 1957, p. 329.

many, Great Britain, Greece, Iceland, Italy, Luxemburg, Malta, Netherlands, Norway, Sarr, Spain (in exile), Sweden, Switzerland, Trieste,
British Cameroons, Gambia, Gold Coast, Kenya, Libya, Madagascar,
Mauripius, Sierra Leone, Tunisia, Ceylon, China (Formosa), Hong
Kong, India, Japan, Korea, Malaya, Pakistan, Philippines, Singapore,
Thailand, Israel, Lebanon, Persia, Canada, Mexico, United States, Brit-
ish Honduras, Costa Rica, Panama, Barbados, Cuba, Dominica, Gra-
nada, Haiti, Jamaica, Puerto Rico, St. Kitts-Nevis, St. Lucia, St. Vin-
cent, Trinidad, Turks Islands, Argentina, Bolivia, Brazil, British
Guiana, Chile, Colombia, Ecuador, Falkland Islands, Peru, Surinam,
Uruguay, Venezuela, Australia and New Zealand.

These two great worldwide organizations, one pro-Communist and the
other anti-Communist, are pitted against each other in a struggle that
has received very little publicity, but which reaches into our own country and certainly into the pacific coast and California where its effects
are felt almost daily.

Philip M. Connelly

Probably the most influential single person in the state of California
insofar as the infiltration of trade unions was concerned is Philip M.
Connelly. At least Mr. Connelly's influence was the result of his publicly known positions, first in the American Newspaper Guild, and sec-
ondly in the C. I. O. high command in this state. During the early part
of his activities, especially in the Newspaper Guild, Connelly posed as a
convivial, innocuous, non-Communist, dedicated liberal. As he espoused
more and more partly line resolutions in Guild meetings, his fellow
members became more and more suspicious of his subversive inclina-
tions. As he participated actively in more and more Communist front
organizations, these suspicions were intensified, but Connelly rose from
mediocrity in the Newspaper Guild to one position of authority after
another. He ultimately became state C. I. O. president, and secretary
of the C. I. O. Council in Los Angeles. Connelly has been identified as
a Communist Party member by many witnesses. He has appeared as a
witness before this committee, and references to his activities and affiliations may be found in our reports as follows: 1951—pages 93, 255,
264; 1953—pages 76, 102, 172, 208, 280; 1955—pages 417, 418, 419.

No sooner had Connelly progressed to a position of authority in the
C. I. O., than he opened its doors throughout the state and admitted
hosts of Communist Party members, fellow travelers and sympathizers.
These, added to the numerous officials of the same political persuasion
who had managed to oust John L. Lewis from his position of authority,
so predominated the entire structure of the California C. I. O. during
the period immediately preceding, during and shortly after Connelly's
tenure, that some of these unions became integral parts of the Communist Party apparatus instead of orthodox trade union organizations.

Connelly received dubious notoriety in connection with the part he
played in the strike that paralyzed the production of military planes

for the defense of this government when the C. I. O. struck North American Aviation shortly before Hitler invaded the Soviet Union and the party line changed. He was excoriated by Los Angeles Municipal Judge Arthur Guerrin in March, 1946, and sentenced to serve 60 days after a jury had convicted him for inciting a riot, disturbing the peace, and violating a court order in conjunction with a strike at U. S. Motors in Los Angeles. He was represented by Leo Gallagher and John T. McTernan, whose names have been repeatedly mentioned in previous reports issued by this committee.

Connelly became eligible for parole in February, 1947, and wires asking clemency in his behalf were sent by Jeff Kibre, William Elconin, and William Brody—all identified as members of the Communist Party. Connelly was released in March, 1947, after having serving 50 days of his 60-day sentence. Among those who greeted him on his release were Joseph O'Connor, of the Marine Cooks & Stewards Union, William Axelrod of the Newsvendor's Union, John Daugherty, of the United Electrical Workers Union, Andrew Barrigan of the Newspaper Guild, and Connelly's wife, Dorothy, who, under the name Dorothy Healey, was then and is still chairman of the Los Angeles Communist Party. Connelly was again convicted in 1947 of driving while intoxicated and served another term at the Los Angeles County Sheriff's Honor Farm. Since his release he has been the Los Angeles editor of the Communist newspaper, the *Daily People's World*.

We cite all of this background material for the purpose of showing how the Communists managed to infiltrate a great trade union organization in this state a few years ago, and we hasten to emphasize that many of the unions then infiltrated and later expelled from the C.I.O. for that reason are still functioning under Communist domination and now constitute a serious threat to our national security and to the welfare of our state. These infiltrated unions that were expelled from their parent labor organizations are still operating under Communist control, and virtually all of them are dealing with industrial matters that are most essential to our continued defense. The International Longshoremens and Warehousemens Union; the American Communications Association; the United Public Workers of America; the United Mine, Mill & Smelter Workers; educational unions such as the Los Angeles Federation of Teachers which was expelled from the American Federation of Teachers because it was found to be Communist dominated—these, and a host of other critical organizations, all heavily infiltrated by Communists who are solidly entrenched at the top in positions of control—pose a constant threat to our continued welfare.

Public Utilities

A few years ago we undertook to find out what measures had been taken by our public utilities in order to protect themselves against Communist or other subversive infiltration. We found that whereas a major part of the aircraft manufacturing industry of the nation is located in southern California, and all of the machinery that actuates these plants is operated by electric energy, and despite the fact that these manufacturing concerns are required by their government contracts to take the most elaborate precautions to screen their personnel for security and to take detailed measures to safeguard the physical attributes of the plant by maintaining a guard services, fences and a system of identification—nevertheless the electric generating plants that provide the vital power for the operation of these enterprises were required to have no security protection whatever.

Each of these public utilities providing such vital necessities as telephonic and cable communications, gas, electrical energy and domestic water, had employed special agents for years, but they were not trained to handle the problem of subversive infiltration. To think that the Communist apparatus, with all of its elaborate machinery, would fail to take advantage of the opportunity to invade these wide open areas is ridiculous. A number of Communists and fellow-travellers *were* found employed in critical positions in many of these California public utilities. A series of conferences between representatives of this committee and representatives of the utilities were held, and as a result of these discussions a series of hearings was held in San Francisco and Los Angeles, and a number of employees were discharged.

Special agents were then employed who had been highly trained in this specialized field. Since that time the incidence of infiltration has sharply declined, although it is a constant problem and will continue to be so just as long as a Communist apparatus exists in the United States.

Anyone who has seen a Communist dominated strike in action realizes that it is quite a different matter than the strikes by non-Communist unions. Lenin once said that every strike is a tiny revolution, and to the Communist leaders these occurrences are not only disputes over wages and working conditions, but embraced a far greater and more deep-seated struggle between the workers on the one hand and the capitalists on the other. The Communist Party of the United States has always called itself the vanguard of the working class, and is always eager to seize the opportunity during a strike situation to propagandize, to recruit, to provoke violence on both sides, and to gnaw away more deeply into the vitals of the American capitalist system which they are dedicated to destroy. In the San Francisco general strike of 1934, in the North American Aviation strike shortly before World War II, in the San Joaquin Valley cotton strikes that were accompanied by angry mobs of rioting workers led by Communist exhorters, in the strike at Warner Bros. studio—and even at the lesser strikes which resulted in the jailing of Philip Connelly and which we have already discussed—undercurrents of viciousness, of hatred toward all non-Communists, and especially the employers, was most discernible. There is a little-known and an exceedingly rare document concerning the San Francisco strike which contains a statement by the Communist

Party and discloses how it was actually fomented and directed by the party. The North American Aircraft strike was directed by Wyndham Mortimer, Philip Connelly, Paul Crouch, and other Communist Party members. Crouch has testified concerning his participation in this matter and has given abundant testimony to establish the Communist direction of this paralysis of one of the nation's most vital aircraft factories. The strikes in the San Joaquin Valley, accompanied by so much violence and bloodshed, were spearheaded by carefully selected Communist agitators and organizers sent from San Francisco and Los Angeles expressly for the purpose of creating class struggle and taking advantage of the depression by developing it into a "revolutionary situation."

The committee has evidence of Communist propagandists smearing babies' faces with molasses in order to take photographs of the flies crawling over the infants' faces, then circulating these photographs for the purpose of arousing the resentment of members of the Workers Alliance and migratory agricultural workers who were living in federal migratory labor camps operated by the United States Department of Agriculture. At that time, as will be seen in a later section of this report, the department was loaded with Communists. The strike at Warner Bros. studios was the subject of prolonged prosecution and litigation during which the Communist nature of the strike leaders was established. Strikes by Communist-dominated unions are unique because they are weapons in the class struggle, and they achieve a special quantity of frenzied hatred and venom that is ominous to behold.

At the writing of this report the Communist Party of the United States has pledged itself to redouble its efforts to infiltrate American labor. This is bound to have extreme repercussions in California, because California and New York are running neck and neck so far as Communist activity is concerned. Until a few years ago the Party organization in New York was far stronger, California being second. Insofar as we can ascertain this is still the case, except that as the population of California has increased and as this state has achieved a more strategic importance insofar as its defense industry and geographic location are concerned, more and more Communist Party members have been transferred from the East and from the mid-West to work among us and two prime goals being the infiltration of labor and education, in that order. In order to document this development, let us see what the Communist Party itself has to say.

As recently as August, 1958, the National Committee of the Communist Party of the United States declared:

> "The Communists strive to win the trade unions to a more consistent program of class struggle and militant action in defense of the immediate interests of the working class. To achieve these objectives they join with other Left forces in the ranks of labor.

* * * In the shops, a growing number of militant workers are shedding their anti-Communist prejudices, and are ready to unite with all forces, including the Left, to fight the company attacks.

* * * *Thousand of union stewards, shop chairmen and other leaders, received their training in the art of organization at the hands of Communists. Much of what was once considered part of the Communists' program has been taken over by the labor movement and thousands were at one time or another members of the Communist Party and contributed to the advance of the trade union movement as Communists.* (Committee's emphasis.)

Yet, while the past year has witnessed a significant reaffirmation of individual liberty by the federal courts and public opinion, trade union leadership still persists in its denial of the right of legal existence to Communists and Left-wingers. Paradoxically, though the trade unions have played an important part in rolling back the McCarthyite ties, they have in this respect succumbed to its vicious influence.

Today, however, our strength and relative position in the trade unions are greatly reduced. It is a difficult matter again to play a role in the labor movement in the spirit of past traditions. The long period of persecution, compounded by our own errors, and the ravages of two years of bitter internal struggle, have had their effects."[42]

There had already been an article in the previous issue of this magazine which, it will be remembered, carries the authentic national Communist Party line month by month, entitled, "On the Communist Party's Political Resolution," by an author who simply signed himself "An American Professor." This anonymous pundit declared that he was not a Communist, and then he made an elaborate analysis of the main political resolution adopted at the national convention of the Communist Party of the United States held in February, 1957. He said, in part, " * * * The theme that dominates the report is the problem of the formation of an anti-monopoly people's party in which American labor would eventually assume a role of leadership." The writer urges development of a national front rather than a popular front; he said the convention should have openly supported Soviet intervention in Hungary, and praised the goal of widespread Marxian education in America.[43]

General Secretary Eugene Dennis of the Communist Party, declared in the August issue of *Political Affairs* that:

"It is through struggle that the working class will come to recognize its true leaders, and repudiate those in labor's top officialdom who helped pave the way for pro-Fascist reaction—for the Taft-Hartley Act and the wage freeze, as well as for the Smith

[42] A Policy for American Labor, by the National Committee of the Communist Party of the United States. *Political Affairs*, Aug., 1958, p. 11.
[43] *Political Affairs*, April, 1958, p. 42.

Act. Nor is it excluded that some reformist labor leaders will themselves 'reform' as the struggle sharpens. We should draw some conclusions from the action taken by certain leaders of the Amalgamated Clothing Workers, to rally the organization and members of that union behind the Sabath bill to repeal the McCarran Act.

Trade-union struggle will go on, in spite of internal 'purges' and F. B. I. 'screening' of the workers in industry. It is going on right now in the maritime industry, and there will be other struggles, other strikes—no matter how many Communists go to jail." [44]

In other reports we have described how Communists in the vital field of communications were found entrenched in the employ of California's public utilities, as well as in the employ of other concerns whose scopes of operation were equally vital. For example, a person under Communist discipline employed in the long distance toll department of a communications concern is obviously in an important position, as is an employee whose knowledge of the overall operation of the concern provides him with the facility to disrupt the entire network. Thus the American Communications Association, heretofore described as having been expelled from its parent organization because it was found to be Communist dominated, is the certified bargaining agent for more than 5,000 employees of the Western Union Telegraph Company in New York City alone, and also approximately 200 employees of the Western Union Cable Company in the same area, and for Radio Corporation of America communications on the West Coast, principally in California and Washington.

The Western Union Telegraph Company maintains its chief office for the transaction of business in its building at 60 Hudson Street, New York City. To this communications network radiate circuits from all major cities in the United States, and a majority of its employees handle messages which flow from various government agencies by the telegraph circuit highlines which connect the main Western Union office with its agencies. This majority of employees is also under the control of the American Communications Association. Some of the more important circuits serviced in this manner are: The United States Defense Department's Signal Center of the First Army Headquarters, Fort Wadsworth; United States Naval Air Station at Floyd Bennett Field, Brooklyn, New York; New York Port of Embarkation, Brooklyn, New York; United States Naval Shipyards, Brooklyn, New York; Sea Transport Station, Atlantic Division, Piers 1, 2, 3, and 4; United States Navy Communications Service, 90 Church Street, New York; Governor's Island and Fort Jay, Second Service Command. [45]

Since these are only a few of the more important government agencies on the east coast which are tied in with comparable agencies on

[44] *Political Affairs*, op. cit., Aug. 1951, p. 9.
[45] Scope of Communist Activity in the United States, part 44, hearings of United States Senate Internal Subcommittee, 1951-1956.

the west coast, it is a very simple matter to understand how a Communist-dominated union that has hundreds of its members employed in this communications system can pose a constant threat to internal security, and it also enables us to understand more clearly why it is important for all public utilities in the critical field to be on the constant alert to protect the public and the nation against subversive infiltration of their facilities. Mr. E. I. Hageman, national President of the Commercial Telegraphers Union, Western Union Division, A. F. L.-C. I. O., Washington, D. C., told the Internal Security Subcommittee that the American Communications Association was still dominated by a group of Communists at the top who managed to perpetuate themselves in positions of control by a system of appointing shop stewards instead of electing them, of rigging a constitution that allows this sort of captivity to be accomplished, and an apathetic membership that suffers such conditions to continue. Hageman declared, " * * * If the Soviet espionage system had access to a hard-core Commie in a telegraph office, there is no question but that they could get information which might be valuable."

This conclusion is, of course, crystal clear, and applies to every public utility that deals with any activity vital to public welfare and security.

Within the past five years every major public utility in California has provided itself with a sound, adequate, efficient group of highly-trained experts in counter-subversion in security matters to take all necessary measures for the purpose of protecting the utility and the public against just this type of infiltration. In a later section of this report we will describe how even the most elaborate protective systems can never be infallible, and we will endeavor to set forth in detail the techniques by which the Communist Party is now sending its most trusted and highly disciplined members into our schools, our universities, our trade union organizations, our public utilities, and many other phases of American life.

Statement by George Meany

We have already set forth a brief description of the two great international labor organizations, the Soviet-dominated World Federation of Trade Unions on the one hand, and the International Confederation of Free Trade Union Organizations on the other. On the domestic scene it is comforting to know that Mr. George Meany, President of the A.F.L.-C.I.O. in the United States, has consistently been an implacable, emphatic and active opponent of Communism, both foreign and domestic, although he pointed out in a recent speech to the members of an F.B.I. Academy that an American Communist is simply a member of an international organization working in this country. Mr. Meany's attitude toward Communism was so forthrightly expressed on such an appropriate occasion and has so much practical effect on labor organizations in this state, that we deem it appropriate to quote from the address mentioned above. Addressing the fifty-seventh graduating class of law enforcement officers at the F.B.I. National Academy in the United States Department of Justice Auditorium, Washington, D. C., Mr. Meany said, in part, that:

"Since the close of World War I, human freedom and individual diginity—which are the very essence of the American way of life—have made much progress in some countries. But human liberty and decency have also been increasingly menaced by a new enemy. This foe of freedom is a total enemy of all of our cherished values and individual dignity. His enmity to free institutions is organized on a total basis. His movements and activities, aspirations and actions are totalitarian in nature. The common aim of all totalitarian governments—whether they be Communist, Nazi, Fascist, Falangist, Peronist or Titoist—is to grab all power for the total destruction of all free institutions and freedom and for the setting up of a dictatorship. This dictatorship is to have total power over every human being in every phase of life—political, economic, cultural, spiritual and what-not.

That such a dictatorship leads to the horrible debasement of society, to outraging every human value, to savage brutality instead of rule by law, was most painfully dramatized in the latest revelations by Khrushchev regarding some of the crimes committed under the instructions of his late mentor and master, Stalin.

Of course, these various totalitarian enemies here and there—or now and then—in the degree of the total power they actually achieve and exercise. They never differ in the degree of total power they would like to wield over the people.

In varying degrees, these sworn enemies of all our democratic institutions pose as militant radicals. They use high-sounding phrases to hide their objectives. But none of them is actually progressive or really radical. One may be a reactionary without being totalitarian. But no one can be totalitarian without being reactionary. There is nothing as retrogressive, as ultra-reactionary, as the totalitarian party organization—or front—whether it be of the red, brown, black or yellow hue.

The Communist brand of dictatorship is—in many respects—the most subtle, sinister and dangerous enemy of freedom. It demagoguely poses as a higher form of democracy. It poses as a political movement, though it is anything but a political party in the normal democratic sense as we know it and live it. Furthermore, it operates as a worldwide conspiracy, as a fifth column, in every free country—with its head and heart in Moscow.

The only patriotism the Communist knows is loyalty to the clique or despot who happens to be at the helm of the Russian dictatorship at any particular moment.

That is why we of American labor have always said: *There are no American Communists—there are only Communists in*

America. These subversives are fanatical believers in the doctrine that their end—Soviet world domination—justifies any and every means.

In view of the illusions some people who specialize in wishful thinking now have about the Soviet orbit moving towards democracy, it is most urgent that we take a sober and realistic look at the Communist 'new look' and 'big smile' tactics. You need no agitation or explanation from me on this score. The Communist criminals, like other dangerous criminals, are no less dangerous when they are well-masked. In fact, when they are well-masked they are even more dangerous. Political subversives who seek to rob the American people of their liberties, are not good citizens or gentlemen merely because they say they are for freedom, or merely because they wear kid gloves in the process of their criminal operations. Well-masked, fully camouflaged Communists, do not make the face of Communism less ugly or its aim less sinister.

Any system of government in which *a party is the government* —particularly when there is only one party with absolute power over every walk of life—*cannot be government by law. And without government by law, there can be no freedom.*

No confessions in New York, no self-denunciation in Prague or Warsaw, no revelations in Moscow, no popular front or united front maneuver can alter this proof. Where the *Party* is the State and has all power, there tyranny is unbridled. Tyranny cannot be reformed. It must be abolished.

Perhaps the most important reason why Communism is the most dangerous totalitarian enemy of human liberty and human decency is because the Communist conspiracy has chosen the ranks of labor for their principal field of activity. The Communists have made the capture of the trade unions their main purpose and the chief road to the seizure of power.

In modern industrial society, in the days of large-scale production and automation—on the threshold of the atomic age—control of the trade unions by Communists would enable the agents of a hostile foreign power to subvert our economic life, impose industrial paralysis on the land and establish a firm foundation for overthrowing our democratic government and replacing it with a dictatorship over all our people—including the workers. This is exactly what happened in Czechoslovakia.

In our own country and in every other land outside the Iron Curtain, the Communist Party and its network of front outfits are a dangerous military installation of a hostile foreign power. Here we have a subversive conspiracy, a fifth column, employing the camouflage of a national political party and masquerading as a movement of social reform.

Can you imagine what chance democracy would have in present day Germany, if the trade unions of the Federal Republic had fallen into Communist hands? Imagine what could happen to human freedom in our own country if the Communists were in control of the A. F. L. - C. I. O. Consider the frightening instability of democracy in France and you will find it is, in small measure, due to the fact that the Communists have won commanding positions in the trade unions of that country.

Here, I must add that thanks largely to the special activities of American labor in support of the democratic free trade union organizations in Italy and France, the Communist grip on labor has been shaken there. These Soviet agents can no longer call the paralyzing political general strikes they used to inflict on the people of France and Italy.

We of American labor approach this Communist program and face the Communist menace as citizens and as trade unionists. We fight this enemy unrelentingly, without a letup. We don't fall for any of the Communists' maneuvers, because we do not believe in doing business with them—on a partnership or any other basis. We fight this enemy with the philosophy of democracy. We fight Communism with practical deeds as well as hard-hitting publications in many tongues. We expose their fallacies and frauds and put Communism in its proper and ugly light by comparing its Soviet paradise with our human American institutions and achievements. They are not always perfect—but they *are* always getting better.

If you will take a look at the Communists in our country or in any other country, on either side of the Iron Curtain, you will see that we are under constant bitter attack. This obviously because our policies and activities really hurt the enemies of freedom everywhere.

Our philosophy as American citizens is that democracy and dictatorship cannot mix. The one is the very opposite of the other. They have nothing in common. They negate each other.

"Our philosophy as trade unionists is that without democracy there can be no free trade unions and without free trade unions there can be no democracy.

To us of American labor, freedom is not only an ideal but a most vital and vested interest. That is why we do not go in for delegation exchanges with Moscow, Peiping, Warsaw or Bucharest. We have nothing to get from them and nothing to sell them. Not until there are free trade unions in these countries will there be freedom in these lands. As we see it, not until the Russians are free to visit each other and exchange opinions and have freedom of communication with each other will it be possible for Russians or Americans to correspond or communicate freely with each other and really get to know each other. That applies to cabinet members and military experts no less than to union officials.''

And in conclusion, Mr. Meany said:

"As we see it, Communism is no longer 'a spectre' in the sense Karl Marx once spoke of it. Communism has become a deadly reality. Millions of Russians, Chinese, Poles, Germans, Balts and others whose unmarked graves have yet to be revealed—tell only a very small part of the gruesome story of the transformation of Communism from spectre to reality. The curse of Communism is not 'cult' of the individual but Communism itself. It is the cult of Communism which is the enemy we face and must vanquish. I am confident American labor will adhere to its principles of devotion to freedom and our free institutions above all else. As long as Communism adheres to the doctrine of world subversion and domination, the Communist powers will constitute a real threat to the way of life, to the progress and even to the very survival of our Country and every other free country. As long as any government is totalitarian, that is—as long as it denies to its own people the enjoyment of democratic liberties, no real and enduring peace—based on genuine mutual trust, can be achieved through agreements with that government.

In our own midst, at home as well as abroad, the Communists have also redoubled their talk of coexistence with the rest of us. In the name of the 'Geneva spirit,' the Communists and their dupes are now calling for an end to every legal effort to curtail their subversive activities and their efforts to infiltrate our free institutions. The Communists like nothing better and want nothing as much as to be given a free hand to use our democratic liberties for the purpose of subverting and destroying our democratic society.

In the interest of self-preservation, governments and societies founded on the principles of liberty must protect themselves by taking measures against subversive movements and their activities. He is no liberal who does not believe in safeguarding democracy and its liberal institutions. True liberalism is the very opposite of every brand of totalitarianism."

The next section of this report will deal with the Communist infiltration of the motion picture industry, and there we shall see how the Teamsters Union was infiltrated during the middle twenties for the purpose of gaining control of everything that moved on wheels within the studio. This powerful organization, the Teamsters Union, has been much in the press during the past several months due to the prosecution and conviction of former president Dave Beck and the congressional investigation of his successor, James Hoffa, because of his associations and activities with known criminals. It is then interesting to note that as recently as June 20, 1958, members of the Teamsters' Union and representatives of the Harry Bridges' International Longshoremens and Warehousemens Union met at the Hotel Statler in Los Angeles to discuss the possibility of co-operating for their mutual benefit. There have been rumors that these two great organizations intend to join forces. A representative of the Teamsters declared after the meeting that, "Our local unions have the necessary autonomy to enter agreements and organize common fronts with whomever they choose."[46]

A similar statement was issued in July, 1958, by representatives of the International Longshoremens and Warehousements Union. The Communist newspaper declared that it understood an organizing meeting of Canadian and American trade unions would soon be held at Windsor, Canada, to lay the ground for a gigantic drive to organize all transportation unions including the Teamsters, Dockers, Seamen, Clerks, members of the National Maritime Union and members of the International Longshoremens and Warehousemens Unions.[47]

The Statler Hotel meeting was under the direction of Louis Goldblatt who represented the ILWU as its secretary-treasurer, and who has also been identified as a Communist Party member by several witnesses who appeared before this and other legislative committees.[48]

This move to amalgamate the Teamsters' Union under the leadership of James Hoffa and the International Longshoremens and Warehousemens Union under the leadership of Harry Bridges and Louis Goldblatt is the most recent major development in California involving unions that are Communist infiltrated, and one that is actually Communist controlled. Since the Teamsters control everthing that moves on wheels, and the ILWU controls a large part of transportation by water, the implications of such an unholy wedlock to the security of the United States is too manifest to need further amplification.

At the last meeting of the National Committee of the Communist Party of the United States all of the emphasis was on the infiltration of American trade unions and American educational institutions. It is now being implemented by direct action. For those who wish further documentation to fully corroborate this conclusion, we refer them to *Political Affairs* for August, 1958, page 11; *National Review*, January 31, 1959, page 491; *Political Affairs*, April, 1958, page 42.

INFILTRATION OF THE MOTION PICTURE INDUSTRY

In 1934 a considerable sum of money was sent by the Soviet Commissar for Heavy Industry, who was then registered at the Claremont Hotel in Berkeley, to a Communist contact in Hollywood. This sum was to be used for the purpose of creating an entering wedge into the motion picture industry. No immediate effort was made at that time to recruit movie stars or technicians into the party, the entire attention of the Communists being concentrated on capturing key trade

---

[46] *Los Angeles Times,* June 18, 1958.
[47] *Daily Worker,* August 3, 1958.
[48] See The Alliance of Certain Racketeer and Communist Dominated Unions in the Field of Transportation as a Threat to National Security, report by the Subcommittee to Investigate the Administration of the Internal Security Act and Other Internal Security Laws to the Committee on Judiciary of the United State Senate, Eighty-fifth Congress, 2d Session, December 17, 1958.

unions. This was the procedure laid down by the Comintern and later set forth in textbooks of the Communist Party. Strong Communist factions were planted and maintained in almost every Hollywood trade union that had jurisdiction over anything in the motion picture studios. The Communist Party working in Hollywood wanted control over everything that moved on wheels—sound trucks, camera platforms, transportation of equipment and personnel to and from locations, and even the tray-dollies in the cafeterias. They soon moved Communist units into those unions having jurisdiction over carpenters, painters, musicians, grips, and electricians. To control these trade unions was to control the motion picture industry.

Next in importance to the Hollywood trade unions working in the industry were the writers, script men and the other professionals having to do with the actual story writing and the production of motion picture plays.

This infiltration, as we pointed out in our 1943 report, pages 93-94, was accompanied by a system of blacklisting for members who had openly opposed Communism or the Communist cliques, and many highly skilled individuals were unable to secure employment because, during these early days of the invasion, they presumed to oppose Communism.

The Painters' Union was captured. So was the Screen Writers Guild, to some extent. The Screen Actors Guild fought so hard to keep out of the Communist clutches that it fell into the pudgy arms of the late Willie Bioff, the mobster from the east who muscled into a top position in the International Association of Theatrical and Stage Employees. After Bioff was convicted for trying to bribe certain studio executives, the Communists renewed their attack and for years the writers were heavily infiltrated. They would have succumbed long ago were it not for the stout resistance of a group of determined, capable, hardhitting patriots who are still very much aware of the never-ending menace.[49]

There was a nucleus of confirmed Marxists already on the Hollywood scene when the Commissar sent the Soviet money to his contact— a Communist who is now working elsewhere but still in the trade union field. Some were writers like John Howard Lawson, who had become fired up with revolutionary fuel in the pro-Communist League of American Writers and has been hissing along under a full head of steam ever since; some were actors like Morris Cornovsky who had been infected in the John Reed Clubs and the Group Theatre.

In its dingy little rooms at 126 West Sixth Street, Los Angeles, the Communist Party issued directions and appointed activists to assist in the task of infiltration, indoctrination and recruiting. Late in July, 1941, this committee questioned Jack Moore, then Secretary of the Los Angeles Communist Party. Since that time many legislative committees—both state and federal—have inquired into the subversive penetration of the glamorous realm of motion pictures, but Jack Moore is

---

[49] See 1943 committee report: also The Red Decade, op. cit., pp. 284-289.

the first highly qualified, authoritative party official to discuss the matter under oath. His testimony was not long or detailed in this regard, but it was crystal clear, solid and unequivocal.

"Q. (by Mr. Combs): Do you know whether or not, Mr. Moore, the Communist International has laid down a policy of capturing, since the May convention, industry; was a method laid down for propagandizing?

"A. No, I don't recall that they ever laid down such a policy.

"Q. I read from the same treatise, page 44, entitled: 'Means of Ideological Influences (a) The Nationalization of Plants; (b) the Monopoly of Book Publishing.'

"The Witness: Pardon me, may I ask a question?

"Mr. Combs: Certainly.

"The Witness: Isn't this the record of the organization of Socialists as it was in Russia after the revolution?

"Mr. Combs: This is 'The Policy and Program of the Communist International.'

"The Witness: It isn't the record of the organization of Socialists?

"Mr. Combs: No (continuing to read): '(c) The Nationalization of Big Cinema Enterprises, Theatres, etc.; (d) The Utilization of the Nationalized Means of Intellectual Production for the Most Extensive Political and General Education of the Toilers and for the Building Up of a New Socialist Culture on a Prolitarian Class Basis.'

"Q. Mr. Moore, do you know whether any efforts have been made in Los Angeles County to get members into the motion picture industry through the craft unions or the trade unions?

"A. In every other industry, too.

"Q. Now, let's limit it in this instance.

"A. The Communist Party tries to recruit members—the motion picture industry as well as other industries. Naturally, we are interested in industrial workers wherever they may be.

"Q. That effort has been made in this Country?

"A. Of course.

"Q. With the motion picture industry?

"A. Yes."

Now, of course, we are quite aware that there was a heavy attempt by the Communists to secure enough control in the industry to eventually use pictures as vehicles for propaganda; to tie up studios by paralyzing strikes; to adorn front organizations with the names of naive stars as bait to attract others. But what else did Mr. Moore tell us? He declared that this program was in accord with a directive issued by the Comintern in Moscow and implemented by obedient action on the part of the Communist Party in Los Angeles County.

John Leech was one of the early functionaries who preceded Moore by several years. He broke with the party and gave a Los Angeles County Grand Jury a voluminous statement naming hundreds of motion picture luminaries from whom he had personally received Communist Party dues. Max Silver came several years after Moore, served as secretary of the party, also dropped out of Communist activities and has testified concerning the same matters. He didn't drop quite as far as Leech, however. Not yet, at least. The Leech document is monumental, has never been made public, and probably never should be. Many of the persons named completely broke with Communism years ago, while others are still active in the underground and unaware that their earlier connections have already been revealed.

The John Reed Club, the Pen and Hammer, the American League for Peace and Democracy, the Joint Anti-Fascist Refugee Committee, the various Soviet Friendship Leagues, and the perennial committees to shore up civil liberties were the first Communist fronts in Hollywood. Then came a host of cultural organizations, then a group for the support of Loyalists during the Spanish Revolution, then the anti-Nazi fronts that sprang up overnight when the Germans violated the non-aggression pact and invaded the USSR on June 22, 1941.

During the era of the first united front, 1935-1945, these fronts multiplied with great rapidity into an intricate and confusing Red network. They had interlocking directorates, traded their mailing lists, exchanged their speakers, aided each other financially, faithfully followed the party line, and were carefully synchronized and manipulated by the local Communist officials from their drab offices on West Sixth Street.*

Some of these fronts were huge. The Hollywood Anti-Nazi League had 4,000 members; the motion picture Democratic Committee, 1,700. Sometimes two or more of the largest fronts joined forces to stage a public affair to exploit a new twist in the party line, raise funds and propagandize. Even by Hollywood standards these affairs were colossal. Usually held at the Embassy Auditorium at Ninth and Grand, these functions jammed the hall with several thousand people. There were impressive settings, klieg lights, a glittering array of stars and rabble-rousing speakers who scoffed and sneered at our American institutions, inflamed racial minority groups, painted ominous pictures of the impending collapse of civil liberties, damned the FBI and legislative committees as Fascist, and sang the praises of the Soviet Union and the party line.

Hundreds of thousands of dollars were collected at these colorful affairs. The agents who covered them were invariably struck by the general resemblance—as to technique—to the Gerald L. K. Smith meetings and newsreel pictures of similar mass meetings held abroad during the war by comparable movements. Throughout the period of the first

---

* Los Angeles Communist Party Headquarters is now located at 524 South Spring Street.

united front these organizations flourished and multiplied, and were enthusiastically supported by prominent film personalities.

During the war Russia muffled the American Communists. We were pouring lend-lease material into that country, taking the pressure off the Eastern front, and flexing our capitalist muscles on behalf of our Communist ally. So that ally deemed it best not to irritate us with the usual subversive actions of its agents in our midst. The Communist-dominated unions turned off the strikes, the fronts reoriented themselves in support of our war effort, and party activity was slipped down into a lower gear.

Then came the battle to oust Communists from their positions of control in the industry shortly after the war was over. A series of hearings was held by this committee, followed by others before congressional committees. The fronts were exposed, the names of the members were published, the Communist control was unmasked and the picture industry began to clean its own house. In 1943, the late James McGuinness, staunch foe of everything subversive and of Communism in particular, started the Motion Picture Alliance for the Preservation of American Ideals. Head of the story department at M. G. M., and highly respected throughout the industry, McGuinness soon put together a hard-hitting and influential organization. Typical of the other members were Sam Wood, John Wayne, Borden Chase, Ward Bond, Adolphe Menjou, Roy Brewer, and scores of prominent writers, directors, actors and technicians. All were and are dedicated to the task of ridding their industry of insidious penetration by Communists.

During the late thirties and early forties V. J. Jerome made several trips to California from New York in his capacity as chief of the party's Cultural Commission. Copies of telegrams that passed between Communist officials immediately before and after his visits show how each was followed by a rash of new activity in the process of subverting Hollywood. As the writer, John Howard Lawson, was moved into position as Jerome's California representative, the boss made fewer trips. Lawson's Communist record has been thoroughly covered in previous reports following his appearance before us several years ago. He has spent much of his time in the east since being exposed, but as this portion of the report is being written he is back with us once more.

By 1945 the infiltration had reached alarming proportions. Once secure in their positions of authority the Communists employed the old technique of promoting each other and smothering everyone else. Just as they had applied this ruthless tactic in the political arenas, the universities and the trade unions, and in the wartime agencies of government, they now utilized it in their penetration of the motion picture industry. When they were exposed, forced to resort to the Fifth Amendment, and were unseated from their vantage places, these Communists pictured themselves as the innocent victims of a blacklist. The difference, of course, was one so very simple that many people accustomed to thinking in more complicated terms failed to grasp it.

The Red Blacklist

The Communists themselves blacklisted all non-Communists because they were operating as agents in a world crusade directed by the international headquarters at Moscow, and this operation was one phase of that crusade. All Communists are imbued with the hate motive of the class struggle and they were carrying out their role in the plan by promoting each other in an attempt to control a vital propaganda medium. The loyal Americans who opposed and exposed them were prompted by patriotism. Yet the latter were accused of blacklisting the former.

By this twisted thinking, every F. B. I. agent who does his duty in removing a Communist from a sensitive government position and thereby protecting his country against espionage, is accused of fostering a blacklist because the subversive employee is flushed out of his position. And every legislative committee that exposes subversive infiltration participates in the blacklist because employers are reluctant to hire people who hate capitalism and are dedicated to the destruction of our government by every foul and unfair means at their command. But this sort of twisted thinking is typical of Communists, and they have used it to convince a great many confused liberals.

Now the plain truth is that in the process of advancing each other and choking all non-Communists, the Party is operating the vilest blacklist of all time. Ask the active anti-Communist professor or trade unionist who has been smeared, undermined, stifled in his work and called a McCarthyite Fascist.

But we are dealing here with motion pictures, so let us examine another actual case. In a major studio a picture was being made that was to achieve Academy Award stature. The producer, director and writer were party members. One of them has since dropped out of all Communist activity. The director was receiving $2,500 per week, and our reports mention him 34 times in connection with Communist affiliations and activities. He taught at the Communist school in Los Angeles—then known as the People's Educational Center. There he met two other party members who needed studio jobs.

During his attendance at the young Communist organization, then known as American Youth for Democracy, this $10,000 per month director met a third party member—also in need of work as a writer.

At meetings of the Progressive Citizens of America, a Communist cultural front, the director discovered four more Communists.

The two teachers from the Communist school went to work at the director's studio. One of them started at $500 a week and was quickly raised to $600 and then $750. The young Communist organization workers sold a 20-page story to the same studio for $25,000. And the front activists went to work at the studio at the insistence of the same director at salaries ranging from $500 to $1,400 per week. As we have said, all were Communists and, with a single exception, far less capable than the non-Communists who were rejected for the same positions.

At the same time, at the same studio, a well-known and thoroughly competent writer contemplated the high salaries being paid this squadron of Red invaders and asked for a $100 raise. He was an anti-Communist, and he was promptly undermined and fired. Thus another vacancy was created. His place was filled by another invader who was immediately given a $750 raise over his original $250 per week salary.

There were many such cases. At RKO the head of the music department refused to use Hanns Eisler as the composer for a picture—simply because he was musically inept. But, Hanns, a Communist, was the brother of Gerhardt Eisler—Comintern boss in the United States, and the producer of the picture was also a Communist. So Hanns Eisler got the job.

By 1945 the infiltration had progressed to the point where propaganda was beginning to appear in pictures and the industry was literally teeming with Communists. So secure was the control of key unions that the party bosses at the headquarters on West Sixth Street decided to make a bold move. They sanctioned a strike at Warner Bros. studio. The Conference of Studio Unions actually manned the picket lines and comprised the painters, set designers, sign writers, screen cartoonists and office employees. The left-wing control of the conference was openly headed by one Herb Sorrell, a large and muscular man with a most aggressive attitude. He has appeared before us and we have heretofore published his record of subversive connections. We have also taken the testimony of two prominent handwriting experts who have authenticated his signature on a Communist membership book.

There was much violence at Warner Bros. during this strike; an average of 50 patients per day were treated at emergency first aid stations; public sidewalks and streets were blocked by 2,500 pickets in the face of a court order against any such mass demonstration. Police cars were upset when they approached the scene—uniformed officers trapped inside. It soon developed that the strikers were represented by a battery of Communist lawyers, Frank Pestana, Ben Margolis, Charles Katz, and Leo Gallagher, all repeatedly identified by witnesses as Communist Party members.

As sheriff's deputies moved in to enforce the court order and prevent the bloody incidents that were occurring with increasing frequency and viciousness; as the strike leaders and their counsel were identified as Communists, the strike lost impetus and sputtered out.

In November, 1950, the National Executive Board of the AFL Painters' Union announced the results of its searching investigation into the affair and declared that Sorrell had "willfully and knowingly associated with groups subservient to the Communist Party line" [50] and ordered him not to hold any union office for five years and not to attend any union meetings during that period. In February, 1952, Sorrell's local union was dissolved and he dropped out of all union activities.[51]

---

[50] Report of National Executive Board, AFL Painters' Union, Lafayette, Ind., Nov., 1950.
[51] *Los Angeles Times*, Feb. 15, 1952.

As resistance to the Red invasion stiffened and as more legislative committees continued to flush out and expose hidden Communists, many courageous former party members scorned to invoke the Fifth Amendment and aided their industry, their state and their country in cooperating fully to combat the infiltration. Witnesses like Edward Dmytryk, Martin Berkeley, Charles Daggett, Leo Townsend, Elizabeth Wilson, Richard Collins, Frank Tuttle—these and many others readily admitted past membership and identified their former comrades. They were supported by the Motion Picture Alliance, thanked by the committees and blasted by the Communists as stool pigeons and traitors.

The effort to inject propaganda into pictures was not really put to much of a test. The strength of the invasion was broken too soon, but experts have explained to us that the approach was exceedingly subtle—and it required a long time to be effective. The Communists realized that blunt, open propaganda would easily be detected; the public would object, those responsible would be eliminated and the party would lose some valuable agents. So, as in the universities, the approach was indirect and slanted with great caution. Writers and directors were instructed to hammer away at the class struggle theme, glorifying the "toiling masses," damning the bloated capitalists. Thus the bank president, the chairman of the board, the department store owner, the wealthy aristocrat or the politician was portrayed as a selfish, venal parasite squeezing dry the underprivileged masses. And their employees or constituents were depicted as lean, underpaid, overworked and most unhappy. This theme, repeated through endless variations, was calculated to create contempt for the free-enterprise system, mistrust of public officials and lack of confidence in the government.

The motion picture industry has demonstrated how determination, organized resistance and relentless exposure can invariably whip the Communists soundly. But it is also demonstrating the lamentable and tragic fact that the indifference of the average American, once he is given a brief respite from the Communist menace, is constantly opening the doors to infiltration once again. We must learn that Communists *never* give up. If only one were left he would devote the whole of his life to the subversion of our government.

As soon as the industry relaxed, the invasion was resumed. New techniques were employed and there are danger signals once again. In September, 1954, Actors Equity voted down a resolution barring Communists from membership; in February, 1959, motion picture producers admitted they had been buying scripts from some Communists who had been fired but who were peddling their wares under false names with the full knowledge of the purchasers. In March, the Academy of Motion Picture Arts and Sciences lifted its ban against making awards to those who had defied legislative committees when asked about their Communist backgrounds. Whenever vigilance is relaxed; whenever executives in the motion picture industry, or regents of a great university, or heads of trade unions show weakness instead of strength and courage and plain patriotism in dealing with this ceaseless threat—then they are becoming the unwitting accomplices in the world drive to soften us up for the eventual kill, and to substitute a Communist regime for the government we should be alert and eager to protect against subversion from within.

INFILTRATION OF THE PROFESSIONS

The Medical Profession

The Communist Party has always been interested in recruiting professional people. Lawyers, engineers and doctors are particularly desired to operate as underground members of the party, not only for the purpose of lending their names to front organizations and thereby giving them a semblance of prestige and dignity, but because, as we shall see, they can perform invaluable services for the advancement of Communism in areas that would be inaccessible for the ordinary rank and file party member.

Thus, when atomic research was commenced at Berkeley, California, in the latter part of 1941 and early 1942, and it was necessary to recruit a number of atomic physicists to work in the radiation laboratory of the University of California, the Communist Party had a nucleus of dedicated scientists all ready waiting for such an opportunity. This was the International Federation of Architects, Engineers, Chemists and Technicians, an organization that was started in the Soviet Union by an American scientist who graduated from the Lenin Academy, and which spread its tentacles throughout the United States and parts of Canada. All of these technical men were recruited into the party and originally placed in a professional unit from which they were detached to do this particular job of espionage.

In order to illustrate the physical organization and activities of a professional section of the Communist Party, we can find no better example than that which was functioning in Los Angeles County in the late thirties. Headquarters for this section was established at 3224 Beverly Blvd., and the section comprised two units of teachers, one of newspaper workers, one of doctors, one of lawyers, two of social workers, one of pharmacy workers, one of engineers and architects, one of theatrical people and musicians, one of writers and artists, and a unit of miscellaneous professions usually referred to in party circles as the hash unit. Unit 131 of this Professional Section, comprising writers who were employed by the Federal Writers Project, undertook to make a historical record survey. Since this project involved the probing into government archives on the state, county and municipal levels, the Communist Party was packing it with its members. Sven Skarr, the California supervisor, was a Communist, and with utter ruthlessness, he demoted and fired employees who were not members of the party in order to create jobs for his comrades. In Alaska, in Hawaii, and in the Philippine Islands, as well as throughout the other 47 states, Communists went burrowing into government records compiling enormous masses of data that were analyzed and correlated for Communist Party purposes, both here and abroad.

The Communists realized shortly after the party was organized in the United States that one of the safest places for the arrangement of important meetings was in a doctor's office. Doctors are protected by law against revealing any communication that passes between them and their patients, the waiting room is an insulating protection against intrusion upon the doctor's privacy, people have a normal reason for coming to and from his office at all times of the night and day, and thus these offices provide a safe place for the transaction of important party business.

In San Francisco, we found a dentist's office being used for such purposes only a few years ago. In Los Angeles, a dentist by the name of V. A. K. Tashjian used his office at 815 S. Hill St., Los Angeles, to masquerade his actual status as head of the Disciplinary Commission of the Communist Party for the entire state.

Another instance of the practical use to which Communist doctors can be put is found in the case of Dr. Samuel Marcus, who was a member of the Professional Section of the Communist Party of Los Angeles County, and at the same time a member of the Los Angeles County Board of Alienists and doing psychiatric work for the Los Angeles Superior Courts. On December 6, 1954, the committee held a hearing in Los Angeles concerning Communism in the Los Angeles County Medical Association, and examined 30 witnesses during a period of almost a week. This hearing was conducted at the request of the Medical Association, some of its officers having become alarmed at the increasing evidence of Communist penetration in its ranks. Some of the officers went to Communist front organization meetings and there saw members of their profession participating in the proceedings in positions of authority. The hearing was described at length on pages 70 to 395 of the committee's 1955 report, and we are happy to state that while a mild problem still exists and will undoubtedly continue to exist so long as medical men prove susceptible to Communist recruiting, the problem of infiltration in the Los Angeles County Medical Association is now comparatively slight.

In the recruitment of doctors the Communist Party places special stress in getting as many psychiatrists and psychologists as possible under party control. This group of specialized professionals are of invaluable benefit to the party in bringing those members who are giving evidences of weakness and straying from the path of Marxian rectitude back into the fold through the application of psychiatric treatment. It should be born in mind, of course, that party members are *ordered* to consult only Communists for their legal and medical problems, and whenever it is necessary to do a job of reindoctrination or to report back to the Communist officials concerning the true mental state of the patient, psychiatrists are most valuable.

Immediately after the invasion of the Soviet Union on June 22, 1941, and the consequent overturning of the international Communist Party line, it became expedient to re-examine the political reliability of those party members who had been assigned to work in the delicate fields of either underground activities or espionage. One of these individuals was Paul Crouch, who had been a party member for 17 years, tried to organize a Communist unit in military intelligence while he was a soldier at Schofield Barracks, Hawaii, was caught and sentenced to a term in Alcatraz Military Prison and later was sent to the Soviet Union for training.

He attended the Frunze Military Academy, which is the equivalent to our West Point, graduated with the rank of an honorary Colonel in the Red Army, reviewed the 40,000 troops which then comprised the Budeny Division, addressed the Balkan countries over the Comintern radio network, and was sent back to the United States to take charge of the infiltration of all of our armed forces with Communist Party members. Crouch served briefly as a member of the National Committee of the Communist Party of the United States, and held top positions throughout the entire country. He headed several state Communist organizations and was in almost constant contact with the highest ranking members of the party's leadership. He had been in California several times, but was assigned to this state permanently in 1939 and ultimately assigned to assume the enormously important command of the Special Section which comprised the engineers and technicians and nuclear physicists that we have heretofore described as belonging to the Alameda County Chapter of the International Federation of Architects, Engineers, Chemists and Technicians, which also included physicists then employed at the University of California's radiation laboratory on secret atomic research.

Crouch reported regularly to his Communist Party superiors, particularly William Schneidermann, the organizer for District 13 whose headquarters were in San Francisco, and was apparently performing his task with his usual efficiency and dispatch and with his usual amenability to Communist Party discipline. His wife, also a party member, carried on her duties at the same time, as did his children who were members of the Young Communist apparatus. Then came the revolution of the international party line in June, 1941, and the re-examination of the reliability of top members by the Communist Party psychiatrists. They evaluated Crouch *negatively* and made their report to the proper Communist authorities. Shortly thereafter—apparently in an effort to test the accuracy of this diagnosis—Crouch and his family were ordered to leave Alameda County and take up Communist work in southern California. Now for 17 years these orders had been accepted by the Crouch family without question. On Communist assignments they had moved from one job to another throughout the length and breadth of the United States, and had never wavered in their immediate acceptance of Communist Party discipline and assignments. On this occasion, however, first Mrs. Crouch and then her husband objected.

The conflict between them and their party superiors mounted in intensity and finally they refused to obey the assignment, dropped out of all party activities, accepted work at Brownsville, Texas, went thence to Miami, Florida, and while there decided to atone as much as they could for their 17 years of attempting to subvert their country. Crouch went to the nearest F.B.I. office and made a clean breast of his 17 years of Communist activity. From that time forward until he died a few years ago, Crouch and his entire family devoted their whole time to assisting their government in every possible way to combat the menace of Communism.

The point of this narrative lies in the accuracy of the psychiatric diagnosis and the illustration of the practical value that Communist psychiatrists can render to the Communist Party conspiracy. Crouch had not been suspected as weakening by any of his superiors, and only when a mass re-evaluation of personnel was conducted because of the changed world situation were these professional men able to probe deep enough and expertly enough to uncover Crouch's increasing weakness and his mounting disillusionment with the party. The point is, obviously, that they were correct, that he *did* break, that he went all the way and devoted the rest of his life to exposing in the greatest detail everything he could think of about the persons he knew as Communists and the techniques and activities of the party.

Thus we see that the effort to recruit doctors occupies a high place on the Communist agendum, and that here is yet another area that demands constant scrutiny and watchfulness in order to effectively resist the ceaseless program of infiltration and recruiting.

The Legal Profession

Lawyers have always been of enormous importance to the Communist conspiracy because they are able to guide it through the labyrinth of its underground activities with a relatively slight degree of interference from the constituted authorities—at least in the United States. We have tolerated this type of activity since the middle twenties, and while we have been sending our counter-espionage agents deep into the heart of the Communist apparatus, neverthless the elaborate precaution with which the party has protected itself against such penetration in recent years has met with considerable success, also. As we shall see later in this section, the Subversive Activities Control Board has been taking evidence in an effort to determine whether or not the Communist Party of the United States is directed from abroad as a preliminary to proscribing its activities in this country, and the Supreme Court has, as yet, refused to let the board know whether it is a constitutional body. Hence, in the event that some day the board may make a report that the Communist Party in this country should be made to register all of its members and conform to all of the provisions of the McCarran-Walter Act, then the Supreme Court could at one stroke destroy all of these years of work, together with the effect of the decision by declaring that the board was unconstitutional from its inception.

This committee has been continuously examining members of the Communist Party and officers of its front organizations for almost 20 years, and we have now become familiar with the same lawyers who represent the same type of clients at almost every hearing this committee has ever held. In an excellent report recently issued by the House Committee on Un-American Activities, dated February 16, 1959, the role of the Communist lawyer is discussed at length, and we have taken some of the material for this portion of our report from that document, which can be obtained by writing to the United States Government Printing Office, Division of Documents, Washington, D. C.

Before discussing in detail the individual lawyers in California who are not only members of the Communist Party but who have devoted their lives to furthering its subversive interests, let us once more place the subject in proper perspective by tracing the development of the legal arm of the Comintern as it stretched out from Moscow and manipulated its puppets in the Communist Parties of the world.

Realizing that Communist subversion in foreign countries must necessarily be a clandestine semi-legal operation, and that the Communists in those countries would inevitably run afoul of the law, one of the most important early subdivisions of the Comintern was known as the International Class War Prisoners Aid Society, designated by the Russian initials for that title, MOPR, and commonly known among American Party members as "MOPER." By 1925, this organization had its branches scattered throughout the world and in America it was known as the International Labor Defense, and had been functioning here since June, 1922. The first international head of this world Red aid organization was Klara Zetkin of Germany, a member of the Comintern Executive Committee. She was followed by Willi Muenzenberg, an unusually facile and imaginative functionary who was the originator of the Communist front and who brought MOPR and its worldwide subordinate organizations to a high state of perfection.

The first director of the American section of MOPR, known as the International Labor Defense, was James P. Cannon, and in California the early ILD organization was headed by Leo Gallagher. The national organization in the United States was later directed by the late Vito Marcantonio, who enjoyed the distinction of being the only member of Congress to actually head a division of an international conspiracy openly dedicated to our destruction.

Under Gallagher's direction, the ILD in California was constantly kept busy protecting domestic Communists and getting them out of jail, as well as representing them in legal proceedings; preventing and delaying the deportation of alien Communist agents and planning the strategy and legal ramifications for the operation of the solar system of Red fronts and propaganda units, as well as the run-of-the-mill every day Communist Party operations. Particularly in the field of political strategy were these legal specialists of great practical value to the party in California.

Although the American Communists tried to operate the ILD like any other front and conceal the fact that it was purely a part of the Communists' far-flung structure, there were occasional slips. One appeared in a highly authoritative Communist publication which declared that the International Labor Defense was far too important an organization to be operated by ordinary functionaries, but must "be guided by the higher committees of the Party." [52]

But only the incredibly naive could possibly have been fooled, anyway. The legal staff of the ILD were all Communists; it only defended Communists and party fronts and foreign party agents; it meticulously followed the party line and said so in its organ, *Labor Defender*. Its members and officers were Communists and it was operated with Communist funds.

Zealous and vigorous in its defense of Communists, the ILD and its successor organizations invariably lose interest when its clients denounce the Communist Party and revert to the business of just being solid American citizens. Take the case of Fred Beal, for a good example. There are other instances, without end, but Beal's was a famous case and he lived in California and discussed the matter with representatives of our committee on several occasions. While he was a party member he participated in the textile strike at Gastonia, North Carolina. There was the usual Communist-inspired violence, during which Beal shot a police officer. The ILD sprang into action and eventually arranged for him to escape to the Soviet Union. Here Beal was hailed as a valiant fighter for the oppressed toiling masses. Particularly so because his victim was a policeman in the bastion of capitalism at the height of a class struggle. So, living in comfort at the Metropole Hotel in Moscow, Beal was busily giving lectures and basking in the fatherland of world Communism.

But soon his propaganda value ran dry, and he was left pretty much alone. He became intensely bored, and after months of such isolation and complaining one of his more influential and sympathetic Communist friends promised to escort Beal through the Lubianka prison.

Situated across the street from the Kremlin and connected with it by an underground passage, this grim structure once housed an insurance company, but after the revolution it became the headquarters of the Soviet Secret Police. Here the more important prisoners were tortured and subjected to interminable interrogation. During the bloody purge trials and executions that swept across the U.S.S.R. from 1935 to 1939, the endless procession of Soviet officials, generals, admirals, diplomats and old Bolsheviks were taken to the Lubianka dungeons and there "persuaded" to sign the most ridiculous and abject confessions of Marxian heresy and collaboration with enemies of the regime. Then they were shot.

---

[52] *The Party Organizer*, Nov., 1945; see, also, The Red Decade, op. cit. p. 95.

When Fred Beal was taken on a tour of this citadel of terror he was being accorded a distinct favor. His guide explained how the prisoners never knew whether they would be allowed to live from one day to the next. The latrines were located at the end of a long corridor, and were constructed of soundproof reinforced concrete. If a prisoner failed to return, this meant he had been shot in the base of the skull, and the body removed through an outside entrance. The psychological effect on the other prisoners was deemed most salutary, from the viewpoint of the Soviet Secret Police.

Beal's doubts about the whole Communist movement had been steadily increasing. This experience filled him with loathing. Watching his chance, he managed to sneak out of the country, catch a boat for the United States, return to North Carolina and there he surrendered himself to the authorities and served a prison term for his offense. The ILD ignored him completely.

This utter hypocrisy is characteristic of every Communist action. The entire movement is based on materialism and has no time to waste on such trivialities as religion or sympathy. The class struggle and hatred is all-important, and the individual is always sacrificed to the relentless advance of the world Communist revolution. The end always justifies the means, and these harsh and brutish concepts are ingrained in the embryonic Communist from the very moment he attends beginners' classes and the tempo is increased throughout his entire membership in the Communist Party.

Red Legal Aid in California

In California there was no difference. Operated from 127 South Broadway, Los Angeles, and staffed by Rose Chernin, Julia Walsh, Leo Gallagher, and other attorneys who will be identified later, the ILD handled strikes by Communist-controlled unions, deportation matters involving foreign couriers and agents, as well as all cases where party members were involved with the law. ILD documents in this committee's files leave no doubt about the invariable practice of utilizing every courtroom proceeding and every legislative hearing as opportunities to spread propaganda, undermine respect for constituted authority, and encourage arrogant defiance of law and order. Courts, law, officers and legislative committees are regarded by all true Communists as part of the decadent capitalist system and weapons of the class enemy—and hence not binding on these soldiers in the Communist ranks who owe their allegiance only to the cause of world revolution.

By 1937, according to the ILD's own records, it had 800 branches scattered through 47 states and claimed a total membership of 300,000. This membership included, of course, highly placed individuals who were considered too important to be formally affiliated with the party, and scores of fellow travelers and members of Communist fronts.

Throughout the period of the party's open activity, heretofore discussed, and also during the period of the first United Front from 1935 to 1945, membership in this organization increased and the branches multiplied because there was a corresponding increase of defiant Communist Party activity and a resurgence of activity among its fronts and propaganda media.

Associated with Mr. Gallagher at the time he was representing the International Labor Defense were Abraham L. Wirin, now general counsel for the American Civil Liberties Union in Southern California, and Grover Johnson, both of whom have specialized in representing Communist Party members and Communist front organizations. There were comparable offices in San Francisco with branches scattered throughout other populous portions of California, but the brains of the ILD were centered in the American Bank Building offices of Leo Gallagher and his associates in the city of Los Angeles, and he traveled all over the pacific coast attending to the duties of his office. One of the principal officers of the organization informed a person who was a member of the Communist Party at the time, that the International Labor Defense was a branch of the Communist Party in the United States, and that all persons who worked in confidential capacities in or for that organization were required to be members of the Communist Party or completely subservient to its discipline.[53]

The principal law firm in San Francisco that handled the ILD matters was headed by Richard Gladstein, and associated with him at various times were George Andersen, Aubrey Grossman, Doris Brin Walker, Harold Sawyer, Herbert Resner, Charles Garry, Francis McTernan, and Robert Treuhaft, although the latter has during recent years confined most of his Red aid activities to the east bay area comprising Alameda and Contra Costa Counties and the area immediately adjacent thereto.

At the conclusion of the first United Front era in 1945, the International Labor Defense had become so thoroughly exposed as a part of the international Communist movement functioning in the United States that it was decided to liquidate it and turn its duties over to other organizations. Accordingly, about the middle of 1946, it was merged with the National Federation for Constitutional Liberties, and then continued its activities under the name of Civil Rights Congress. Needless to say, the National Federation for Constitutional Liberties was also a well-known Communist front, and Rose Chernin, who had directed the ILD activities in Southern California under the supervision of Leo Gallagher's office, headed the new organization, as well. The national director was Elizabeth Gurley Flynn, a charter member of the Communist Party of the United States, director of its Women's Commission, a member of its National Committee, and an expert in drumming up legal aid for party members and front organizations. We will see in a subsequent section of this report dealing with the decisions of the United States Supreme Court affecting internal security how Elizabeth Gurley Flynn is still extremely active in undermining the public confidence in the Federal Bureau of Investigation, in legislative committees, and in taking credit for having brought about the astounding change in the legal precedents that had been established by the Supreme Court in cases involving the Communist Party and its manifold activities. In launching the Civil Rights Congress as a new Communist front to replace the ILD, Mrs. Flynn was aided by William L. Patterson and George Marshall.

In California the newly-organized Civil Rights Congress got under a quick start. Rose Chernin was replaced by Marguerite Robinson, who established offices in room 709 at 326 West Third Street in Los Angeles, and so built the membership of the organization that by August 5, 1951, when a meeting was held in the Embassy Auditorium in Los Angeles, there was a crowd of at least 1,200 people present, including prominent Communist Party members who addressed the audience. They included John Howard Lawson, Ben Margolis, and Don Wheeldin who recently resigned from the Communist Party but is typical of the "fallout" mentioned earlier, and has not as yet broken so completely that he is willing to assist his government in frankly and publicly disavowing the Communist movement in its entirety.

.When this committee held its public hearings about the infiltration of the Los Angeles County Medical Association and questioned some of its members about their affiliations with the Civil Rights Congress, witnesses invariably invoked the protection of the Fifth Amendment. Such witnesses included Dr. Thomas L. Perry, Dr. Morris R. Feder, Martin Hall, Dr. Murray Korngold, Kenneth Hartford, Dr. Richard W. Lippman, Dr. Saul Matlin, Dr. P. Price Cobbs, Dr. Wilbur Z. Gordon and Dr. Marvin Sure. Dr. Mardin Allsberg who for many years has demonstrated his patriotic, courageous and forthright anti-Communist attitude as a member of the medical profession, testified that he had attended a Communist Party rally and was later astounded to see the same members of the medical association attending meetings of the Civil Rights Congress and other fronts.

No sooner had the Civil Rights Congress commenced to function than legislative committees began to probe into its antecedents and its methods of operation. It soon became evident that it was staffed by the same Communist Party members, supported by the same enthusiastic fellow travelers who consistently affiliated with the various Communist front organizations, defended no one except Communist Party members and Communist organizations and was, indeed, nothing more than a continuation of the International Labor Defense under another name. The same attorneys rendered the same type of service, and these facts were soon being made public on a wide front by state and congressional committees on un-American activities. As the publicity began to have its effect on the public at large and the true nature of the Civil Rights Congress became known, it experienced trouble in raising funds and in recruiting. It was then listed by the Attorney General of the United States as a Communist dominated organization, following the usual exhaustive study by the F. B. I., and this exposure withered up its source of revenue, whittled down its membership, and reduced its effectiveness to the point where it eventually disbanded. Then the defense of the agents of internal Communist subversion was taken up by the National Lawyers Guild, while the Citizens Committee for the Protection of the Foreign Born redoubled its activities to protect alien Communists, under the direction of Rose Chernin who by now had gained considerable experience in this type of work.

We need say very little about this latter organization, since it was infiltrated by Marion Miller acting as an undercover agent for the Federal Bureau of Investigation, and her testimony and her appearance on a national television program left no vestige of doubt about the Communist nature of this front.

In a previous report we have discussed the National Lawyers Guild at considerable length. By way of brief resume here it is only necessary to point out that the Communist nature of this organization was established by Earl Browder himself, who, while General Secretary of the Communist Party of the United States, stated under oath that the National Lawyers Guild was nothing more than a Communist transmission belt.[54] And Louis Budenz, former editor of the Communist *Daily Worker*, declared that, "In the National Lawyers Guild there is a complete duplicate of the Communist Party's hope and aspirations in that field, although there are a number of non-Communists in the National Lawyers Guild. In fact some of their lawyers locally are no Communists, but they play the Communist game either wittingly or unwittingly." [55]

National Lawyers Guild

The National Lawyers Guild is nothing more than an offshoot of the International Labor Defense, and while it likes to create the impression that it was started in order to counteract the "reactionary" nature of the American Bar Association with a freewheeling, liberal association of attorneys on a national basis, its complete subservience to the Communist Party line, its consistent activities in performing exactly the same sort of services for the Communist Party, its members, its front organizations and its propaganda media that were performed by the I. L. D. and the Civil Rights Congress, together with the fact that all of its officers with any importance or authority have either been party members, ardent fellow travelers, or under Communist discipline, establishes the organization than nothing more than another front, and a very potent one, indeed.

Selma Mikels attended the University of California at Berkeley, graduated from its law school, passed the bar examination and started practicing her profession in Los Angeles. She was, at the time, affiliated

---

[54] Report on National Lawyers Guild, Sept. 17, 1950, p. 2, House Committee on Un-American Activities.
[55] The Techniques of Communism, op. cit., p. 180.

with the Communist Party. In 1940, the California State Relief Administration was investigated by an Assembly committee because of widespread allegations that it was heavily infiltrated by Communists. Among the many witnesses examined by this committee, which was the forerunner of the subsequent committee on un-American Activities, was one Bronislaus Joseph Zukas. He was at that time employed by the S. R. A. at Visalia, and was also the financial secretary of the local chapter of the State, County & Municipal Workers of America. A subpoena *duces tecum* was served on Mr. Zukas calling for him to produce the records of the local. This he refused to do, and was prosecuted for contempt. At his jury trial at Visalia, he was defended by Abraham L. Wirin, heretofore mentioned as having been associated with Leo Gallagher, and since leaving the Gallagher office having been general counsel for the Southern California American Civil Liberties Union, and Selma Mikels. Miss Mikels was, at the time, engaged to be married to the late Lee Bachelis. Mr. Bachelis, until the time of his death, was the most important cog in the Civil Rights Congress organization, since he was in charge of its bail fund. This accumulation of money was used to secure the freedom of Communist leaders who were arrested and prosecuted under the provisions of the Smith Act. Thus, since 1939, Selma Mikels Bachelis has been a member of the Communist Party, constantly devoted to furthering its interests and using the legal education she gained at the State University for the purpose of aiding the agents of a foreign government to destroy us.

Esther Shandler has also devoted her legal talents to the same purposes. She was admitted to the State Bar in December, 1945, started to practice her profession in April, 1946, and one of her first appearances in public on behalf of a Communist client was before this committee in connection with the death of Everitt Hudson, the student who was recruited into the Communist Party while attending Stanford University and murdered while he was attending U. C. L. A. Representatives of the committee had contacted one of the persons who had information about the Communist activities of the decedent, had been with him at a Communist meeting the night preceding his death, and had expressed a willingness to testify fully concerning the circumstances surrounding this tragic case. A committee representative was en route to see the witness when he discovered she had been contacted by attorneys for the Communist Party and terrorized to the point that she was afraid to testify. She was nevertheless compelled to appear before the committee as a witness, and sat next to her attorney, Esther Shandler, who would not permit her to do more than invoke the Fifth Amendment over and over again. Immediately after this episode the witness, Lola Whang, married Joe Price, another U. C. L. A. student who had also attended the Communist meeting heretofore mentioned. Neither of them has ever revealed any facts concerning the Communist meeting, or the movements of young Hudson during the period immediately preceding his death.

Miss Shandler has appeared on behalf of the Committee for the Protection of the Foreign Born, the Civil Rights Congress, and has been identified as a Communist Party member by several witnesses who were in the party with her.

Pauline Epstein has been practicing the legal profession in Los Angeles since 1933, has also devoted her time to the representation of Communist Party members, is retained by the Committee for the Protection of the Foreign Born, and was considered sufficiently eminent in aiding the cause of Communism that she was selected to speak at the American Russian Institute program celebrating the thirty-sixth anniversary of the Soviet Union in November of 1953. She was Treasurer of the Los Angeles Chapter of the Lawyers Guild during 1951 and 1952, and served on its national executive board in 1956 and 1957.

J. Allen Frankel, during his 48 years as an attorney in Los Angeles, has consistently served the Communist cause. He, too, worked for the Committee for Protection of the Foreign Born, the International Labor Defense, Civil Rights Congress and Lawyers Guild. He has been a Communist Party member for many years.

Charles Katz has practiced law in Los Angeles for more than 20 years, and, in addition to his activities in the Lawyers Guild and the other familiar fronts, has acted as counsel for some of the more notorious party functionaries. He has specialized as somewhat of a Marxist theoretician, and was a member of the executive board of the Arts, Sciences and Professions Council and the Jewish People's Fraternal Order. Mr. Katz has also been unmasked and his Communist affiliation disclosed.

Ben Margolis has been exceedingly busy as a Communist and a member of the State Bar. He was treasurer of the San Francisco Lawyers Guild in 1937, has taught in Communist schools, belonged to all of the important fronts, was associated in the same law office with Leo Gallagher and Charles Katz, and has recruited many other lawyers into the party.

John L. McTernan is a Communist lawyer in Los Angeles, has been active in the Lawyers Guild and the other fronts that proved so attractive to his legal comrades.

John W. Porter was admitted to the bar in 1935, and has since followed the familiar pattern of activity: Lawyers Guild, Committee for Protection of the Foreign Born, and Civil Rights Congress. He also served in several federal agencies: Department of Labor, National Labor Relations Board, Department of Justice, Office of Price Administration and War Labor Board. He has been a member of the Communist Party for many years.

Rose S. Rosenberg, another Los Angeles Communist, has devoted her legal talents to composing and submitting briefs to the United States Supreme Court in an effort to influence it in favor of Communist interests. She is a prolific circulator of open letters, petitions and resolutions, and was especially active in behalf of Julius and Ethel Rosenberg, who were executed as atomic spies.

Seymour Mandel, identified as a Communist lawyer in Los Angeles, served as executive secretary of the Lawyers Guild in that city and has acted as attorney for both of the Communist legal fronts—the Committee for Protection of the Foreign Born and the Civil Rights Congress. Mr. Mandel's specialty, however, seems to have been in representing aliens who have been charged with subversive affiliations or activities and who were being processed for deportation by the United State Immigration and Naturalization Service.

Samuel Rosenwein served as general counsel for the Civil Rights Congress, has affiliated with many Communist front organizations, and in 1949 acted as chairman of the Civil Liberties Committee of the National Lawyers Guild. He has also been identified as a Communist Party member.

Richard L. Rykoff practices law in Los Angeles. According to sworn testimony he affiliated with the special lawyers group in that city, which is the modern counterpart of the old lawyers unit of the Professional Section that we have earlier referred to, and which provides an organizational unit within the party structure that serves to bring together various professional groups in order that they can better correlate and execute their party assignments and activities. On several occasions Rykoff telephoned to Mrs. Anita Schneider in San Diego. He knew her as an active member of the party in that city and sent her directions from time to time. On one occasion he advised her to evade the law by making false representations to the State Department in applying for a passport to travel behind the Iron Curtain, and on another occasion he advised her concerning the exhibition of Communist propaganda films to the members of a party-dominated front organization in San Diego. Unfortunately for Mr. Rykoff, he was unaware that at the time he was having these transactions with Mrs. Schneider believing her to be a loyal member of the Communist conspiracy, that she was actually an undercover agent for the Federal Bureau of Investigation. Rykoff has represented the Los Angeles Committee for protection of the Foreign Born, has filed briefs before the United States Supreme Court in an effort to influence its decisions, has represented the Civil Rights Congress and has been affiliated with the National Lawyers Guild.

In the northern part of the State, particularly in the San Francisco bay area, both in San Francisco and Alameda Counties, the Communist lawyers followed the same general pattern as their comrades in the south. Aubrey Grossman and Richard Gladstein were the legal kingpins in the Communist machinery for that region, and while we have already alluded to the latter, we have not yet given any details about the activities of Mr. Grossman although we have mentioned him from time to time in various reports during the last 18 years. Grossman is a graduate of the University of California at Berkeley and attended its law school.

He affiliated with the Young Communist League while still a student, and, according to the testimony of one of his law school faculty members, was so busy with Young Communist League activities while studying law that he had some difficulty in maintaining the necessary scholarship average prerequisite to his graduation.[56]

Grossman's record is both long and interesting. As we stated in our 1943 report, he graduated from the University of California in the winter of 1932, and from the law school of that institution three years thereafter, being admitted to practice his profession in this state in May, 1936. In 1934, Grossman participated in a long series of Communist line activities at the university. He appeared as a speaker at many protest meetings held at Sather Gate, and was active in the students' strike at the university which was sponsored by the Communist Party through one of its fronts known as the National Student League. On July 3, 1935, he participated in another Sather Gate meeting called by the Communist Party to incite students to proceed to San Francisco and take part in a "bloody Thursday" parade commemorating the Communist-directed general strike of 1934. He has been associated with the National Student League, the Student Rights Association, the Social Problem Club, the American Youth Congress, the Anti-War Committee, the Anti-ROTC Committee Youth Section—all while he was still a student, and with virtually every major front organization in the United States since that time. His application for admission to the State Bar of California was accompanied by a vigorous protest filed by the American Legion, and shortly after his admission the *Western Worker*, then the Communist newspaper in this State and lineal ancestor of the *Daily People's World*, announced that Grossman was the lawyer who would work in behalf of International Labor Defense.

Minutes of the Communist Party state convention held in San Francisco, May 14-15, 1937, in the committee's files, reflect that Grossman was elected a member of the State Committee of the Communist Party and pledged himself to recruit at least 10 new members. As early as 1941, two former Communist Party members, one of them the head of the entire East Bay Communist organization, testified before this committee that they had known Grossman as a member of the Young Communist League and the Communist Party during the time he was a student at the university.[57]

In 1936, Grossman associated himself with Richard Gladstein, Ben Margolis and Harold Sawyer—all Communists, and started his long career of devoting his education and his license to practice law for the benefit of the international Communist conspiracy. He and Gladstein acted as attorneys for some of the defendants in the notorious King-

[56] See testimony of the late Prof. Max Radin before the California Joint Fact-finding Committee on Un-American Activities, San Francisco, Dec. 3, 1941, Transcript Vol. VI, pp. 1768-1783.
[57] See testimony of Miles G. Humphrey, California Joint Fact-finding Committee on Un-American Activities, Transcript Vol. V, pp. 1616-1631; testimony of Donald Morton, Transcript Vol. VI, pp. 1793-1794.

Ramsay-Conner murder case, which involved the slaying of George Alberts, engineer for a vessel known as the *Point Lobos*. Since King, Ramsay and Conner were identified as Communists, and since one of the other defendants, George Wallace, turned state's evidence, the entire Communist apparatus in the Bay area was alerted to whip up propaganda in behalf of the defendants. That is, all of the defendants except Mr. Wallace, whom they ignored. Earl Warren, now Chief Justice of the United States Supreme Court, was then the District Attorney of Alameda County, and he personally prosecuted the case. This was Mr. Warren's first head-on clash with the Communist Party, and he said many unpleasant things about it and its methods.

The murder occurred in 1937, and shortly thereafter Mr. Warren was elected Attorney General of California. We have already alluded to the fact that the Communists capitalized on the liberal administration of Governor Culbert L. Olson and managed to infiltrate the state government to the extent that they literally surrounded him with undercover party members. When he exercised his high office to parole King, Ramsay and Conner but left George Wallace, the non-Communist who had turned state's evidence, to languish in the penitentiary, Earl Warren became greatly incensed. This committee, then known as the California Joint Fact-Finding Committee on Un-American Activities, held a long and detailed hearing in San Francisco. Earl Warren appeared as a witness before us, and the transcript of his testimony is most illuminating. He described the Communist propaganda machinery that was mobilized to protect King, Ramsay and Conner, described the role of George Wallace in aiding the prosecution but being ignored by both the Communists and the Governor, and said a great many heated and emphatic things against the Communist movement in general and its antics during the *Point Lobos* trial in particular. We will allude to this episode later in this report when we discuss the recent decisions of the United States Supreme Court in the field of internal security.

The first time Aubrey Grossman ever stepped on a witness stand before a legislative committee investigating subversive activities was before this committee about 18 years ago. On that occasion he denied that he had ever been affiliated with a Communist front organization, the Young Communist League or the Communist Party. In 1945 his efforts on behalf of the Communist movement were such that he was rewarded by being made Educational Director of the Communist Party of San Francisco, and the committee files contain letterheads of that organization with Mr. Grossman's name prominently displayed thereon. He has attended both state and national Community Party conventions; he had represented many Communist-dominated unions, and he was appointed Director of the Civil Rights Congress for the entire Pacific coast region shortly after that organization was launched in 1946. Under his direction this legal branch of international Red aid flourished so successfully that he was called to the east in order to assist in developing it in other parts of the country. In 1950, he became National Organizational Secretary of the Civil Rights Congress, and a year later was in sole charge of the entire structure nationally.

During the late forties this committee held a series of hearings concerning the Civil Rights Congress, the American-Russian Institute and the California Labor School, the Communist educational institution in San Francisco. Immediately Grossman alerted his organization of Bay area lawyers for a series of lectures calculated to teach prospective witnesses before the committee how to conduct themselves when on the witness stand. Mr. Richard Gladstein participated in such a panel as its presiding officer at the California Labor School in 1951. In 1953, Grossman decided to resume his private law practice and associated himself with Bertram Edises and Robert Treuhaft in Oakland. Both of his new associates have been identified as Communists, and their firm also had an associate by the name of Robert L. Condon who had been a member of the California State Assembly, was elected to Congress, started to go to Nevada to view an atomic bomb test, but was prevented from doing so by the government because he was deemed a security risk. Condon is also a graduate of the University of California, and was formerly employed by the government as chief enforcement attorney for the Office of Price Administration of Northern California in 1942. One of the attorneys who worked under him was Mrs. Doris Brin Walker, who will be mentioned later in this section and who received considerable attention in our 1955 report. At the present writing, Mr. Grossman is still enthusiastically devoting virtually all of his time and talents to traveling about the country on behalf of the Communist Party and its front organizations.

We have already alluded to Mr. Richard Gladstein at some length in this and preceding reports. He was admitted to the Bar in 1931, has acted as attorney for the Communist-infected Marine Cooks & Stewards Union before that organization was expelled from the CIO in 1950, has been counsel for the Committee for Protection of the Foreign Born, the Civil Rights Congress, and a wide variety of Communist fronts and Communist-dominated unions. Doris Brin Walker, while an attorney for the Office of Price Administration, lined up a job with the firm of Gladstein, Grossman, Sawyer and Edises to specialize in the handling of labor cases. All Communists, as we have said, will resort to every possible artifice, ruse, strategem, and even lies for the purpose of promoting each other. An example of this sort of practice is to be found in the action of Francis McTernan, who deliberately falsified material facts on the application of Doris Brin Walker for a job with Cutter Laboratory. This matter was thoroughly covered in our 1955 report, heretofore mentioned.

George R. Anderson has also been repeatedly identified as a Communist, and was one of the first lawyers in San Francisco to take a particularly active part in the International Labor Defense. He also was prominent in helping to organize the International Juridical Association, which was a division of the ILD to which a great many Communist lawyers throughout the United States were attracted. Anderson has also been identified with practically every major Communist front in the bay area, has acted as counsel for various Communist-dominated unions, and has been prominent in his legal work for the Committee for Protection of the Foreign Born, the National Lawyers Guild and the Civil Rights Congress.

Anderson, during one phase of his career, devoted a great deal of time to the representation of Communist members of various waterfront unions who had been arrested for resorting to violence against non-Communists in their organization. These cases would invariably arise from severe beatings and attacks by the Communist element against anti-Communist individuals, generally referred to along the waterfront as "dumpings."

Anderson was quite successful in getting his clients off with either no punishment at all, or extremely mild fines and a few days in jail. He was a frequent spectator at many of our earlier hearings in the bay area, but invariably stated that he represented no client but was merely attending as an interested visitor. He would take a seat in the front of the room and when a witness gave the slightest indication of co-operating with the committee by revealing some of his experiences while a Party member, Anderson would glare at him—presumably in an effort at intimidation—and while the practice seemed to have little practical effect, nevertheless it was such a studied pattern of activity that it intrigued the interest of the committee members.

Charles R. Garry, also identified as a member of the Communist Party, has been practicing law in San Francisco since about 1938. He has represented the Civil Rights Congress, the Committee for Protection of Foreign Born, has been affiliated with a wide variety of Communist fronts, has acted as counsel for a number of Communist-dominated unions, and has, in short, followed the general pattern of activity that runs like a common denominator through the careers of the other lawyers in this State who have been identified as party members. He, of course, belongs to the National Lawyers Guild, having joined it immediately upon being admitted to the Bar, has served as its executive board member in San Francisco, as President of the San Francisco Chapter, as a delegate to its national convention, and a member of its national executive board.

In 1948, Mr. Garry was a candidate for election to the House of Representatives from the Fifth Congressional District on the Independent Progressive Party ticket. It will be recalled that this organization was described in the first section of this report, and was headed statewide by Mr. Hugh Bryson, former president of the Marine Cooks & Stewards Union.

Mr. Garry has, like his comrades in the legal profession, sent numerous petitions to the United States Supreme Court in an effort to influence its decisions. Obviously, all of these petitions sought to mold the court's opinions in consonance with the Communist Party line, and while some of the other Communist lawyers sent an occasional petition, Mr. Garry's have been especially numerous and vehement. He has taught in the Communist school in San Francisco, has also been quite active in the International Workers Order, a sort of Communist insurance concern operated on a nationwide basis which attracted a great many racial minority groups. This organization, though now defunct, was an extremely rich and potent organization. While it was being suspended from operating in California because of its subversive nature, and pending a revocation of its certificate of operation, its entire file was stolen from the office of the California Insurance Commission, and so far as we know it has never been recovered.

In the 1955 report, we devoted a section to the case of Doris Brin Walker who, by misrepresentation on her employment questionnaire, obtained a position with the Cutter Laboratories in Berkeley, California, and who was discharged after the employer discovered her Communist affiliation. Mrs. Walker brought a suit against the company for reinstatement, and the matter was taken up to the Supreme Court of the United States after which Mrs. Walker was compelled to seek employment elsewhere.

At the University of California in Berkeley she maintained such an excellent scholarship average that she was elected to Phi Beta Kappa, she was graduated from the law school of that institution, worked with the Office of Price Administration, as has been mentioned in connection with Aubrey Grossman and Richard Gladstein, she also was associated with their firm after she left government service, and despite her status as an attorney and her record as a brilliant student, she deliberately worked at jobs that were entirely incompatible with her background.

Commencing in 1946, and continuing until 1950, Mrs. Walker worked for the H. J. Heintz Company, the Bercut-Richards Packing Corporation and the Cutter Laboratories. She was also an active member and a minor officer of the Communist fraction in the Cannery Workers Union and the United Office and Professional Workers of America, which was almost as Communist-saturated as was the old Marine Cooks & Stewards Union. Commencing in the latter part of 1948, Mrs. Walker became interested in politics to the extent of lending her services to the Independent Progressive Party, as well as to the Civil Rights Congress, the Committee for Protection of the Foreign Born, the National Lawyers Guild, the *Daily People's World*, and the usual wide variety of Communist front organizations and activities that are characteristic of the other Party members whose records are outlined above.

Mrs. Walker, who is also known as Doris Marasse, has been repeatedly identified by sworn testimony as a member of the Communist Party—a fact which was thoroughly established during her legal controversy with the Cutter Laboratories—and is presently the wife of Mason Roberson, a reporter for the *Daily People's World*.

It will be recalled that we have explained how, some 18 years ago, Abraham L. Wirin came to Visalia with a young woman graduate of the University of California Law School by the name of Selma Mikels, who assisted him in the defense of Bronislaus Joseph Zukas. In 1958 Abraham L. Wirin went to San Francisco to defend John Powell, his wife and his associate, who were arrested by the United States Government and charged with printing false accusations against the armed forces of this country, charging them with the use of germ warfare during the war in Korea. He was also assisted by another woman graduate of the University of California Law School—Doris Brin Walker, also known as Doris Marasse, and also known as Mrs. Mason Roberson.

These are only a few of the members of the California State Bar who have been positively identified as Communists. There are many others: men like Lawrence R. Sperber, Fred H. Steinmetz, and Jack Tenner—but there is little to be gained at this point by mentioning all of them, except to point out that they all belong to the National Lawyers Guild, which is a Communist-dominated organization, that they prostitute their profession by giving clandestine aid and support to the Communist Party by teaching in its schools, recruiting lawyers as its members, using the representatives of its lawmaking bodies, both federal and state, and its courts for the purpose of emitting the most defiant and militant Communist propaganda; by aiding the international conspiracy on all fronts and in every possible manner during the whole of their time and in a manner wholly inconsistent with their solemn obligation to support and defend the state and nation where they are privileged to practice their profession.

It is little wonder that the Communist Party has placed such enormous emphasis on the recruitment of lawyers to its ranks, and that it leans so heavily upon them for guidance, advice and protection. Since the International Labor Defense changed its name to the Civil Rights Congress, and since that organization was exposed and withered away, the Lawyers Guild, the Citizens Committee for Protection of the Foreign Born and, in some localities, the American Civil Liberties Union, are carrying forward the work. All of these lawyers are constantly bombarding the federal courts, and particularly the United States Supreme Court, with petitions and writs of all sorts and are seeking to intervene as friends of the court for the purpose of influencing its decisions so the Communist conspiracy can proceed unhampered to whittle away at our governmental institutions and soften us up for the eventual kill.[58]

COMMUNIST FRONT ORGANIZATIONS

The origin of the Communist front is credited to Willi Muenzenberg, who developed it as an efficient weapon of deceit. We have stated many times in many reports that no one should be accused of subversion or

[58] For a detailed discussion of the role of the Communist lawyer, see: Communist Legal Subversion, report by the Committee on Un-American Activities, House of Representatives, Eighty-sixth Congress, First Session. Feb. 16, 1959.

should be called a fellow-traveler merely because he unwittingly joined one or even two of these organizations. They are, by their very nature and operation, calculated to appeal to the unwary liberal who affiliates with no idea that the organization is in fact directed by the Communist Party, and serves as a recruiting medium and a means of expressing the current party line. There were innumerable fronts designed to appeal to the emotions of all types of American citizens. There were fronts for the trade unionists, the racial minority groups, the actors, the writers, the do-gooders, the too-poor, the too-rich, atomic scientists laboring in the rarified atmosphere of profound research, teachers, professional men, and even little children.

Some of these organizations were so cleverly camouflaged that many joined and participated in the activities of the group for a considerable length of time before they realized it was being manipulated by Communists from concealed positions. Obviously, an individual who drifted into one or two of these organizations, discovered their true nature and got out should not be a target for criticism. But it is a relatively simple matter to follow the progression of the indoctrinated individual from one front organization to another on an ascending degree of virulency. First joining a relatively innocuous group, then falling for the sugar-coated recruiting propaganda, then being drawn into several more front organizations, then beginning to assume positions of authority as an executive secretary, a treasurer or an organizer, then speaking before groups of front organizations, then participating in a whole galaxy of fronts—it is not difficult to determine at what point in this career the individual has become indoctrinated. The party has, of course, gone to the greatest lengths to protect its members against exposure. Consequently the counter-subversive agencies can get an excellent idea of whether a person is a Communist by the number of fronts in which he participates, the length of time he has been engaging in such activities, his persistent following of the inconsistencies of the Communist Party line, his long and persistent association with known members of the Communist Party, his subscription to Communist Party literature, his attendance at Communist functions, and his efforts to indoctrinate others and spread the Communist creed. So, membership in a procession of Communist front organizations, while not necessarily proof of membership in the party itself, nevertheless provides a reliable indication of a strong tendency in that direction.

As early as 1922, one of the charter members of the Communist Party of the Soviet Union, an old Bolshevik later liquidated in the purges of 1935-1939, had this to say about the methods of the United Front and its complicated array of organizations: "It is easier and pleasanter to smash things, but if we have not the power to do so, and if this method is necessary, we must make use of it . . . in the firm trust that this method will do harm to social democracy, not to us . . . and in the conviction that we *shall crush them in our embrace*.[59]

---

[59] The Red Decade, the Stalinist Penetration of America, by Eugene Lyons, op. cit., p. 47.

Among the earliest Communist fronts was the John Reed Club, named after the American journalist who visited Russia immediately before, during and after the revolution of 1917. Always an earnest liberal, Reed waxed enthusiastic about the implications of the revolution, and wrote a book that was widely published throughout the world, particularly in this country, called "Ten Days That Shook the World." John Reed Clubs sprang up like mushrooms all over the United States, and the ultra-liberals flocked to them in droves. Then came the Friends of Soviet Russia, then Friends of the Soviet Union, then the various subdivisions of the Comintern, including the International Labor Defense, already described, then the Anti-Imperialist League; the League Against War and Fascism; the League for Peace and Democracy; the American Peace Mobilization, a host of fronts through which propaganda and aid was channeled to the Spanish Loyalists who were fighting in the revolution, then the Friends of the Abraham Lincoln Brigade; Joint Anti-Fascist Refugee Committee; National Council of the Arts, Sciences and Professions; Mobilization for Democracy; the Anti-Nazi League; the League of American Writers; International Workers Order; The Workers Ex-Servicemens League; the National Student League; the Labor Research Association; the National Committee for the Defense of Political Prisoners; the Workers School; the Workers Book Shops; the International Publishers; the Workers Library Publishers; the Pen and Hammer Club; the Film and Photo League; the National Youth Congress; American Youth for Democracy; the Labor Youth League; the Civil Rights Congress; the League for Women Shoppers; the Tom Mooney Labor School; the California Labor School; the Peoples Educational Center; the Twentieth Century Book Shop; the Progressive Book Shop; the International Book Shop; the American Writers Union; Committee for Defense of Mexican-American Youth; Labor's Nonpartisan League; United Organizations for Progressive Political Action; Independent Progressive Party; the Actors Laboratory Theatre; the Hollywood Writers Mobilization; Northern California Committee for Academic Freedom; the American-Russian Institute; the National Lawyers Guild—all of these and many times this number of Communist controlled organizations were flourishing in California at one time or another.

In addition, there were the sporadic and temporary fronts whipped up to plug for a temporary switch in the party line, such as the clamor for the opening of a second front during the early stages of World War II, the fronts that proclaimed "the Yanks are Not Coming," that were active just before the Soviet Union was invaded and went out of existence the day afterwards, and other fronts to bring the troops home from Korea immediately, to get out of Formosa, to recognize Communist China, to scrap all of our atomic weapons, and for the defense of numerous Communist functionaries and notables like the functionaries who were convicted under the Smith Act, indeed, every important Communist who became embroiled with the law had a "defense committee" that sprang into action to provide funds and stir up sentiment in his behalf.

The Attorney General's List

So far as we know there has never been published a reliable explanation of how the government uses membership in front organizations for the purpose of evaluating the loyalty of its prospective employees in sensitive positions. In June, 1957, the Commission on Government Security published its 807-page report at the conclusion of two years of intensive analysis of the entire security posture of the United States. This survey included the civilian loyalty program, the military personnel program, the document classification program, the atomic energy program, the industrial security program, port security, international organizations (including the United Nations), passport security, civil air transport security, immigration and nationality program, the Attorney General's list of front organizations, the right of persons accused of disloyalty to be confronted with witnesses against them, the subpena power of the government in loyalty cases, and the privilege against self-incrimination.

The Attorney General of the United States, acting on field investigations by the Federal Bureau of Investigation, compiled a list of Communist front organizations and disseminated it throughout all of the government offices where it would be of practical value in insuring the loyalty of employees. Since the Commission on Government Security made an intensive study of this entire matter, and since it has never before been presented, and because it has a decidedly practical application in California, we quote from the report herewith.

In June, 1941, Congress appropriated $100,000 for the Federal Bureau of Investigation to "investigate the employees of every department, agency, and independent establishment of the Federal Government who are members of subversive organizations or advocate the overthrow of the Federal Government," and directed the bureau to report its findings to the agencies and to Congress. (Public Law 135, Seventy-seventh Congress.) In 1941 also, Congress began the practice of attaching riders to the regular appropriations acts—a practice which continued during World War II and for a number of years thereafter—barring compensation to "any person who advocates, or who is a member of an organization that advocates the overthrow of the Government of the United States by force or violence; provided, that for the purpose hereof an affidavit shall be considered prima facie evidence that the person making the affidavit does not advocate, and is not a member of an organization that advocates, the overthrow of the Government of the United States by force or violence; provided, further, that any person who advocates or who is a member of an organization that advocates the overthrow of the Government of the United States by force or violence and accepts employment, the salary or wages for which are paid from any appropriation contained in this act, shall be guilty of a felony, and, upon conviction, shall be fined not more than $1,000 or imprisoned for not more than one year, or both.''

The appropriation for the Federal Bureau of Investigation pointed up the questions raised by this series of acts: What organizations were ''subversive'' and who was to determine that fact? It will be noted that Congress included no organizations by name in the acts, except in the Selective Service and the Emergency Relief Appropriation Acts; nor did it set up machinery for a definition of ''subversive'' which would be binding on all departments; nor did it name or empower any specific agency to make a determination.

In order that the Federal Bureau of Investigation might carry out its mandate to investigate despite the omissions in its appropriations act, the then Attorney General, Francis Biddle, in June 1941, advised the Federal Bureau of Investigation that the Communist Party and the German-American Bund, named in the acts mentioned above, and seven other organizations came within the congressional intent.[60] This intent appears to have been made out from the language in the act dealing with advocacy of overthrow of the Federal Government, together with the legislative history of the act.

On March 16, 1942, the Civil Service Commission, pursuant to Executive Orders 9063 (7 f. r. 1075) and 9067 (7 f. r. 1407), adopted War Service Regulation II, Section 3 (7 f. r. 7723), providing that an applicant might be denied appointment if there is ''a reasonable doubt as to his loyalty to the Government of the United States,'' and stating this matter might be considered in determining whether removal of an incumbent employee will ''promote the efficiency of the service.'' These regulations were rescinded in 1946, with the cessation of armed hostility.

The Attorney General's list, as it came to be called, made its first public appearance on Sept. 24, 1942. On that date Congressman Martin Dies of Texas, in reply to statements made as to the usefulness of the investigation carried on by the House Committee on Un-American Activities, read on the floor of the House of Representatives excerpts from what he termed a ''photostatic copy'' of the confidential memorandum which was distributed to the heads of the respective departments, in which the Attorney General branded 12 organizations as Communist controlled. Each of the excerpts, headed ''strictly confidential,'' began with the following caveat:

''Note.—The following statement does not purport to be a complete report on the organization named. It is intended only to acquaint you, without undue burden of details, with the nature of the evidence which has appeared to warrant an investigaiton of charges of participation.

60 Memorandum, the Federal Loyalty-Security Programs, submitted to Commission on Government Security by Attorney General Brownell under covering letter dated Dec. 11, 1956.

It is assumed that each employee's case will be decided upon all the facts presented in the report of the Federal Bureau of Investigation and elicited, where a hearing is ordered, by the Board or Committee before which the employee is given an opportunity to appear.

Please note that the statement is marked 'strictly confidential' and is available only for use in administration of mandate Public Law 135.''

It then went on to describe at some length the organization, membership requirements, history, leadership, and program of the named organization, and to discuss the extent of Communist control over it. The organizations mentioned were: American League Against War and Fascism, the American League for Peace and Democracy, the American Peace Mobilization, the League of American Writers, the National Committee for Defense for Political Prisoners, National Committee for People's Rights, the National Federation for Constitutional Liberties, National Negro Congress, Washington Cooperative Book Shop and Washington Committee for Democratic Action.

On February 5, 1943, President Roosevelt issued Executive Order 9300, citing as his authority therefor Title 1 of the First War Powers Act, 1941, and his powers as President. This order established within the Department of Justice a new interdepartmental committee on employee investigation, composed of five members appointed by the President from among the officers or employees of the "departments, independent establishments, and agencies of the Federal Government.''

Executive Order 9300 remained in effect until March 21, 1947, when President Truman revoked it and issued Executive Order 9835, which instituted the so-called loyalty program. Citing as authority the Constitution and Statutes of the United States, including the Civil Service Act of 1883 (22 Stat. 403), as amended, and Section 9-A of the Act approved August 2, 1939 (18 U.S.C. 61 (i)), and his powers as President and Chief Executive of the United States, the order set up a loyalty review board and, in Part III, Section III, directed:

"The Loyalty Review Board shall currently be furnished by the Department of Justice the name of each foreign or domestic organization, association, movement, group or combination * * * which the Attorney General, after appropriate investigation and determination designates as totalitarian, Fascist, Communist, or subversive, or as having adopted a policy of advocating or approving the commission of acts of force or violence to deny others their rights under the Constitution of the United States, or as seeking to alter the form of Government of the United States by unconstitutional means.

"(a) The Loyalty Review Board shall disseminate such information to all departments and agencies.''

The list was forwarded by the board in December, 1947, and made public by printing in the Federal Register on March 20, 1948. (13 F. R. 1471.); at that time it comprised 82 organizations, 35 of which were named for the first time.

The list as disseminated after October 21, 1948, did, in a sense, characterize the organizations, for they were listed under the six headings set up by the order. Those names ranged from the Ku Klux Klan and Silver Shirt Legion of America, to the Communist Party, U. S. A.; and the Jefferson School of Social Science. The practice of using descriptive headings was abandoned when Executive Order 9835 was revoked by Executive Order 10450 in April, 1953.

The first, and thus far the only, real Supreme Court review of the list came in 1951 in *Joint Anti-Fascist Refugee Committee* vs. *McGrath*. (341 U. S. 123, 1951). In this case the Refugee Committee, the National Council of American-Soviet Friendship and its affiliates, and the International Workers Order sued in Federal District Court for injunctive relief. They recited irreparable damage from being listed without hearing, both in terms of public support and harrassment by administrative agencies of state and federal governments with which they dealt. The District Court granted the Attorney General's motion to dismiss on the grounds that no claims were stated on which relief could be granted. The Court of Appeals affirmed.

Justice Burton announced the judgment of the Supreme Court, but no opinion, in itself, commanded a majority. Five justices held that the plaintiffs had standing to sue, although there was disagreement whether this arose from injury to the organizations or from a standpoint of vindicating the rights of their members. Four justices agreed that listing without notice at the hearing was improper, either on constitutional grounds or as a violation of Executive Order 9835. Justice Burton held that the government's motion to dismiss admitted, for purposes of the decision, that the Attorney General had acted arbitrarily, and took no position on the broader issue. Three dissenting Justices (Reed, Vinson and Minton) would have upheld the judgments of the courts below. Justice Clark did not participate in the case.

On remand to the District Court, cross-motions of both the plaintiffs and the Attorney General for summary judgment were denied, as was the plaintiffs' petition for a temporary injunction. In this action, the Attorney General filed long affidavits giving reasons for listing each of the organizations; these are summarized in the opinion. He also argued that security regulations would not permit disclosure of many confidential reports and sources of information on which his determinations were based. The District Court did not resolve this issue in its opinion. Certiorari directly to the Supreme Court to review the denial of the temporary injunction was denied; appeal to the Courts of Appeals resulted in affirmation of the denial. In the same opinion, the Appellate Court reversed a subsequent dismissal of the suit because of mootness; the Attorney General, in the meanwhile, had set up the hearing procedure outlined below, and had argued that the court case was moot pending the plantiffs availing themselves of this administrative procedure. The Appellate Court ordered the District Court to reinstate the case and give the plaintiffs time to ask for a hearing under a new procedure. They did not file for such a hearing within the 10 days allowed, however, and the District Court held that their failure to act constituted acquiescence in the designation. This decision was affirmed by the Circuit Court of Appeals on February 28, 1957. The International Workers Order forwarded a letter of protest to the Attorney General on June 12, 1953, indicating that the organization neither acquiesced in the designation nor wished to participate in a hearing.

It appears that as a result of the opinions expressed by members of the Supreme Court in the *McGrath* case, Attorney General Brownell published on May 6, 1953, Attorney General's Order No. 11-53, which provided, in part:

"(b) Whenever the Attorney General after appropriate investigation proposes to designate an organization pursuant to Executive Order 9835 or Executive Order 10450, or both, notice of such proposed designations shall be sent by registered mail to such organization at its last known address. If the registered notice is delivered, the organization, within 10 days following its receipt or 10 days following the effective date of Executive Order 10450, whichever shall be later, may file with the Attorney General * * * a written notice that it desires to contest such designation. If the notice of proposed designation is not delivered and is returned by the Post Office Department, the Attorney General shall cause such notice to be published in the *Federal Register,* supplemented by such additional notice as the Attorney General may deem appropriate. Within 30 days following such publication in the *Federal Register,* such organization may file with the Attorney General * * * a written notice that it desires to contest such designation. Failure to file a notice of contest within such period shall be deemed an acquiescence in such proposed action, and the Attorney General may thereupon after appropriate determination designate such organization and publish such designation in the *Federal Register.*"

The Commission on Government Security pointed out that widespread public knowledge of the list's contents may have served a useful purpose in putting citizens on notice of possible loss of employment from too active membership in one of the named organizations. The activities of the Subversive Activities Control Board, which is designed to make judicial determination, with attendant safeguards, and require public registration of organizations and their members, may eventually replace this function of the Attorney General's list. The tremendous time and effort required for hearings before this board, together with possible necessity of disclosing confidential information or informants, should be borne in mind, however, in view of the fact that some 20,000 new employees are hired each month.[61]

The commission recommended that the Attorney General's list be continued, but a statutory basis for its maintenance and the listing of organizations should be authorized only after a full F. B. I. investigation and an opportunity for the organization to be heard by examiners of a central office which the commission urges be established, with right of appeal to a central review board. Decisions of examiners in the field and the central review board would be advisory only so far as the Attorney General's office is concerned.

This recommendation, if adopted, will correct misuse of the Attorney General's list of subversive organizations by laymen. There has been a tendency on the part of some employing concerns to assume that anyone who has been affiliated with any of these organizations on the list must have subversive tendencies. Actually, unless one has the necessary experience and information to realize that these organizations vary from the relatively innocent to the extremely dangerous, he is not in a position to evaluate the record of any of his employees. Literally thousands of sincere and loyal persons were attracted to various front organizations during the period of open party activity, and particularly during the era of the United Front from 1935 to 1945. Since the entire Communist Party line is carefully groomed and tailored to exert the widest possible appeal, it exerts a powerful attraction to opponents of racial and religious discrimination, proponents of better housing and working conditions, supporters of an idealistic world government, pacifists, those who wish to immediately discontinue all atomic weapons tests and who yearn for peace at any price, and a widely assorted group of ultra-liberals.

These non-Communists made up the bulwark of membership in all of the front organizations during the period of open party activity, since there were not enough party members to keep the organization financed and active. The effect of these highly articulate Communist fronts on American public opinion is simply incalculable. By exchanging their membership lists. it was. possible for petitions, telegrams and letters bearing thousands of names to be mustered almost over night and channeled into the offices of state and federal legislators to influence their votes in subtle conformity with the existing party line.

A recent example of the effectiveness of this type of propaganda is seen in the actions of an extremely liberal minority of the World Order Study Conference, which met under the sponsorship of the National Council of Churches of Christ in November, 1958. This minority persuaded the conference to adopt a resolution urging the United States to immediately recognize Communist China and to admit it to membership in the United Nations with full privileges. Then a cleverly worded statement was released to the press, pointedly inferring that

---

[61] See report of the Commission on Government Security, issued pursuant to Public Law 304, Eighty-fourth Congress, as amended, June, 1957, Washington, D. C., pp. 645-655.

these matters were passed, not only by the conference, but by the national council, which represented a majority of American Protestants. Rev. Daniel A. Poling, and the Rev. Norman Vincent Peale, having taken the trouble to learn something about the Communist techniques of propaganda and front organization activities, became suspicious and began a poll of 45,000 Protestant preachers. Of the 8,572 answers already received, 87 percent voted *against* the resolution, 11 percent in favor of it and 2 percent expressed no opinion.

Most of the largest and active front organizations that flourished during the period of the party's open activity have been quietly liquidated. This was caused by persistent and constant exposure of their concealed control by the many hearings conducted by committees on un-American Activities, by hearings before the Subversive Activities Control Board and publication of the Attorney General's list of subversive organizations. This sort of exposure, as we have pointed out, hoisted the warning signals for all to see and took away much of the camouflage that had been concealing the Communist character of the organizations from public scrutiny. This stripping aside of the protective coloration also took away much of the excuse from even the most naive liberals for affiliating with these movements innocently. And after the Khrushchev speech at the Twentieth Congress of the Communist Party of the Soviet Union in February, 1956, the signal was given for the launching of the Second United Front period and the Communists throughout the world began to function through existing non-Communist organizations of a liberal character, rather than through its own galaxy of front organizations.

At the present time we still have a few of the more potent front organizations doing business on a rather active scale. The Citizens Committee for Protection of the Foreign Born is especially active in Los Angeles and San Francisco; the Citizens Committee to Preserve American Freedoms is also active in both cities, but especially in Los Angeles; the American-Russian Institute, which seeks to foster trust and confidence in all things Soviet, is still active, as is the Emergency Civil Liberties Committees which was created in 1951, after the American Communists began to retreat to underground positions. We have already described the National Lawyers Guild, and we should not conclude this section without referring to the Los Angeles Chapter of the American Civil Liberties Union.

· In previous reports we have traced the origin and development of the American Civil Liberties Union as a national organization. We have also, from time to time, discussed the activities of its branches in San Francisco and Los Angeles. During the middle thirties and for a short period in 1946 and 1947, we received evidence that we believed justified the statements appearing in our 1943 and 1948 reports to the effect that the American Civil Liberties Union in California had become a transmission belt for the dissemination of Communist propaganda. We do not believe that the American Civil Liberties Union nationally is in any sense subversive; a part of its function is the protection of civil liberties of all people, regardless of the fact that some of them may be members of the Communist Party or other subversive organizations. The American Civil Liberties Union has also defended the right of Gerald L. K. Smith to make public addresses, and during the last war it performed similar services in defending the rights of members of the German-American Bund, especially on the Pacific coast and particularly in California. The Southern California chapter of this organization has, however, devoted an unusually large part of its time and energies to the protection and defense of Communist Party members, and to the support of Communist organizations and fronts.

It is difficult to make a firm and permanent evaluation of an organization like the Southern California Chapter of the American Civil Liberties Union. As its personnel fluctuates, so does the ideological character of the institution itself. The national organization has a policy that no member of the Communist Party can hold an office. This move, obviously motivated because of a realization that the Communist Party is a subversive organization and that it poses a constant and deadly menace to the preservation of all of our cherished institutions, has not been reflected by the activities of its Southern California branch in recent years. We make no criticism, of course, because the Los Angeles Chapter, like the other chapters of the American Civil Liberties Union, protects the civil rights of Communists as well as other people. It is a fact, however, that in addition to carrying out the regular functions of the organization, some of its representatives and some of its officers have persistently attended Communist front meetings, have joined many Communist fronts, and have participated at banquets and receptions honoring some of the leading Communists of the United States. Such activities are hardly in conformity with the anti-Communist policy of the national organization and most of its chapters throughout the United States.

Several years ago a schoolteacher in the northern part of the state was accused of being subversive by a radio commentator whose broadcast alleged that she was a member of the United World Federalists, which he described as a Communist dominated organization. As a result of these broadcasts and criticisms the teacher was discharged. She brought a suit for reinstatement and for damages against the commentator and the radio station that employed him, and a representative of this committee went to San Francisco as an expert witness. He testified that we had never listed the United World Federalists as a subversive organization, had no evidence that it was Communist controlled, and that we did have evidence that it was *not* a Communist front. Such an organization is an obvious target for Communist infiltration, but by the same token so is the American Civil Liberties Union, because it espouses the defense of unpopular causes and members of unpopular organizations; and so is every trade union because through control of industry a country can be paralyzed; and so is every educational institution because they are lush fields for indoctrination and recruiting and provide future intellectual leadership for the Communist Party. Some chapters of a national organization may be penetrated at one time or another to such an extent that they become transmission belts for the Communist Party line; at the same time, other chapters of the same organization may be militantly anti-Communist. One of the most militantly anti-Communist chapters of the American Civil Liberties Union, indeed, is situated in Washington, D. C., and the National Director of the ACLU, Mr. Patrick Murphy Malin, is certainly no friend of Communism. The Los Angeles Chapter of the American Civil Liberties Union, by permitting its officers and official representatives to participate in Communist front meetings and propaganda activities, is hardly being objective, and if it resents charges of partiality towards the extreme Left, these criticisms are generated by its own activities and it has no one to blame but itself.

The Communist Book Stores

Before concluding this section on Communist front organizations, we should say a word about the two major propaganda outlets in this state: The International Book Store in San Francisco, and the Progressive Book Store in Los Angeles. The former is located at 1408 Market Street near the Fox Theater, and the latter is located at 1806 West Seventh Street. Such stores are nothing more than Communist fronts, since they carry and disseminate party literature and propaganda material from all over the world. In these stores one can purchase propaganda material from Red China, from all of the Iron Curtain countries, from North Korea and North Viet Nam, from Indonesia, from the Middle East countries, from Africa, from England, Italy, France, Germany, Mexico, South American countries, and inordinately large amounts from India. In addition, one may purchase current editions of the weekly Communist newspaper printed in California, *the People's World,* also copies of the *Daily Worker* from New York, copies of *Political Affairs,* the ideological publication of the National Committee of the Communist Party of the United States from which we have already quoted extensively, *Masses & Mainstream,* a cultural publication under Communist auspices; and the theoretical organ on Marxism called *Science and Society,* which is published in New York. In addition, there are publications of the National Council of American-Soviet Friendship, the Emergency Civil Liberties Committee, *Facts for Farmers,* and the publications of a great many Communist dominated trade union organizations. We have also received considerable testimony of indisputable accuracy showing that from these two main outlets for Communist literature the various units of the Communist Party organization throughout the pacific coast are kept supplied with material for study and research.

The person who is usually in charge of the Progressive Book Store in Los Angeles is Frank Spector, a Russian Communist who has been defying efforts to deport him for a good many years, and who has appeared before this committee as a witness. Until the "secret" Khrushchev speech in February, 1956, the contents of this book store were uniformly and militantly Communist. Thereafter a few books began to appear on the shelves that in the old days would have been considered completely heretical. For example, before the publication of Dr. Zhivago by Boris Pasternak, there was a book called Not by Bread Alone. Dudintsev, the author, held a prominent place in the literary fraternity of the Soviet Union. During the Stalin regime and until the Khrushchev speech heretofore mentioned, the clamps of rigid censorship had been tightened to such an extent that no Soviet writer dared to produce anything that was not in strict conformity with the Communist line, and certainly he would never dare publish a single word that was even inferentially critical of the Soviet regime. But in the Khrushchev speech there was a promise that these old rules should be relaxed, that criticism should be invited, that Bolshevik self-criticism was an excellent thing, and that writers should be free to publish their true feelings. This book, Not by Bread Alone, was certainly critical of the Soviet regime and it rocked the intellectual foundations of the country. Yet it was being sold in the Progressive Book Store in Los Angeles by Frank Spector. In addition, even after he had been imprisoned in Yugoslavia for such rash heresy, Milovan Djilas' book, The New Class, was also sold in the Progressive Book Store, as were copies of the Pasternak book, Dr. Zhivago. No such attitude was taken in the San Francisco outlet, the books in the International Book Store clinging steadfastly to the Communist cause, and carrying no item that was critical of the Soviet regime or the party line. We almost neglected to say that in addition to the three books already mentioned that were sold in Los Angeles, there was another, even more indicative, called The Naked God, by Howard Fast. This book, which is a garbled but nevertheless angry and vehement criticism of the Communist Party of the United States published shortly after Fast left the organization, was roundly lambasted in Political Affairs by a reviewer under the title, "The Nakedness of Howard Fast." Yet this book was sold with the three companion volumes heretofore mentioned under the direction of Frank Spector in the Progressive Book Store in Los Angeles.

Why this sudden deviation from the old and rigid Party line? Obviously, the cause is attributable either to the fact that the Progressive Book Store wants to divert suspicion from itself or because it has made a sincere and pronounced deviation from the path of Communist rectitude. We believe it has done the latter, that it has received great criticism because of this deviation, and we will set forth our reasons in detail in that section of the report which is entitled, "Current Communist Techniques."

THE PARTY GOES UNDERGROUND

During the second World War, Russia received such staggering quantities of material from the United States, and was so anxious for the Allies to open a second front and relieve the pressure of the German attack against the Soviet Union that it was expedient to soft-pedal the activities of the Communist Party and the hordes of Soviet agents that had successfully infiltrated some of the most sensitive positions in our government. Consequently Earl Browder, then the head of the Communist Party of the United States, was allowed to change the policy of the party, toning down its brash and defiant activities and urging Communist collaboration with capitalist powers; changing the name of the Communist Party to the more innocuous Communist Political Association, and in general to adopt a soft policy of collaboration. This continued until some months after the war was over, when it became desirable—from the International Communist standpoint—of getting affairs back to normal; that is, back to an old anti-capitalist, militant Communist line. Browder was considered expendable for the achievement of this purpose. He was criticized by the French theoritician, Jacques Duclos, when the latter returned from a Moscow conference, and shortly thereafter was expelled from the Communist Party of the United States. That organization immediately resumed its old militant tactics on an even more ambitious scale, and thus invited counter-measures on the part of our own government officials.

Smith Act prosecutions were commenced after painstaking and characteristically thorough investigations by the Federal Bureau of Investigation. It is a well-known fact that the leaders of the American Communist Party have occupied their positions of authority for many years, perpetuating themselves in office over and over again. Consequently when these leaders were convicted and taken out of circulation, the party was temporarily demoralized. At the same time there was a marked acceleration on the part of legislative committees in exposing the front organizations and propaganda media throughout the country, and these organizations and party organs began to suffer from a lack of membership and a lack of funds.

It is obvious, of course, that the Communist Party had prepared itself to some extent for these exigencies. Second- and third-string squads of leaders had been selected, and the party had also followed the Kremlin's order to the letter in preparing a parallel underground party organization that could be activated at a moment's notice. The federal judiciary was uniformly upholding convictions for contempt by legislative committees when witnesses arrogantly shouted epithets at members of federal and state legislatures, and stubbornly refused to answer the most fundamental questions about places of birth, places of residence, occupations, and marital status. A long string of unbroken judicial precedent resulted in fines and jail terms for these recalcitrant witnesses; the front organizations were running shy of members and funds, the leaders of the Communist Party were serving terms in federal penitentiaries after having been convicted in a series of Smith Act prosecutions—and the federal judiciary had established solid legal precedent upholding these actions against the leaders of the Communist conspiracy that was seeking to destroy us and had been openly proclaiming that purpose for 30 years.

So effective were these counter-measures on the part of our own government that the Communist leaders issued defiant statements. Eugene Dennis, General Secretary of the Communist Party of the United States, made an angry declaration after being released from a federal prison. He had prepared the address for delivery at a meeting of a Communist front, the Committee to Reverse the Smith Act, sponsored by the Civil Rights Congress, attended by 3,500 people and held at the Rockland Palace in Harlem. He was unable to deliver the speech at the meeting on June 26, 1951, because of illness, and on July 2, of that year he and six other members of the National Committee of the Communist Party of the United States began serving their five-year sentences after having been convicted for violating the Smith Act by a federal jury. Since some of the remarks contained in this speech not only established the fact that when Communist leaders print this sort of material in their official ideological publication it is not to be taken lightly, and because some of the statements reflected the party's retreat to underground positions and its war to bring about a change in the judicial precedent that was hamstringing its activities, we quote it liberally. Dennis said:

"Friend and foe alike know that this is an important turning point in the life of the Communist Party. Never before in the 30 stormy years of our Party's history have 11 of its national leaders faced long prison terms. Never before have lawyers been jailed for courageously defending Communists in court. Never before has the organizing of the vanguard Party of the American working class been unconstitutionally declared an act of 'criminal conspiracy.' Never before has our Party—or any other American political party—been deprived by judicial edict of its legal rights and constitutional liberties.

These facts are well known. Nobody has any doubts that we Communists find ourselves in a new situation. And there is much speculation about what we are going to do now.

But not everybody has grasped the cardinal truth that the American people are in a new situation. Many who are far from happy about the Vinson decision [a decision by the U. S. Supreme Court upholding the validity of the Smith Act prosecutions] have not yet awakened to the fact that this turning point in the life of the Communist Party is also a critical turning point in the life of the Nation.

Many who have been alarmed at the step-at-a-time advances of Fascist-like reaction over the postwar years are still not aware that the process of Fascization and advanced war preparation in the U. S. A., are now undergoing a *qualitative change.*

The Vinson decision nullifies the First Amendment and its guarantees of freedom of speech, press, and assembly. This is a drastic, pro-Fascist encroachment upon the democratic gains and traditions of the people.

But the Vinson decision does more.

It signalizes the blotting out of constitutional guarantees and threatens the breakdown of *all* institutions of bourgeois democracy.

The *Wall Street Journal* felt obliged to chide Felix Frankfurter for letting the cat out of the bag. The rule of expediency, Justice Frankfurter declared in his concurring opinion, is to become the supreme law; it is no longer necessary to conform to the Constitution. Six judges have changed the rules to meet the needs of the Sixty Families of Big Capital. Now Wall Street's government needs no longer to worry about constitutionality. It is free from all restraint, except that imposed on it by the people themselves.

The Vinson decision affects all Americans, because it is a major victory for pro-Fascist reaction. It gives warning that the war-mad monopolists mean to lose no time in stepping up the tempo, expanding the scope, increasing the ferocity of repression.

This victory for the pro-Fascist forces immeasurably increases the dangers of Fascism and world war.

* * * if the Vinson decision is not effectively challenged, we are going to have even more rigid thought control than that already plaguing Americans in every walk of life. But we are also going to have far more rigid controls over wages, and over the economic and political activity of the trade unions. Hand in hand with this will go still greater license for the war profiteers, big business, exploiters and big-time crime syndicates.

If the Justice Department is permitted to carry out its threat of mass frameup arrests and prosecutions, many who are far from being Communist sympathizers will be taken as 'prisoners of war' —along with the Eleven, the Seventeen, and other Communist leaders. But those who retain their liberty will not escape new hardships. The frameup will become a device for imposing ever more brutal speedup, ever-rising living costs, and ever-declining of real wages. Those responsible for mounting inflation will not be among those arrested, nor will the war profiteers. The tax burden will grow and grow.

Every casualty we Communists may suffer will be duplicated many times over by the people as Wall Street wreaks its vengeance on the working class and the camp of peace.

Our Party is the vanguard of the Negro people's struggle for equality and national liberation. If the Communist Party is driven underground, every lynch-minded white supremacist will come out

in the open. If Henry Winston and Ben Davis, as well as Eugene
Dennis and Gus Hall, go to jail, police brutality against Negroes
and legal lynchings will mount. If judicial edict can outlaw the
party of Negro-white unity, this same edict can be used to outlaw
all united struggle against discrimination. * * *

Under conditions of legality, we Communists have been working with some success to win millions to our immediate aims and
programs. That aim is the establishment of a broad peace front,
opposed alike to the war policies of the war-partisan Truman administration, MacArthur's 'loyal opposition' and the so-called
'isolationists' like Hoover and Taft.''

Then, after repeating his previous criticism of the Supreme Court
decision upholding the Smith Act conviction, reiterating his propaganda against the capitalist enemy, and quoting from a book written
by William Z. Foster, Chairman of the American Communist Party,
Dennis continued:

*"The economic royalists have succeeded in depriving our Party
of its constitutional rights, and now they are determined to im-
prison its leadership and drive the Communist Party underground.*

*We are going to fight for the liberty of our leaders. We are
going to resist being driven underground. But wherever we are we
are going to be with and among the masses."* (Committee's italics.)

  *   *   *   *   *   *   *

"But no matter what happens, our Communist Party is not
doomed to burrow in the dark like a blind mole. To the extent that
we may be driven underground, we carry the beacon light of
Marxist Science with us. Its study and mastery will guide us
under all conditions and constantly replenish our leadership.

Every Communist worthy of the name will be able to lead
broad masses—under any and all circumstances. The more difficult
the conditions imposed on us become, the more essential it is for
every member of our Party to become a better Marxist, in order
to guarantee that the working class and people may have their
path of struggle illuminated by its light.

Marxism imbues us with working-class principles which are
universal, general, and beyond compromise under any circumstances. Marxism enables us to have a clear perspective at all
times, and to care for the future of our class while championing its
present and immediate interest and those of all the people.''

  *   *   *   *   *   *   *

"Trade-union struggle will go on in spite of internal 'purges,'
and F.B.I. 'screening' of the workers in industry. It is going on
right now in the maritime industry, and there will be other struggles, other strikes—no matter how many Communists go to jail.''

  *   *   *   *   *   *   *

"Certainly, the struggle for peace cannot be brought to a close
by any court edict. Recognition of the Chinese People's Republic,

peaceful negotiation to end the war in Korea, a halt to Anglo-American moves to complete the rearming of Western Germany and Japan, a five-power pact of peace—these are slogans of action around which increasing millions of Americans are going to rally and organize—Smith Act or no Smith Act!

We Communists are going to fight to the last ditch for our constitutional and inalienable right to participate openly in these struggles.

But if we are driven underground—our enemies will not be able to prevent us from moving ever deeper into the thick of the people's mass movement.

The forms of struggle may change, to accord with new and more difficult conditions. But as Marxists we know that the struggle will go on. And now, even more than before, the struggle will decide everything. (Committee's italics.)

Our Party was born in struggle, steeled and educated in struggle. We thrive and grow in struggle which brings to our leadership and ranks the best men and women the working class, the negro people, and all other sections of the population can produce.

But, as we face up to the manifold problems and difficulties of this new situation, we recognize the struggle will now bring new hardships to all of us—and our families.

Under these circumstances, courage of course is indispensable. And I am confident that, individually and collectively, we Communists have plenty of courage. But personal courage in itself is not enough. We need the kind of courage that flows from steadfast conviction and fidelity to principle. We need the courage that is not to be confused with recklessness, that shows concern for people and care for the integrity and welfare of the Party as a whole. We need courage that is accompanied by flexibility and tactics, by skill in fighting *the enemy.** (Committee's italics.)

I am confident that our Party, its leadership and its membership, will rise to meet this new challenge and give a good account of itself before the American working class to which it is responsible.

But I would remaind you that our Marxist Science warns us at all times to be on guard against those Right and Left dangers, to wage the struggle for our correct line and policy always on two fronts. Now more than even [sic] we must struggle against *both* panic and complacency, against sectarianism and adventurism, and against capitulation and liquidationism.

I think I have already made it clear that there is no ground now for complacency. And all thoughtful Americans, recalling the

---

* By "The Enemy" Communists express the class struggle which is a basic and indispensable part of Communist ideology, and the enemy refers to every person and institution that is not pro-Communist, and in particular the judiciary which upheld the convictions of the Marxian leaders, and the "repression" by the FBI, the legislative committees, and all other governmental agencies engaged in an effort to protect our country from internal subversion.

catastrophe ushered in by Hitler's Nuremberg decrees, found the warning of the grave dangers which the Vinson decision holds for our working class and people." [62]

The F. B. I. had for years been sending its undercover agents deep into the heart of the American Communist Party. Even as the Russian espionage apparatus had managed to place its agents, largely recruited from the ranks of the American party, in many sensitive government positions, so was the Federal Bureau of Investigation able to place many of its undercover agents in extremely high and responsible positions in the Communist movement. Consequently, when the time came to launch the Smith Act prosecutions, case followed case until the first, second and third string groups of Communist officials were behind bars and the party was—for a time—greatly demoralized. This resulted in a retreat to underground positions accompanied by a grim resolve to bring about a change in the law which permitted this disruption of the party program by locking up the leadership, and also an equally deadly resolution to fight to the death both the Federal Bureau of Investigation and legislative committees on un-American Activities. These were no idle gestures. The party was desperate and it was engaged in a fight for its very life. The intention to wage warfare on these three fronts, viz., against the legal situation that permitted repressive measures against the party, against the F. B. I., and against the legislative committees, was, as we shall see, expressed in such angry, vehement and unmistakable terms that even the most gullible manic-progressive could not have the slightest doubt about what the party intended to do.

The phenomenal growth of California since the end of the last war, the rapid multiplication of its defense industries, its importance as a communication and transportation center, and its enormous strategic importance by reason of its physical situation have combined to make it especially attractive for Communist activity. Consequently, Communists from all over the United States, and particularly from the Middle West, have been coming to this state in great numbers. In addition, the fact that California is contiguous to Mexico gives it an espionage significance that we cannot afford to overlook. Intelligence officers who have had practical experience in the counter-subversive field have known for years that the espionage activities of the Communist movement in America have been directed both from Canada and from Mexico, but during the past several years Mexico has achieved a much greater significance. It was not illogical, then, for the Communist Party of the United States to plant the nerve center of its underground apparatus in this state.

---

[62] "Our Cause Is Invincible," by Eugene Dennis. *Political Affairs,* August, 1951, p. 1-11.

Underground, But Not Deep Enough

From the state capitol at Sacramento a motorist can proceed in a general northerly direction through magnificent mountain scenery along State Highway 40 to a little community called Twain Harte. This part of the state is sparsely settled, and in the summer time caters to fishermen, hunters and tourists. In a small and isolated cabin in the vicinity of Twain Harte the Communist Party concealed the center of its nation-wide underground apparatus. The location had been picked with great care, both because of its isolated position, because a party of four or five men and three or four women going in and out of the area would create no suspicion, and because it would be relatively simple for them to pose as a party of tourists. Communication with the other segments of the underground organization was maintained by courier, as was contact with the two segments of the California Communist Party, both that which functioned in a relatively open manner, and that which was a part of the underground. Supplies of food and other necessities were regularly brought to the cabin, there were very few visitors, and those responsible for Communist security felt that they had not only followed all of the basic directions established by such Soviet experts as B. Vassiliev, and his Soviet disciple in the United States, J. Peters, but had also obtained the benefit of the best specialists the party could produce for the purpose of implementing these basic precepts and taking every possible precaution to insure the continued secrecy of this very vital center.

But the Federal Bureau of Investigation, now being subjected to a vicious and widespread attack by the American Communists and their stooges, was alert to the situation. A number of agents were sent from the San Francisco field office to northern California, and while posing as fishermen and tourists maintained a close surveillance on the establishment and even closer surveillance on every one who entered or left the premises. There was a good deal of communication between the F. B. I. field office and Washington headquarters for the purpose of perfecting devices whereby our government could obtain information about the conversations that were occurring between these underground leaders, about their plans for implementing the secret organization, concerning strategy and tactics to be placed in operation, and concerning the nature of the rest of the underground structure. A detailed discussion of these precautions and of the devices employed by the F. B. I. in this particular instance have no place in this report. They would, however, make fascinating reading, and if they can ever be disclosed they would provide further prestige to an enormously successful and magnificent organization that has stood like a tower of strength between the Communist agents in this country and their persistent and ever-continuing efforts to subvert us. The F. B. I. is not prone to defend itself from attack or to sing its own praises, but most assuredly the unmasking of this nerve-center of the Communist underground was one of its most distinguished contributions.

When the proper time came the agents descended upon the Twain Harte cabin and arrested the occupants. These security experts of the Communist underground were ignominiously taken to San Francisco, fingerprinted and booked, then, in due course of time, prosecuted in the United States District Court in San Francisco. They were represented by Richard Gladstein, together with several of the other Communist lawyers who have been discussed earlier in this report. Since the defendants preferred not to testify, and steadfastly refused to even admit their true identities, it became necessary for the United States Attorney to establish their identity for the benefit of the court and the jury.

At this stage of the proceedings an elderly man was called to the witness stand, identified as an F. B. I. fingerprint expert who had been flown here from Washington, and he proceeded to qualify himself as a fingerprint and identification specialist of more than 20 years practical experience. He then introduced a sackful of empty beer cans that were taken from the Twain Harte cabin at the time the defendants were placed under arrest, and produced large sheets of transparent plastic material on which had been superimposed the fingerprints taken from· the beer cans and enlarged to the size of an average office desk top. These fingerprints and the enlargements were made under the supervision of the expert witness, who then produced the actual fingerprints of the defendants themselves that were taken at the time they were booked. These had also been enlarged to the exact and precise dimensions of the latent fingerprints that had been taken from the beer cans. These actual prints were also on transparent plastic material of the same dimensions as the latent prints taken from the cans. After having identified each one of the defendants together with his actual fingerprints, the sheet containing those prints was placed over a sheet of latent prints, and every irregularity, every minute loop and whorl corresponded perfectly. This procedure was followed with each one of the defendants whose prints were taken at the time of the booking, and in each instance the fingerprints taken from the beer cans not only matched perfectly; but the presentation was so graphic and so unassailable that there could be no possible doubt about the establishment of identity.

This was, of course, one of the basic elements of the case, and the trial terminated in the conviction of the principal Communist functionaries, and in addition produced what was probably a far more important result; it indicated to the Communist Party and to its Soviet bosses the efficiency of the Federal Bureau of Investigation and its ability to penetrate into even the murkiest depths of the American Communist underground despite every precaution to insure against such discovery and exposure.

We cannot refrain from stating parenthetically that even one of the present Justices of the United States Supreme Court, while traveling through the Middle East during this period of the Communist retreat to

underground positions, found a parallel situation in many of the countries he was visiting and also discovered that the party organization
there had been broken up into small units of not more than five people
and usually only three, for purposes of security. This indicates that the
Communist Parties of the world were following the same basic principles of security organization in maintaining their underground apparatus, that retreat to such positions was carefully being co-ordinated
and directed by a central agency, and that this agency could only be
the Soviet Union which devised the basic strategy for the maintenance
of underground organizations and expressed those principles in a document from which we shall shortly quote. The Supreme Court Justice
who made this trip was Justice William O. Douglas, and he described
his impressions as follows:

> "* * * Today they are mostly underground. They meet se-
> cretly; there are three at a meeting and a meeting lasts perhaps ten
> minutes—just long enough to exchange confidences, bolster up
> courage, and decide on the party line." [63]

The Communist Party of the United States was, at the time Justice
Douglas' book was published, ever since has been and still is broken up
into units of not more than five and usually three individuals for
security purposes, and meetings are held at card tables in private
homes, in restaurants and other public places, and only one individual
in each of these triangles knows who to contact in the triangle above
and the triangle below. Since we have discussed this organizational
structure in previous reports, there is no necessity to elaborate further
on it here.

The Vassiliev Document

In 1948 this committee participated in a seminar on counter-subversive activities and techniques at the Presidio of San Francisco. Approximately 800 people attended the series of lectures for two days, and they
included intelligence personnel from both the Army and the Navy,
representatives of the Federal Bureau of Investigation, members of the
California Peace Officers Association, representatives of various District Attorneys, together with agents of the Office of Special Investigations, the Civil Service Commission, the Immigration Service, and all
other official agencies that were legitimately interested in counter-
subversive problems. Former members of the Communist Party addressed the gathering, as did other lecturers, including Senator Burns,
the chairman of this committee, and R. E. Combs, its counsel.

On that occasion both Senator Burns and Mr. Combs quoted from a
document that had long been in the committee's possession, and which,
so far as we know, had not previously been released. It was known as
the Vassiliev Document. Part of it had appeared in the Communist

---

[63] Strange Lands and Friendly People, by William O. Douglas. Harper & Bros., New
York, 1951, p. 3.

press in 1931, and ever since that time it had been used and is still being used as a basis for underground organization by the Communist Parties of the world. The author, B. Vassiliev, was an instructor in these matters at the Lenin School in Moscow, which we have previously described as a training center for carefully selected Communists from the various parties throughout the world who went to the Red academy and prepared themselves for espionage work for three or four years during which they listened to lectures by experts such as Vassiliev, witnessed techniques that were most effective in blowing up steel supports for high voltage electric transmission lines, tunnels, bridges, railroad tracks, and other bourgeois targets. There were also classes in the effective sabotaging of food stuffs, radio stations, steamships, reservoirs of domestic water supply, coupled with courses in high-level political activity designed to accomplish the most effective infiltration of large masses of people, especially in the backward countries of the world.

We realize that these matters are completely outside the orbit of the average American's activities. But they have been established by the unshakeable testimony of individuals who attended these courses and since defected from the party; the Vassiliev document has been thoroughly authenticated and is in the archives of the committee. Fragments of it have been, since 1948, published by various other agencies— but since there is an active Communist underground in California, and since it is slavishly following the directions established by the Vassiliev document, and since the nerve center for the entire Communist underground was located in this state, and because we believe the members of the California Legislature and people of this state should have an adequate understanding of the techniques being employed by the Communist agents in our midst, we believe it highly desirable and practical to reproduce portions of the Vassiliev document herewith.

As was pointed out by Ralph de Toledano, the author of Seeds of Treason, the definitive work on the Alger Hiss case, and an authority in the counter-subversive field:

> "The underground Party is organized on Bakuninist lines, concretized by one B. Vassiliev in 1931, under the title: *Organizational Problems and Underground Revolutionary Work.* This Communist outline runs to five pages. It merits serious study. Vassiliev directed:
>
> 'In proportion as the legal apparatus of the Party is liquidated, the directing functions will inevitably require a regrouping of Party forces. This reconstruction of the work will pass more and more to the illegal apparatus.'
>
> This has been going on, carefully and methodically, since the inception of the cold war." [64]

---

[64] This We Face, by Ralph de Toledano. *American Mercury,* April, 1959, p. 38-41.

The pertinent parts of the Vassiliev lecture to students of the graduating class at the Lenin School in Moscow is as follows:

"In * * * conditions of growing economic crisis and heightened threat of war against the U.S.S.R. all measures will be taken by the ruling classes of the capitalist countries to guarantee their rear before declaring war; that is, everything will be done by them to weaken, disorganize and, as far as possible, liquidate completely all revolutionary proletarian organizations, and in the first place the Communist Parties.

If until recently it was necessary to talk of the campaign of the ruling classes against the Communist Parties, and of the Parties having to prepare for transferring to underground work, now all parties are facing an extermination in the preparation which has been carried out. In the first place the Communist Parties of the advanced capitalist countries must now have a concrete plan of what to do if the country should be declared under martial law and a beginning made dealing with Communists according to military law. At the same time the U.S.S.R. enlarged plenum of the ECCI, [Executive Committee of the Communist International], demands from the Communist Parties that they should undertake such forms and such a pace of Party work as to allow them in spite of all repression, in spite of mass arrests of leading workers and rank and file members of the Communist Parties, in spite of the suppression of the legal Party press, to strengthen to the maximum degree their mass work, so as to draw the broadest proletarian masses into the revolutionary struggle." *

" * * * With regard to the meetings of the Party Committees it is still essential to have in view the following rule, which is absolutely binding for illegal Communist Parties. At the meeting of the Party Committee, or in any case at the plenary meeting at which representatives of the rank and file Party activists take part, those members must not be present in whose hands are the connections with Party organizations, addresses, etc., because if the police arrest such a meeting, then the whole Party Committee will be arrested, and to reorganize the Party organization after all the addresses, connections and so on, have been lost, is naturally very difficult. It is necessary that at least one comrade who keeps the addresses, connections, etc., should not come to the meetings of the Party Committee and that at the moment of the meeting of the Party Committee he should take special measures of precaution to avoid the arrests, which usually follow on the rounding up of a Party Committee by the means of those addresses and connections which the police get hold of in the course of the same.

* Compare with the statements contained in the address by Eugene Dennis, quoted above.

Before big revolutionary demonstrations and mass proletarian actions, which are being prepared by illegal Communist Parties, this rule must also apply to all illegal Communist Parties.

What should be the distribution of work within the Party Committee? The following are the most important functions. First, the Secretary of the Party Committee. Not only is it not necessary for the Secretary of the Committee of a Communist Bolshevik Party to be the political leader of the committee, but as a rule he should not be a political leader * * * In the Russian Party the Secretary of the Committee is at the same time the leader of the Party Committee. But in the underground party the position was quite different. Then the Secretary was never the leader of the Party Committee. He was a comrade who was responsible for connections with the Party organizations above and below; for conversations with comrades who were in need of this or that advice or information from the Party Committee, and so on.

Why is such a rule essential? It is important because the Secretary of the Party Committee in illegal and semilegal conditions is the person on whom, above all, the blow of action will fall. If that person is the political leader of the Party Committee then naturally his arrest will affect very harmfully all the work of the Party Committee. The political leader of the Party Committee should not perform secretarial work and in general, as a rule, should not be connected with the technical functions of the Party apparatus. I think this rule of Bolshevik underground work should now be transferred completely into the practice of all our Communist Parties.

The responsibility for the publication and the distribution of illegal literature should be placed upon one member of the Party Committee. This function should now be absolutely obligatory for all Communist Parties, including legal Communist Parties, beginning with the Central Committee and ending with the District Committees. We now have it as a general rule that on the eve of big revolutionary actions legal Communist literature is forbidden, confiscated or in the best case censured in such a way that all the Communism is washed out of it. As, for example, in Czechoslovakia. Therefore, if the Party does not have an illegal printing press for the preparation of a political campaign and does not at the same time prepare the publication of illegal literature, then at the most critical moment the Party remains without literature, as happened, for instance, with the Czechoslovakian Communist Party.

* * * All Communist Parties must without fail have an extensive apparatus for the publication of illegal Party literature: printing plants, various kinds of rotary machines, copying machines, mimeographs, and simple hectographs in order to publish illegal literature, newspapers, leaflets, etc. In particular it is absolutely

essential that the local Party Committees should guarantee the publication of the factory papers for the factory cells of the big enterprises, especially in connection with the carrying out of the campaigns. * * * With regard to illegal literature it is also necessary to have ready arrangements for its distribution. For that it is essential to have a *special* apparatus for distribution which must not, as a rule, coincide with the general apparatus of the Party Committee. (Committee's italics.) * Special comrades must be brought into this end, there must be special addresses for the safe-keeping and conveyance of literature from the printing press to the district and from the districts and localities to the factories for distribution among the workers. * * *

One of the members of the committee should undertake the duty of the organization of proletarian self-defense. This is now beyond all doubt essential. There is a great deal of talk about proletarian self-defense, and if all these conversations were brought together they might annihilate the bourgeois by their sheer weight; but the practical results are not worth a halfpenny. There is a certain amount of work on proletarian self-defense in Germany, the Chinese comrades work well, too, they having quite different conditions of work, but about the other Parties it is unfortunately impossible to say anything good. Resolutions are passed, but all the same there is no proletarian self-defense. So, it must become a rule that every Party Committee appoint a special comrade to take charge of this work. This comrade must, by the way, definitely arrange a special training for members of the organization of proletarian self-defense, in order that these organizations may be real self-defense organizations—not the present meetings of comrades which call themselves self-defense organizations. The practice of the proletarian self-defense detachments during recent demonstrations shows that the comrades from the sections of self-defense do not have the slightest conception of any kind of self-defense. When the police attacked them they did not know how to resist. They didn't understand the tactics of street fighting; didn't even know how to box, and as a result in certain cases one policeman broke up dozens of sections of proletarian self-defense, because our comrades waved their arms about aimlessly while the policemen were quite confident and used all the skill of well-framed boxers.

*   *   *   *   *

"At present the question of proper arrangement for learning about the work of our opponent the Social-Fascist, the Fascist, discovering the plans of police with regard to breaking up demonstrations, etc., assumes very great importance. Every Party Com-

---

* We have previously referred to the Aesopian language commonly used in party literature. This language has a peculiar meaning for Communists, and is usually quite unintelligible and confusing to the layman. In Communist parlance the world over, the word "special" refers to underground or espionage activity.

mittee should clearly look at this side of every day Party work; should place on one of its members the special duty of organizing work in this direction and should systematically check how this work is being carried out and what are the pressing concrete tasks.

How can Party Committees be elected in illegal Parties? Naturally, in an illegal Party elections cannot take place as they do in legal Parties, but nevertheless they are possible. That is to say, that the forms of electing Party committees in illegal Parties should be different from those used in legal parties. For example, the election of Party committees at aggregate meetings, at wide conferences, cannot in any case be allowed in illegal parties. There the elections must take place in narrower conferences. The measure of representation at these conferences in illegal Parties must of necessity be very compressed. Moreover, the elections themselves in illegal Parties must come as a rule, take place in such a way that even the members of the conference do not know who is elected on the Party Committee. At the present time two methods of electing leading organs in illegal parties are practiced. The first method: the Party conference elects a special commission for counting the votes cast for candidates for members of the Party Committee. Then the candidates are named and the election of the Party Committee proceeds by secret vote. The commission checks the result of the voting, while it does not report to the conference as to the personnel elected. Another method of election: the conference elects a narrow commission in which a representative of the higher Party Committee takes part, and this narrow committee elects the new Party Committee. In strictly illegal Parties, as for example the Italian Communist Party, the latter method of election is the only one which guarantees more or less strict conspiratorial conditions.

The most important element of successful working of the Party Committee—the one on which during the checking of its work the most serious attention must be concentrated—is the question of connections of· the Party Committee with the higher and lower Party organizations, especially with factory cells and the fractions in the mass non-Party organizations. This question now has a decisive importance, especially in the legal and semilegal Communist Parties. The illegal Communist Parties have already worked out a whole number of measures and methods in order to keep their communications with the lower organizations and with separate members of the Party, in spite of the severest police repression. But with the legal and the semilegal parties there is bad work all the time along this line.

What are the most important methods of communication that is essential to foresee? It is essentially important to have a well-laid-out method of live communication. Live communication is kept

going by the help of the system of so-called appearing or reporting places. What is a reporting point? A reporting point is this:
The Party Committee establishes special addresses or flats or other
places where on certain days at a certain time representatives of
the cells and fractions of the mass organizations must appear.
There, also, representatives of the Party Committees appear. Representatives of the cells and fractions make reports on what has
happened in the factory, what the cell has done, what it proposes
to do, and so on, and representatives of the Party Committee,
having received the report, advise the cell how it should act, passes
on to it the directions of the higher Party organ, and so on. *This
system of appearing places must without fail be established in all
Parties without exception, legal and illegal* (committee's italics),
while the legal Parties a double system of reporting places must
without fail be established—a system of legal and illegal appearing points.

*　　*　　*　　*　　*

"If the Party has already more or less seriously and funda-
mentally gone over to underground conditions, and the shadowing
of leading active Party members has begun, and the Party members are being arrested in the streets, then it is very important
that special signals should be established for the appearing flat,
showing in the first place the safety of the flat; second, showing
that exactly those people have come who were expected, and that
these comrades who have come are talking with exactly those comrades whom the observer is coming to see. In order to show that
the reporting places are in working order—for example, a flower,
a flower pot was placed in the window, the comrade came, saw
that the flowers were there, knew that it was safe, and entered.

For verifying those who come to the reporting places, a system
of passwords is established. The comrade comes to the reporting
point and he says some agreed-upon sentence. They answer to that
agreed-upon sentence with another agreed-upon sentence. So both
comrades check each other. In Russian underground conditions
very complicated passwords were sometimes used in the central
appearing places. This was called for by the circumstances that
different workers passed through different reporting places; rank
and file workers from the cells, district and central Party workers.
Accordingly, one password was picked for the rank and file workers, and more complicated ones for the district workers and a still
more complicated one for the central workers. Why was this necessary? It was necessary for conspirative reasons, since only certain things could be said to the rank and file worker while perhaps
other things could be said to the district worker while you could
speak with full frankness about the whole work of the illegal organization to the representative of the central committee.

Besides flats for reporting points, connecting link flats are also needed for communication by letter, and these flats must in no case coincide. And finally there must be flats for the sheltering of illegal comrades, comrades whom the police are looking for, comrades who have escaped from prison, etc. For all our legal Communist Parties the question of addresses and flats now play the role of first importance. * * * It is essential for all Parties to occupy themselves now in the most serious way with the solution of the 'housing' problem.

It is also necessary to give the most serious attention to the problem of the organization of letter communication. In checking the work of the Party Committee it is necessary to consider this question especially. Does the Party Committee have addresses for communicating by letter with the higher and lower Party organizations, and how are these communications put into practice? Now, even for the legal Parties, the firmest rule must be established that all correspondence concerning the functioning of the Party apparatus must without fail go by special routes guaranteeing letters from being copied in the post. All kinds of special circulars, general information reports on the condition of the Party in legal Parties can go through the ordinary post to legal Party addresses, but everything concerning the functioning of the Party Committee, even in legal parties, must without fail go by special route. In the first place, the use of special courier must be foreseen, who will personally carry letters, not trusting these letters to the state post. Here the Parties must make use of connections which they have with post and telegraph and railway servants, connections with all kinds of commercial travelers for traveling firms, and so on. All these connections must be used in order that without extra expense responsible Party documents can be transported. Further, every Party should take care that every letter, apart from whether it goes through the state post or by courier, should be written in such a way that in case it falls into the hands of the police it should not give the police a basis for any kind of arrest or repression against the Party organization.

This makes the following three requisites. First requisite: the letter must be in code, i.e., all aspects of illegal work are referred to by some special phrase or other. For example, the illegal printing press is called 'auntie;' type is called 'sugar,' and so on. A comrade writes: 'Auntie asks you without fail to send her 20 pounds of sugar.' This will mean that the press is in need of 20 pounds of type. Or a comrade writes: 'We are experiencing great difficulty in finding a suitable flat for our aunt.' That means it is a question of finding a location for the illegal printing press.

Second requisite: besides the code, as above, ciphers are used; illegal parts of letters being put not only into code but also into ciphers. There are many different systems of ciphers. The simplest and at the same time the most reliable is the system of cipher by the help of a book. Some book or other is agreed upon beforehand then the cipher is made in this way: simple fractions or decimals are ciphers. The first figure of the first fraction shows the page of the book. Then further comes the actual cipher. For the numerator of the fraction we must take a line counting from above or below; for the denominator that counting from either the left or right which it is necessary to put into the cipher. For example, we need to put into the cipher the letter 'A.' We look in the book and see that this letter is in the third line from the top, the fourth letter from the left towards the right, then we cipher three over four (3/4), that is, the third line from the top, fourth letter from left to right. Also on this method: for example, counting the line not from above but from below, then the three will not be the third line from above but the third line from below. You can agree to count the letter in the line not from left to right but from right to left. Finally, for greater complexity in order to keep the sense from the police, you can also add to the fraction some number or other. Let us say the numerator is increased by three and the denominator by four. In this case, in order to decipher, it will be necessary first to subtract in the numerator and denominator of every fraction. A whole number of similar variations can be worked out to complicate the ciphers. The advantage of such a cipher is that it is not only very simple but also each letter can be designated by a great number of different signs and in such a way that the cipher designation of letters are not repeated. The book cipher can be used without a book. In place of a book, some poem or other can be chosen, learned by heart and the deciphering done according to it. When it is necessary to cipher or decipher, the poem must be written out in verses and then the ciphering or deciphering done and the poem destroyed.

The third requisite which is also recommended should be used in correspondence, is writing with chemical inks—that is, with such inks that are impossible to read without special adaptation. If a secret Party letter falls into the hands of the police written in invisible ink, the open text of such letters must be made to appear perfectly blameless, for example, a son is writing to his mother that he is alive and well and of the good things he wishes her. Not a word about revolution. The police must guess first of all that under this apparently innocent text there is a hidden text. Having discovered this secret, the police tumble against a cipher. If they succeed in deciphering the cipher, they stumble up against a code and they still have to decipher that code. But all this takes time in the course of which the police can do nothing. If the police succeed in reading it in the course of two or three weeks, then by that time the Party organization has been able to cover up all the consequences of the subject which was written about in the letter.

What kind of invisible ink should be used? Invisible inks exist in very great number. They can be bought in any chemists shop. Finally, comrades must use the latest inventions in chemistry in this direction. The simplest invisible ink which can be recommended and which can be found everywhere, is, for example, onion juice and pure water.

If we consider legal parties which are being driven underground, the question can be put in this way: the Party should fight to the very last to retain all existing forms of the legal working class movement; for the legal existence of the Communist Party; for legal Communist literature; for legal trade unions; for other legal unions of mass organization. In the process of this struggle the Communist Parties of these countries, however great the democratic freedom is at the given moment, however easy at any given moment it may be for them to get permission to publish legal Communist papers, or organize demonstrations, etc., must at the same time construct and strengthen their illegal apparatus from top to bottom. All legal parties are now under the greatest responsibility in respect to the creation and strengthening of an legal party apparatus. All of them must immediately undertake measures to have within the legally-existing Party Committees an illegal directing corps. The illegal part of the Party apparatus must be separated from the legal apparatus of the Party Committee, and a part of the members of the Party Committee must already now be made illegal. Such comrades as Comrade Thaleman [German Communist functionary] cannot go underground. It would be completely stupid for him to be underground at the present moment. Comrade Thaleman and other prominent leaders of the Communist Party must have the possibility of quickly passing underground at the necessary moment; must have the necessary living accomodations for this; must have facilities for quickly changing their names, and all other means of swiftly avoiding the pursuits of the police, so that the police should look for them in quite a different direction to the one in which they have gone.

Besides leaders like Comrade Thaleman who are well known to the whole working class, there are a number of leaders in all Communist Parties who are less well-known or completely unknown to the broad mass of the working class and in wide police circles, but who are well tried in practical Party work. It is very important to bring to leading work those who are unknown to the wide masses and to the police, but who have been tried in the process of every day Party work as good organizers, good conspirators, and completely devoted to the cause of Communism.

Cells of illegal directing organs must be created from among these activists and along with the increasing repression those sections of the Party apparatus which are most susceptible to repression should be handed over to their charge, as well as the more important Party documents, etc. At the same time the legal exist-

ence of the Party Committee and the legal use of the names of
members of the Central Committee and other Party units who
can still legally speak in the name of the Party Committee, etc.,
must be preserved until the last. If this work is properly arranged,
then the police on arriving and securing members of the Central
Committee, district and other Party committees who are known
to it, and seizing the premises of the Party Committee, will seize
only the premises in which there are no Party documents and only
those comrades who do not longer hold in their hands the most
important threats of the Party apparatus. The Party apparatus
carried underground in such cases, at once begins to function,
guaranteeing uninterrupted direction of Party work * * *

Most important and fundamental legal or semi-legal cover for
an illegal Communist Party is the trade union. Therefore, illegal
Communist Parties must give the utmost serious attention to the
trade unions, and must fight with all their strength and by all
means possible for their open existence. Practice has shown that,
for example, in Rumania and even in Yugoslavia, with its violent
Fascist terror, the open existence of Red trade unions under a
strong Communist influence is possible.

* * * The most important question of all Party work is the
question of the active core of the Party. Putting every Party member, every Party worker, in his most suitable place—that is the
kernel of the question, as Lenin liked to put it; and the Party
organizer in order to hit the nail on the head must learn to put
every Party member in his right place, while remembering that
Party members cannot be shuffled around like pawns or children's
bricks, which can be placed in any direction. One Party member
is suitable for the organization of an illegal printing press—he
must be used for this, but he may not be suitable as a propagandist,
and if he is sent to carry on propaganda this will prove of such a
kind that two other propagandists will have to be sent to put his
work right. Another comrade, a fine propagandist and educator,
who knows how to explain in the most popular way the most
difficult political problem, or the most complicated political slogan,
is a bad conspirator if he is on conspirative work and will bring
harm to the Party. Therefore, the Party organizer must in the
most careful way study the human material with which he has to
deal, in order to know for what concrete task that human material
can best be made use of * * * *We must be very bold in making
use of the creative experience of the revolutionary proletarian
masses; this experience has been and will always be the most decisive in the work of the Communist Parties and the whole of the
Communist International.*" (Committee's italics.)

The last sentence quoted above, which we have italicized for emphasis, points up the slavish devotion by all foreign Communist Parties
to the Soviet prototype. The names of the party officials and the duties

imposed on each, the physical organization of the party and its fronts, the security measures of the underground apparatus, even the peculiar Aesopian language employed in communicating between party members—all of these are patterned on the Soviet model. And so inflexible and absolute is Communist Party discipline, that orders issued from above must be carried out without the slightest hesitation or question, and this is particularly true when the orders come from a *Soviet* Communist rather than down through the chain of command that exists in a foreign Communist organization.

In a previous report we have explained how a school for underground organization and activity was maintained in Alameda County at Orinda, and we quoted from the experiences of students who, while devout Communists, attended these classes. They were instructed how to carry on illegal communications, and how to make and operate an illegal printing apparatus from materials found in most kitchens. The use of meeting places and appearing points, the exchange of passwords, the arrangements of flowers as a signal to visitors that they could safely enter may all seem somewhat cloak-and-daggerish to the average reader of this report. We assure you in all sincerity that this is not the case. We have interviewed dozens of former Communist Party members who have actually participated in this sort of activity, and if our readers wish to pursue the matter any further and completely corroborate the fact that the underground in California is today slavishly following the instructions laid down by such experts as B. Vassiliev, we refer them to the books that are cited in the footnote.*

There are many other books, all reliable, dealing with experiences of the authors in the Communist underground in the United States. The cumulative effect of these treatises completely corroborates the fact that the Vassiliev document is being followed by the Communist Party underground in the United States at the present time.

Attention may also be directed to an address made by Dr. J. B. Matthews on the occasion of the thirty-second annual meeting of the American Legion, Department of Connecticut, Hartford, Connecticut, on August 19, 1950. The title of Dr. Matthews' address was, "The Communist Underground," and he made specific reference to the Vassiliev lecture. Dr. Matthews said: "There is no doubt about the complete authenticity of this document. The details of the order amounted to a blueprint of the Communist undergrounds in all countries outside the Soviet Union, the United States of America included. The order embodying these details is a veritable primer for Americans who want to understand the true nature of the Communist Party." As Matthews points out, the Communist Party of the United States has quit issuing membership books or cards and has entrusted knowledge as to the membership of the party to individuals who are not only highly trusted but who pass the information on cards from one place to another

---

* (My Ten Years as a Counter-Spy, by Boris Morros; Witness, by Whittaker Chambers; This Masquerade, by Angela Colamiris; Out of Bondage, by Elizabeth Bentley; Empire of Fear, by Vladimir and Evdokia Petrov.)

for security reasons, and the offices in Los Angeles and San Francisco are completely devoid of party records and documents of any kind. This is in strict accordance with the directions issued by Vassiliev. Complete files of Communist Party membership in the United States have been taken out of the country and kept, at one time or another, in both Mexico and Cuba. Vassiliev's order that places be prepared for the housing of illegal printing plants is reflected in the school established at Orinda where precise instructions in the greatest detail for the maintenance and operation of undercover printing facilities were taught and discussed. The lecture also pointed out the necessity for reserve leadership of the party, and we saw that leadership take over when Smith Act prosecutions placed the regular party officials behind bars.

Vassiliev also urged that the party remain above ground and legal until the last possible minute—and this is reflected by the defiant statements of the party's General Secretary, Eugene Dennis, which we quoted earlier in this section of the report. The material in the Vassiliev lecture concerning letter drops, meeting places, passwords, and clandestine communications, is all amply verified by an examination of the reading sources that we have already mentioned. Any readers who may wish to pursue the subject further will be provided with a reliable list of supplementary sources if they will make the request in writing to this committee in care of Senator Burns.

The reader will recall that toward the end of the Vassiliev document there is an injunction to the leaders of the underground to mobilize the services of the "less well-known or completely unknown" Communist activists "who are well tried in practical Party work * * * unknown to the wide masses and to the police, but who have been tried in the process of everyday work as good organizers, good conspirators, and completely to the cause of Communism." This is the type of hard-core, highly indoctrinated party member who has survived the downgrading of Stalin, the revolts in Hungary and Poland, and who is unshaken in his determination to further the cause of world revolution at all costs. Throughout the United States and in California the party *has* mobilized its relatively unknown membership. It is making use of the lethal fall-out of party members we referred to earlier; it is alerting its "sleeper apparatus" composed of individuals who have been secret party members for many years but who have never paid dues, never attended a meeting, never associated with Communists, but who have wormed their ways into positions of trust and confidence and influence and are now secretly working in behalf of the Communists' objectives. Then, too, there are the captives who once made the mistake of affiliating with the Communist Party, dropped out, climbed to positions of power, prestige and high position over the intervening years, and are now subject to blackmail by their old party contacts who threaten to expose them and ruin them unless they agree to perform little favors upon request.

The fight against Communism in this state is far more challenging, far more difficult and far more necessary than ever. The party is now beginning to pick up additional membership. The deviationists are being forced out of the organization, new leadership is being prepared, new funds are becoming available, and meanwhile the party is still concentrating on the penetration of trade union organizations and educational institutions. It is implementing the Khrushchev directive to create a second and wide United Front by sending its members into mass liberal organizations and seeking to warp them to the Communist way of thinking.

We must constantly bear in mind that we are charged with the duty of protecting the innocent liberal against unjust accusations of subversive activity and affiliation, we must observe the rules of the game, scrupulously protect the civil rights of all who appear before the committee and at the same time endeavor to report to the legislature and to the people concerning the true nature of subversive activities and propaganda within our borders. On the other hand, the Communist Party is bound by no rules of morality, law, decency, or ethics. To the Communist the end justifies the means in all cases, he is disciplined to instantly carry out his assignments, as a witness he is recalcitrant, stubborn, abusive, and does little more than repeatedly invoke the protection of the Fifth Amendment. The challenge is a great one indeed. It is so great that every educator, every trade union official, should take the time to thoroughly inform himself about Communist tactics, and then join the ranks in a broad co-operative effort to stem the infiltrators.

President Eisenhower recently visited the hospital to see Secretary of State John Foster Dulles, who was then recuperating from X-ray treatment for cancer. By the side of Mr. Dulles' bed was a copy of the book by Harry and Bonaro Overstreet, entitled What We Must Know About Communism, W. W. Norton & Co., New York, 1958. The Secretary of State recommended that the President read this volume, and it is now being serialized in the *Los Angeles Times* and other newspapers of wide circulation. While certainly not the best book that has been written about Communism, it is a popular one, and contains much excellent material. Mr. Overstreet and his wife are capable writers, and he learned something about Communist front organizations at first hand, having been lured into a number of them from time to time. Mr. Overstreet is an example of a non-Communist liberal who was attracted to a few of these front organizations, found out what they were all about, and had the courage to do something about the problem instead of shrinking away from the experience and remaining silent. Many people who have had similar experiences—in fact the overwhelming majority of them— are content to remain silent, when by speaking boldly they could strike an effective blow against the menace that

attracted them to its periphery. Writing about the Communist underground, the Overstreet book had this to say:

"It is in the theory of the state once more, that we find the
rationale of one of Lenin's basic edicts: namely, that Communists
in non-Communist countries must maintain both a legal and illegal
apparatus. They must be able to work in the open—through a legal
Party, where this is allowed and through as many fronts as possible
—in order to give 'vanguard' leadership to the masses and to
politicalize their struggles. But also they must be able to work in
the underground, carrying on activities that are patently outside
the law of the land but are called for by the long-range purpose
and 'monolithic unity' of the world Communist movement. Such
double organization, Lenin specified, is necessary in any 'bourgeoise' country—which is to say, any 'enemy' country—just as it
was necessary for the Bolsheviks in Tsarist Russia.

The C. P. U. S. A. has always—or, at least, since it first affiliated with the Comintern—maintained the requisite double apparatus. Between 1920 and 1935, it scarcely bothered to conceal its
double character; or, during those years, it was always seeing the
revolution just ahead. Thus, we have only to turn to early issues
of *The Communist*—forerunner of *Political Affairs*—to read the
record of legal and illegal organization. The October, 1921, issue,
for example, states without equivocation, 'The center of gravity of
our activities is not fixed. It is constantly shifting; sometimes in
the direction of the legal organization, sometimes in the direction
of the underground organization. This center of gravity is at all
times determined by the ever-changing realities of the actual class
struggle.'

An equally frank statement appears in the July, 1922 issue:
'A truly revolutionary (i.e. Communist) party can never be
"legal" in the sense of having its purpose harmonize with the
purpose of the laws made by the capitalist state. * * * Hence, to
call a Communist Party "legal" means that its existence is tolerated by the capitalist state.' The article then goes on to say that
since the 'legal' political party thus exists by 'enemy' tolerance,
the revolutionary cause can never be entrusted to it alone.

As late as 1934, the manifesto of the eighth convention of the
C. P. U. S. A. said that, in view of the 'growing danger of illegal-
ity,' the Party must tighten its discipline, combat spies, and 'insure the secret functioning of the factory nuclei.' "

　　　*　　　　*　　　　*　　　　*　　　　●

"The United States is by no means alone in having to cope with
the problems attendant upon the legal-illegal operations of the
Party. Every non-Communist country in the world faces this same
problem— and deals with them as it thinks best. But no country
has solved them." [65]

---

[65] What We Must Know About Communism, op. cit., pp. 23-35.

Infiltration of Federal Government

Several years ago the committee issued a report in which we earnestly endeavored to describe the international Communist movement, tracing the history of the Russian revolution, the foundation of the Comintern, the establishment of the Communist Parties of the world, history of the Communist Party of the United States, and a history of its activities in California. We did this because we wished to indicate that the movement is international by its very nature, and that a resident of Michigan who was active in Communist activities there on Monday can well be active in California two days later. This elastic, international, ever-shifting and changing aspect of Communism cannot be viewed by focusing a microscope on the activities in California alone. The Communist Party of this state, both above and underground, acts according to the dictates of the Soviet Union. It has always been thus and it ever will be. The party line is carefully timed and correlated like a finely syncronized mechanism, and operates on a global scale. To act provincial about a problem of Communism is to demonstrate a hopeless lack of knowledge concerning its true nature and an equally hopeless ineptitude in analyzing its activities in California with any degree of accuracy. Nevertheless, we were lambasted soundly by some of the more "progressive" members of the press for straying so far afield.

It will be interesting if we receive the same sort of critical treatment from the same sources because we undertake in this report to mention a document like the Vassiliev lecture, to link the second United Front with the Khrushchev speech of February, 1956, and trace the development of the international Communist front organization to Willi Muenzenburg.

The Communist underground in California today is extremely active and it could not possibly be understood unless one is not only familiar with the establishment of the underground headquarters near Twain Harte, but also with the international nature of the Communist movement, and with a document as vital as the Vassiliev lecture. It is the underground organization, for example, that would handle political infiltration and endeavor to control elected officials by placing undercover Communist secretaries in their offices to read their mail, make their appointments and arrange their engagements and speaking dates. It is the underground organization that would contact the unknown party members or "sleepers" in lofty positions and urge them to use their prestige and influence for the benefit of the party. It is the underground apparatus that gives a nudge here, a shove there, applies a deft touch of propaganda at the precise moment when it will be of the greatest effect, that flatters liberals into conformity with the party line, and manipulates the naive do-gooders into positions of unwittingly performing the party's work.

In many situations, indeed, the underground organization of the Communist Party of the United States and its espionage operations are virtually identical. To those of us who may have become complacent, weary of hearing about Communism so frequently, and who have become apathetic and little concerned with this problem, we direct attention to a thoroughly reliable and accurate partial list of employees in high places who were either members of the Communist Party, espionage agents, who invoked the Fifth Amendment when questioned under oath about their Communist activities and affiliations, or were proven to have collaborated with the Communist Party or the Soviet agents in the United States. It will be noted that many of them moved from one important government agency to another through years of infiltrating activity. The staggering damage they did to the security of the United States will probably never be known, but it was obviously tremendous. The partial list is as follows:

State Department

Alger Hiss, head of the Department of Political Affairs.
John Carter Vincent, head of the Far Eastern Division.
Robert T. Miller, Assistant head, Division of Research and Publication.
Maurice Halperin, head of the Latin-American Division.
Laurence Duggan, head of the Latin-American Division.

Henry Collins, Jr.
Leo Drozdoff
Harold Glasser
Irving Goldman
Stanley Graze
Julian Friedman
Mary J. Keeney
Carl Aldo Marzani

DEPARTMENT OF THE TREASURY

Harry Dexter White, Assistant Secretary of the Treasury
Harold Glasser, Director of the Division of Monetary Research and Chief Financial Advisor to the Economic Board following the invasion of North Africa, and Treasury representative to UNRRA.
Frank Coe, Director of the Division of Monetary Research.
Abraham George Silverman, Chief Economist, French Purchasing Mission.
Soloman Adler, Official Treasury Representative to China.
Bela Gold, Division of Monetary Research.
Irving Kaplan, Division of Monetary Research.
Victor Perlo, Division of Monetary Research.
William Ludwig Ullman, Division of Monetary Research.
Edward Fitzgerald
Stanley Graze
William Taylor

DEPARTMENT OF JUSTICE

John Abt, Special Assistant to the Attorney General.
Alger Hiss, Special Assistant to the Attorney General.
Irving Kaplan, Special Assistant to the Attorney General.
Norman Bursler
Donald Hiss
Judith Coplon

DEPARTMENT OF AGRICULTURE

John Abt
Julia Older Blazer
Henry Collins, Jr.
Harold Glasser
Bela Gold
Alger Hiss

Charles Kramer
Victor Perlo
Margaret Bennet Porter
Lee Pressman
Julian Wadleigh
Nathan Witt

RESETTLEMENT ADMINISTRATION

William Ludwig Ullman
Lee Pressman

Nathan Gregory Silvermaster

WORKS PROGRESS ADMINISTRATION

John Abt   Lee Pressman
Harold Glasser

NATIONAL RESEARCH PROJECT

Irving Kaplan, Associate Director   Harry Magdoff
Edward J. Fitzgerald   Harry Ober
Charles Flato   Herbert Schiemmel
Jacob Grauman   Alfred Van Tassel

NATIONAL LABOR RELATIONS BOARD

Nathan Witt, Secretary   Charles Kramer
Edwin Smith   Allan Rosenberg

DEPARTMENT OF LABOR

Henry Collins, Jr.   Donald Hiss

FEDERAL WORKS AGENCY

Edward Fitzgerald   Irving Kaplan

FEDERAL SECURITY AGENCY

Edward Fitzgerald

FEDERAL ECONOMIC ADMINISTRATION

Edward Fitzgerald

EMERGENCY DEFENSE AGENCY

Victor Perlo

DEPARTMENT OF COMMERCE

Edward Fitzgerald   Victor Perlo
Harry Magdoff   William Remington

SECURITIES EXCHANGE COMMISSION

John Abt

SOCIAL SECURITY BOARD

Joel Gordon   Irving Kaplan

TENNESSEE VALLEY AUTHORITY

William Remington

NATIONAL YOUTH ADMINISTRATION

Charles Kramer   Leon Elveson

NATIONAL RECOVERY ADMINISTRATION

Henry Collins, Jr.   Victor Perlo

HOME OWNERS LOAN CORPORATION

Victor Perlo

BOARD OF ECONOMIC ADMINISTRATION AND FOREIGN ECONOMIC ADMINISTRATION

Frank Coe, Assistant to the Executive Director of the Board of Economic
  Administration.
Laughlin Currie, Deputy Administrator of the Foreign Economic Administration.
  (Later an administrative assistant to the President of the United States.)

Bela Gold   Philip Keeney
Michael Greenberg   Nathan Gregory Silvermaster
Irving Kaplan   Allan Rosenberg
Mary J. Keeney   Julian Wadleigh

FEDERAL EMERGENCY RELIEF ADMINISTRATION

David Weintraub, Assistant to Harry Hopkins, the Director.

CIVIL SERVICE COMMISSION

Benjamin Wermiel   Irving Schiller

NATIONAL ARCHIVES
Irving Schiller

OFFICE OF EDUCATION
Alice Prentiss Barrows

CO-ORDINATOR OF INTER-AMERICAN AFFAIRS
Robert T. Miller, Head of Political Research.

Joseph Gregg   William Park
Irving Goldman   Bernard Redmont

CO-ORDINATOR OF INFORMATION
Julia Older Blazer

UNITED STATES RAILROAD RETIREMENT BOARD
George Silverman

WHITE HOUSE
Laughlin Currie, Administrative Assistant to President Roosevelt.

OFFICE OF WAR INFORMATION
Joseph Barnes   Adam Tarn
Julia Blazer

OFFICES OF STRATEGIC SERVICES

Lt. Col. Duncan Chaplin Lee, Legal Advisor to the Commander of the O.S.S., Major Gen. William J. Donovan. Maurice Halperin, Head of the Latin-American Division. Jack Sargeant Harris, Head of Military Intelligence for South America.

Carl Aldo Marzani, Deputy Chief of the Presentation Division. Leonard Mins, assigned to the collection and analysis of information on Soviet Russia.

George Vuchinich, (also spelled Vucinich) formerly with the Abraham Lincoln Brigade and who worked with Tito during World War II.

John K. Fairbank, China Division.
Helen Tenney, Spanish Division.
J. Julius Joseph, Japanese Division.
Milton Wolff, former Commanding Officer of the Abraham Lincoln Brigade.
Leo Drozdoff
Irving Fajans
Irving Goldman
Paul Martineau
Philip Keeney
Donald Niven Wheeler
David Zablodowsky

OFFICE OF PRICE ADMINISTRATION

Helen Kagen   William Remington
Charles Kramer   Doxie Wilkerson
Victor Perlo

OFFICE OF WAR MOBILIZATION

Jacob Grauman   Harry Magdoff
Irving Kaplan

WAR PRODUCTION BOARD

Edward Fitzgerald   Harry Magdoff
Harold Glasser   Victor Perlo
Stanley Graze   William Remington
Jacob Grauman   Alfred Van Tassel
Irving Kaplan   David Weintraub

OFFICE OF SURPLUS PROPERTY
Nathan Gregory Silvermaster

CONGRESSIONAL INVESTIGATIVE COMMITTEES
Senate Committee to Investigate Munitions Industry

Alger Hiss
John Abt
Charles Flato

Charles Kramer
Allan Rosenberg

Subcommittee on Civil Liberties of the Senate
Committee on Education and Labor

Harry Collins, Jr.
Charles Flato

Sonya Gold
Herbert Schimmel

Select Committee on Interstate Migration of Destitute Citizens

Frederick Palmer Weber
Henry Collins, Jr.

Harry Magdoff
Alfred Van Tassel

Special Committee to Study Problems of American Small Business

Henry Collins, Jr.

Charles Kramer

Subcommittee on Technological Mobilization of the
Senate Military Affairs Committee

Frederick Palmer Weber

Charles Kramer

Senate Subcommittee on Wartime Health and Education of the
Senate Committee on Education and Labor
Frederick Palmer Weber

UNITED STATES NAVY

Naval Bureau of Ordnance

Max Eltcher and Morton Sobell, together with eight to ten other members, disclosed during the Rosenberg Atomic Bomb espionage case.

Record Management Section of the Navy
Irving Schiller

Office of Naval Intelligence

Emmanuel Larsen

Andrew Roth

UNITED STATES MARINE CORPS
Brig. Gen. Evans F. Carlson

UNITED STATES ARMY
(SCAP) Military Government in Japan

Philip Keeney
Andrew Grajdanzev

T. A. Bisson

OMGUS (Military Government in Postwar Germany)
Major Henry Collins, Jr.

Air Corps

George Silverman, Economic Advisor and Chief of Analysis and Plans, Materiel and Service, Pentagon, Washington, D. C.

William Ludwig Ullman, Materiel & Service Section, Pentagon Washington, D. C.

Signal Corps

Sidney Glassman, Signal Corps Inspector

Julius Rosenberg, Signal Corps Inspector

Aberdeen Proving Grounds

Herman Landeau

Vincent Reno

MILITARY INTELLIGENCE

Psychological Warfare Division
Peter Rhodes

Troop Information and Education

Sgt. Luke Wilson

Lt. Col. Julius Schreiber, Psychiatrist.

Lt. S. M. Fischer, former reporter on the *San Francisco Chronicle* who admitted he was a Communist Party member while a student at Columbia University in 1940, and thereafter until he entered the Army in 1941, when he testified he dropped out of active Communist Party work.

Karl Fenichel, who also testified that he dropped out of the Party when he joined the Army.*

Simon W. Gerson, Legislative Director of the Communist Party of New York.

Sgt. William Gandall, former member of the Abraham Lincoln Brigade, trained by Soviet Military Officials.

UNITED NATIONS

The following employees of the United Nations have invoked the Fifth Amendment against self-incrimination when questioned under oath about their Communist affiliations and activities:

Alfred Abel

Frank Carter Bancroft

Julia Older Blazer

Frank Coe

Ruth E. Crawford

Leo M. Drozdoff

Dorothy Hope Tisdale Eldridge

Leon Elveson

Eda Glaser

Sidney Glassman

Joel Gordon

Stanley Graze

Jack Sargeant Harris

Harry Ober

Jerome A. Oberwager

Jane M. Reed

Irving T. Schiller

Herbert Schimmel

Alexander H. Svenchansky

Alfred Van Tassel

Eugene Wallach

Benjamine P. Wermiel

Herman Zap

Marjorie Zap

Jacob Grauman

Sonia Gruen

Helen Kagen

NOTE: When this list of United Nations employees was brought to the attention of former Secretary General of the United Nations, Trygve Lie, they were shortly discharged.

We wish to emphasize that this list is partial and contains only some of the names of individuals who were engaged in pro-Communist activities, invoked the Fifth Amendment when asked about their subversive affiliations, were identified as Communist Party members, or as collaborators with Soviet agents or American Communists. The list was compiled as part of a valuable work by Ronald W. Hunter, a recognized expert in the counter-subversive field who has had practical exeprience as a government agent, and whose work is entitled, *Russian Conspiracy in the United States, a History of Domestic Communism.* The work is thoroughly documented, and the listings are corroborated by official documents which are in the public realm. None of the material in Mr. Hunter's work is classified and the commercial reproduction of any of its contents is protected by common law copyright.

For those who wish to pursue the study of underground operations of the Communist Party in more detail, we refer them to our report on the International Federation of Architects, Engineers, Chemists and Technicians, Berkeley Chapter, that acted as a cover for scientific espionage in connection with atomic bomb research during the early forties, and to the testimony of the late Paul Crouch, who headed the special section of the Communist Party in Berkeley and Oakland, the membership of which was comprised of research scientists and nuclear physicists. We trust that this exposition will convince the reader that

---

* Evidence produced before a wide variety of official investigative agencies has established that the uniform Communist Party practice was to automatically expel all persons when they joined the Armed Forces and to automatically reinstate them when they were discharged and returned to private life. The individuals mentioned under this section all testified that they followed this procedure, but refused to do anything but invoke the Fifth Amendment when questioned the period of their active Communist Party activity. They were, to all intents and purposes, assigned to underground activity during the period of their service in the Armed Forces.

there is much more to the Communist menace than a lot of imbalanced individuals who plod along the picket lines and dabble in Marxism.

In June, 1947, J. Edgar Hoover, Director of the Federal Bureau of Investigation, summarized the distinction between Communist members of the open or above-ground organization and members of the underground and described fellow travelers and the amoral character of the party in general in an article which originally appeared in *Newsweek* on June 9, 1947, and was reproduced in *Case and Comment*, the lawyers' magazine, November-December, 1947, page 21. He said:

"Our surest weapon is truth. The Communists cannot endure the searching gaze of public observation. Their most effective work is carried on under a cloak of secrecy. Lies and deceit are their principal tools. No trick is too low for them. They are masters of the type of evasion advocated by that great God of Communism, Lenin, who observed: 'Revolutionaries who are unable to combine illegal forms of struggle with every form of legal struggle are very bad revolutionaries.'

* * * The known, card-carrying * Communists are not our sole menace. The individual whose name does not appear on party rolls but who does the party's dirty work, who acts as an apologist for the party and who rises in its defense and spearheads its campaign in the numerous fronts, is a greater menace. These are the 'Communist sympathizers,' 'fellow traveler,' and 'Communist stooges.' To prove their evil intent is at times difficult but they brand themselves by shifting and turning as the party line changes to meet new situations. Whether they be innocent, gullible, or willful, makes little difference, because they further the cause of communism and weaken our American democracy.

The Communists are now carrying on a vigorous campaign to bring their total membership in the United States up to 100,000. This figure, however, does not reveal their actual strength. Conservatively, there are an estimated 1,000,000 others who in one way or another aid the Communist Party.

* * * We cannot hope successfully to meet the Communist menace unless there is a wide knowledge and understanding of its aims and designs.

* * * If there were to be a slogan in the fight against Communism it should convey this thought: Uncover, expose and spotlight their activities. Once this is done, the American people will do the rest—quarantine them from effectively weakening our Country." †

---

* The Communist Party ceased issuing membership books or cards in December, 1947.
† Mr. Hoover amplified these matters and brought a description of Communism in the United States down to date in his recently published book, Masters of Deceit: The Story of Communism in America and How to Fight It, by J. Edgar Hoover. Henry Holt & Co., New York, 1958.

CURRENT COMMUNIST TECHNIQUES

The present activities of the Communist Party in California, the current party line, the character of the physical organization of the party apparatus may all be attributed to the events that occurred in 1956. The years 1939 and 1941 were also critical in the world Communist movement, because they produced not only profound changes in the international Communist Party line but a complete reversal of Communist thinking almost overnight. Prior to August, 1939, the Communists had been taught to hate Hitler and everything he represented. For years they had espoused the cause of racial minority groups the world over—hypocritically, but nevertheless vociferously. They had deplored Fascism, and Hitler not only provided much grist for the Communist propaganda machinery by his repression of the Jewish minority in that country, but his ruthless and brutal reign through the instrumentality of the Gestapo and his role as an arch Fascist and threat to world peace and security had been used in Communist propaganda publications ever since he was released from Landsberg prison. Then, in August, 1939, and without previous warning, Hitler and Stalin signed a non-aggression pact. The stunned Communist Parties throughout the world dutifully changed their propaganda line, but their confidence was undeniably shaken. From the time the non-aggression pact became effective until it was violated on June 22, 1941, the line was at least a toleration of the Hitler regime. Then, after June 22, 1941, the international line was to hate Hitler again but with far greater venom than ever before because he had now attacked the fatherland of the world Communist movement. In 1956, the Kremlin again paralyzed the thinking and the propaganda viewpoint of the Communist Parties of the world when Khrushchev made his "secret" speech in February, 1956, and ripped to shreds the reputation of the dead Stalin.

We have previously described Stalin and the role he played in the Communist revolution of 1917, his rise to power, and the method by which he managed to get himself deified throughout the country that he ruled with all of the tyrannical attributes of Peter the Great. Statues and pictures of Stalin appeared in all public places; the history books were filled with outrageous distortions for the purpose of sublimating him as the brains of the revolution, the leader of the Red Army, the originator of all diplomatic strategy, the architect of the world Communist movement, the omniscient leader—in short, superhuman attributes were ascribed to this man who launched the most horrible blood purges from 1935 to 1939 that the world had ever seen, and whose obsessive vanity and lust for absolute power turned him into the warped and tyrannical figure that American anti-Communists had proclaimed him to be almost from the time he came to power by undermining all his real or fancied opponents and climbing over their dead bodies until he became the absolute master of the Russian Communist Party, the head of its secret police, and therefore the master of the Soviet Union and of world Communism. Thousands of deluded fellow travelers who persistently clung to the front organizations that flourished during the period of the first United Front, and, indeed, thereafter until a few years ago, angrily retorted that all of these attacks on the Soviet leader were capitalist propaganda, the product of misinformation and downright lies. So accustomed had the Communist propaganda machinery in this country become to extolling the virtues of Stalin and lambasting his critics that it became almost automatic for all Communists and their supporters to praise everything Stalin did, and to brand every critical remark against him as an outrageous falsehood.

This, then, was the situation that had existed for a period of almost 30 years when, with the Khrushchev speech of February, 1956, came another shattering blow that stunned the Communists of all countries, but particularly in the United States, France and Italy. Khrushchev proclaimed that Stalin had been a megalomaniac butcher, a figure who scorned the protection of civil liberties, gloried in unleashing naked terror, and that he was, in short, all of the unpleasant things the anti-Communist critics had said he was during all of these years.

The effect of this speech was to brand as utterly unreliable all of the Communist propagandists and fellow travelers throughout the world, to highlight their complete hypocrisy, to completely clinch the assertion that in Communism the end justifies the means, and—this was perhaps most astonishing of all—it necessarily included a tacit admission that in his acts of butchery and insensate brutality, Stalin had been aided and abetted by the members of the Communist Politburo who now attacked him, including Khrushchev, the butcher of the Ukraine, Mikoyan, the apostle of terror, and every other Soviet leader who participated in these activities over so long a period.

Khrushchev, at the same time, declared that the time had come to ease the tensions for which Stalin had been responsible. Writers should be permitted to publish their real beliefs; criticism against the Soviet regime should be encouraged; in foreign countries the Communist Parties should be allowed to proceed toward their respective goals in conformity with the peculiar situations of their several environments, instead of slavishly following the dogmatism of an inflexible set of rules that had hampered the individual development of these parties instead of having encouraged it. Obviously, these relaxations of the old repressions were made because the new leaders in the Kremlin sensed that the death of Stalin had symbolized a firming up of the smoldering resentment of the Russian masses against regimentation, discipline, brutality, and terrorism that they had been compelled to endure since the Communists came to power. The old methods of the Soviet Secret Police would no longer work, rumblings of counter-revolution had been heard among the intelligentsia of the country and had seeped down into the working masses. Some of the Kremlin leaders were old Bolsheviks who had gone through the revolution of

1917, and they remembered how the oppressive measures of the Tsar had been endured for many years, until finally a spark of revolution was started, quickly gathered strength and electrified the entire country until almost as one man the people rose and toppled over the decaying regime.

Counter-revolution has always been the one thing that the Kremlin leaders fear above all others, hence the maintenance of the Soviet Secret Police as an instrument of terror to be used by the Communist minority to subjugate the masses of the people, hence the one-party control of the means of communication and transportation, to say nothing of the instrumentalities of education, the labor unions, and all of the other vital institutions in the country. And this, as we have said, was the reason for the effort to relax the Stalinist repression and give the people some new freedoms in order to avert a counter-revolution.

Then came the books by Dudintsev and Djilas. Then came the sharpening of the breach between Tito and Khrushchev. Then came the revolts in Poland and Hungary, where the smoldering embers of resistance burst into flame and the same Mikoyan who recently came to spread light and sweetness in consonance with the appeasement line of the Soviet Union toward the United States, was sent into Hungary, backed up by the armored might of Russia, and ruthlessly mowed down the citizens of that country as though his dead master, Stalin, were personally directing the affair. Mikoyan had learned his lesson well, because he assured the Hungarian leader of safety, persuaded him to come to start peaceful negotiations, and when the Hungarian arrived he was immediately liquidated.

China was not immune from the stirring of the masses of oppressed people in resentment against the iron regime which ground them into obedience, and mowed them down in a bath of blood. They were encouraged to criticize the Chinese Communist regime, the move by Mao Tse-tung being alluded to as the "policy of the hundred flowers," but when some of these flowers presumed to stick their heads above the others and take advantage of the invitation to express their disagreement with some of the policies of the Red Chinese regime, they were summarily extinguished.

All of these matters played their part in driving wedges of doubt and dissidence deep into the hearts of many of the Communist Parties of the world. Italy, where the party enjoyed more members than any foreign party in the world—that is any party organization outside of the Soviet Union—immediately experienced a pronounced decline in membership. To a lesser degree the same thing was true in France. In the United States the party was divided into cliques and splinters of party leaders in angry disagreement. John Gates, the former editor of the *Daily Worker* of New York, resigned in disgust and disillusionment when he was unable to persuade his comrades that the party organization in this country had outlived its usefulness and should be disbanded. He resigned, but his resignation is too recent to enable him to completely break the Red cord that, while somewhat frazzled and tenuous, nevertheless still binds him to the Communist cause. It caused the resignation of Howard Fast, the darling of the American Communist cultural set, whose books contained effective party propaganda and who was hailed and praised uniformly in Communist circles until the time of his defection, when the same voices that sang his praises the day before now arose in a strident and angry chorus of criticism and abuse.

Why do we place so much emphasis on these events? We do so because it is necessary to understand them in order to appreciate what has happened in our own state as a result of these things that occurred in countries thousands of miles away. It serves to emphasize the fact that Communism is inevitably and innately an international movement, and that nothing can happen of any consequence in any Communist country, especially the Soviet Union, without producing an immediate reaction in the United States on the part of every fragment of the party organization. We heretofore stated that in the Communist bookstore in Los Angeles we were recently able to purchase the books by Dudintsev and Djilas and Boris Pasternak. These are actually anti-Communist works, and the fact they are now being sold in the Communist book store in the City of Los Angeles is indeed a startling development. It points up the fact that in the International Book Store in San Francisco none of these books are to be found, the Communists in the north being more dogmatic and loyal to such national leaders as Foster and Dennis, while the Communists in the southern part of the State have become increasingly independent of that leadership.

The answer to this situation is to be found in the fact that the leader of the Southern California division of the Communist Party is Dorothy Healey. She first appeared before our committee when she was a field examiner in the State Department of Labor in December, 1941. Several times married to Communist functionaries, and now the wife of Philip M. Connelly, Dorothy Healey in 1941 was a pert, vivacious, attractive, but completely indoctrinated Communist. She came into state employ during the penetration of our government by Communists who flocked into their positions during the late thirties, and particularly as a result of the election of 1938. Dorothy Healey was typical of scores of undercover party members who managed to entrench themselves deep in the heart of our State Government.

Participating in strikes, lending her considerable organizational talents to the creation and operation of front organizations, directing the preparation and distribution of propaganda, Dorothy Healey rapidly rose in the ranks of the Communist Party until finally she emerged as a member of its National Committee and the head of the organization for all of Southern California. But Dorothy Healey was also caught up in the developments of 1956. We should say at this juncture that many of the party members who either defected in 1956 or shortly thereafter, or who veered sharply to the right and attacked their superiors who still clung to the old dogmatic Communist ideas, had gradually been going through a process of disillusionment for a great many years. In many cases this occurred unconsciously, but people with any semblance of judgment can hardly justify a long period of complete contradictions in the Communist Party line, and find their ideals and beliefs blasted overnight without realizing that no one single thing has actually caused them to leave the movement. So when the events of 1956 occurred, for many individuals it was simply the final nudge necessary to complete disillusionment and a break with the party. Some individuals, of course, left the movement completely. Some remained true to Marxism, but left the party organization for one reason or another. Others remained in the party and fought to put over their own relatively conservative ideas against the stubborn party leadership represented by William Z. Foster. Dorothy Healey belonged to the latter group. Her battle with Foster was vicious and heated. It boiled over into the pages of *Political Affairs* and threw the southern California party organization into a turmoil. This is the reason for the presence of the anti-Communist books in the Progressive Book Store on West Seventh Street, and it also underscores the contrast between this propaganda outlet and the store in San Francisco where no such literature is to be found. In both stores Communist books and other materials are on sale, but in Los Angeles the party member can buy literature on both sides of the question. At 1408 Market Street in San Francisco, no such choice is available.

We have it on very good authority, which we are unable to disclose for public scrutiny, that Dorothy Healey is in very bad graces with the Communist high command, and that she will either be brought back into the path of strict obedience and rectitude or compelled to leave the party. In the meantime, efforts have been made to restore discipline among the rank and file membership in Los Angeles, and this effort has met with considerable success.

We sincerely hope that by describing the troubles that are besetting the Communists in the United States, and especially in the southern district of California, that we do not convey the impression that the party has suddenly become weak and impotent. On the contrary, the dedicated nucleus of party members who remain active, together with the greatly expanded underground organization, comprises those individuals who have weathered all the storms of contortion in the party line, are more firmly dedicated to their cause than ever before, and who are now operating an organization that has rid itself of the weaklings and the expendables. The party has activated its sleeper apparatus, and the greatest weapon it now possesses is the unfortunate apathetic attitude of many American citizens who have deluded themselves into thinking that the trouble from internal subversion is ended.

Members of this committee, together with such eminent authorities as J. Edgar Hoover, the Attorney General of the United States, the head of the Department of Justice's Division of Internal Security, the members and staffs of the congressional committees and those of the various state committees, undercover agents of the F. B. I., experts who have published books on the subject such as the Overstreets, Eugene Lyons, Elizabeth Bentley, Louis Budenz, Whittaker Chambers, Hede Massing, Benjamin Gitlow, Howard Fast, Boris Morros, Robert Morris—and too many others to list here, are unanimous in their estimate that the Communist Party in this country is now a more challenging menace than ever before. We must always remember that the American party is simply an organization of Soviet agents operating in this nation to accelerate our destruction. So successful has been the technique of internal subversion, not only here but throughout the free world, that subversion by force has largely been discontinued by the international Communist movement.

"* * * dependence of the Communists on direct armed aggression has in recent years been lessened. The emphasis today is on indirect aggression. That type of aggression places a much heavier reliance than heretofore on subversion and espionage and on all forms of political education and political propaganda.

The principal instrument of the Soviet Communist for carrying on these tactics of subversion and political agitation abroad is, of course, the apparatus of the international Communist conspiracy." [66]

And as Mr. Hoover stated in his book, Masters of Deceit, the retirement of the Communist Party to previously prepared underground positions and the liquidation of most of its front organizations, together with its cleverly contrived propaganda, has tended to convince a great many American citizens that the party has all of a sudden become too weak to constitute any serious threats.

Any person who doubts the design of the international Communist movement to subvert and conquer us, has only to take the time to read the authoritative Communist literature on the subject. It is not necessary to use any sources except those of the highest Communist authorities, since their avowed and steadfast purpose has been expressed many times in terms much more clear and emphatic than anything contained in the writings of the late Adolf Hitler. As Nikita Krushchev recently declared: "But of course we must realize that we cannot coexist eternally. One of us must go to his grave. We do not want to go the grave. They don't want to go to their graves, either. So what must be done? We must *push* them to their graves." [67]

Dmitri Z. Manuilsky was a prominent functionary assigned by the Communist Party of the Soviet Union to play a leading role in the organization of the Comintern's far-flung international organization. His statement about the inevitability of war between the Communist and free worlds has been cited many times, and we have referred to it

---

[66] Department of State bulletin, Dec. 1, 1958, pp. 880-881.
[67] Speech by Nikita S. Khrushchev, reported in *American Mercury*, Feb., 1959, p. 95.

in preceding reports. But the Manuilsky statement, because of his high position in the Soviet hierarchy, and because of the tendency toward apathy on the part of the American people today, is now more pertinent than ever. Mr. Manuilsky was a presiding officer in the United Nation's Security Council in 1949. In 1931, he made a speech at the Lenin School of Political Warfare, during which he said:

> "War to the hilt between communism and capitalism is inevitable. Today, of course, we are not strong enough to attack. Our time will come in 20 to 30 years. To win we shall need the element of surprise. The bourgeoisie will have to be put to sleep. So we shall begin launching the most spectacular peace movement on record. There will be electrifying overtures and unheard of concessions. The capitalist countries, stupid and decadent, will rejoice to co-operate in their own destruction. They will leap at another chance to be friends. As soon as their guard is down, we shall smash them with our clenched fist."

Petition for Communist School

We have also mentioned the California Labor School in San Francisco as a Communist school which we exposed in the late forties. It had been known as the Workers School, the Tom Mooney Labor School, and the California Labor School. A hearing on behalf of the Subversive Activities Control Board was held in San Francisco for the purpose of deciding whether or not the institution was in fact controlled by the Communist Party. The decision that it was so controlled was arrived at after the taking of considerable testimony, and this conclusion was sent to the Board in Washington. Immediately the party apparatus began to solicit petitions, letters, telegrams, and all sorts of pressure tactics by its fellow-travelers, party members and sympathizers, together with a smattering of gullible liberals, and in the process filed a petition with the Subversive Activities Control Board asking, in effect, that this Red School be permitted to continue its operations. Signers of this petition included: Dr. Frank Weymouth, Professor Emeritus of Philosophy [sic] at Stanford University; Dr. Percy M. Dawson, Los Altos; Harriet E. Eddy, Librarian Emeritus at the University of California; Rev. Stephen H. Fritchman, Pastor of the First Unitarian Church, Los Angeles; Mrs. Helen Freeland Gibb, Berkeley; Richard Lynden, San Francisco; Bishop Edward Lamb Parsons, San Francisco; Prof. Ira B. Cross, Berkeley; Rockwell Kent, New York; Rev. Harry F. Ward, New Jersey; Dr. Jacob Auslander, New York; Prof. Robert Morss Lovett, Chicago; Attorney Daniel G. Marshall, Los Angeles; Prof. Albert Guerard, Stanford University; Dr. C. L. Collins, Vallejo; Dr. Wilbur F. Swett, San Francisco; Dr. Joseph Kaufman, San Francisco; Mildred Rosenthal, San Francisco; Dr. Mary A. Sarvis, Oakland; Rev. Dryden L. Phelps; Clarence M. and Harriet Vickland, Oakland;

Dr. Ann Maryin, Berkeley; Rev. Clarence B. Aggriott, Berkeley; Dr. Ephraim Kahn, Berkeley; Prof. Bayard Quincy Morgan, Palo Alto; Prof. C. Alvarez-Tostado, Palo Alto; Gertrude Luehning, Palo Alto; Prof. George H. Colliver, Stockton; D. Harding, Brisbane; Prof. Curtis MacDougall, Evanston, Ill.; Prof. Karl De Schwienitz, Sr., Evanston, Ill.; Prof. Ambert W. Herre, Seattle; Henry Wilcox, South Norwalk, Connecticut; Pauline Taylor, Youngstown, Ohio; Dr. W. E. B. DuBois, Brooklyn, New York; Kumar Goshal, Brooklyn, New York; Herbert Aptheker, Brooklyn, New York; William L. Patterson, Brooklyn, New York; Earl Robinson, Brooklyn, New York; Rev. William H. Melish, Brooklyn, New York; Elizabeth Moos, New York City; Robert W. Dunn, New York City; Prof. Henry Pratt Fairchild, New York City; Dorothy Brewster, New York City; Hugh Hardyman, La Crescenta, California; Clinton D. Hollister, Santa Barbara; Morton Dimonstein, artist; Ben Margolis, Attorney, Los Angeles; John T. McTerman, Attorney, Los Angeles; Leo Branton, Jr., Attorney, Los Angeles; Mrs. Charlotta Bass, Los Angeles; Dr. Joseph Hittelman, Los Angeles; Rev. D. V. Kyle, Los Angeles; A. Soundel Becker, Los Angeles; Dr. Sidney S. Cole, Los Angeles; Stanley Moffett, former Judge, South Gate; Rev. Emerson G. Horgan, Long Beach, and Charles S. Litwin, Long Beach.

We can anticipate no legitimate protest to the publication of these names, since they were appended to a petition which was filed as a public document with the Subversive Activities Control Board in Washington, and certainly the signers of the petition would hardly have appended their signatures to the document unless they had known something about the character of the California Labor School. It would have been a very simple matter to review the testimony of the hearing in San Francisco, together with a number of hearings and reports by this committee, as well as other official agencies. Needless to say, all of the agencies, together with the Subversive Activities Control Board examiners in San Francisco, agreed that the organization was completely under Communist control. A cursory review of its genealogy would suffice to establish that purpose. An examination of the cumulative index covering this and previous reports will indicate that most of the signers of this petition have been referred to on many occasions in our reports.

Although the California Communists are still suffering from the effects of internal warfare between the Stalinists and the extreme right and left wings, the dissident groups have now been largely eliminated, and the difficulties have largely been resolved. We see evidences of this in the resumption of the old militant attitude, the tapering off of the feud between Dorothy Healey Connelly and William Z. Foster and their respective followers, in the renewed interest in the domestic political situation, and an acceleration in recruiting and infiltration of the two major targets: trade unions and educational institutions.

As J. Edgar Hoover remarked at a national convention of the American Legion:

"* * * The F. B. I. investigations have shown that there is a hard core of conspiratorial Reds unaffected by Party differences and controlled by the heavy hand of Moscow. As long as this undercover 'apparatus' exists, the Communist threat cannot be brushed aside as trivial or fanciful. It is a continuing, aggressive force constantly at work to suborn and subvert the American people. * * * The influence of the subversive conspiracy has been almost unbelievable—reaching deep into practically every walk of life. To gauge the effectiveness of this campaign, we need only to note the widespread and vociferous clamor raised whenever our government attempts to deal firmly in self-defense against the subversive threat.

Certain organizations obviously dedicate their efforts to thwart the very concepts of security. They vehemently oppose methods to gain this security and it is obvious that their aim is to destroy it. They protest that they are fighting for freedom, but in reality they seek license. They hypocritically bar Communists from their membership, but they seem to hate all persons who abhor Communists and Communism. They claim to be anti-Communist but they launch attacks against Congressional legislation to curb Communism. They distort and misrepresent and ridicule the government's security program. They lobby and exert pressure on the leaders of government both in the legislative and executive branches."

There is little need now for the Communists to use one of their own front organizations, or to create a new one for the purpose of fomenting a protest march against one of the government's atomic research establishments in order to highlight a desire to scrap our atomic defense program. Such a march was led a year ago against the establishment at Livermore. It originated in Palo Alto, gathered a group of pacifists, peace-at-any-price enthusiasts, party liners and fellow travelers, and this small but determined cavalcade took the road for Livermore under the leadership of Dr. Linus Pauling, who spends some of his time in scientific research at Cal Tech, but who apparently devotes most of his energies to attending Communist front meetings, following the party line in general, and urging the discontinuance of our atomic research for defensive purposes in particular. The Communist Party has little need to mobilize its membership to throw picket lines around premises that are being subjected to a Communist-supported strike because there are enough unions—most of them expelled from their parent organization—that are Communist dominated to provide this sort of manpower. There is little need for the Communist Party to finance propaganda publications when a magazine like *The Nation*, or one published in California like *Frontier*, will attack the F. B. I., support the Communist fronts, editorialize sympathetically in behalf of witnesses that appear before legislative committees, and generally parrot the party line for nothing.

Party techniques have changed several times since this committee was established in 1940. But, as we have pointed out many times, a party member who remains completely inactive is of little use to the movement, and the instant activity is started, then the anti-Communist techniques that have been changed to meet the situation also become effective. The accumulation of documentary information over a period of almost 20 years provides information of inestimable value; continuous practical experience for that length of time is even more valuable, and new sources of information are being constantly developed. With the defections that have been caused by the occurrences of 1956, many disillusioned former Communists have come forward to volunteer their information. But it must be remembered that the party foresaw this sort of development as early as 1931, when Vassiliev issued his famous lecture on security and underground organization. Since the party reorganized itself several years ago on an underground basis, no former member can describe the activities of any unit except that to which he belongs. This information would entail the identities and activities of a very few individuals, and since the front organizations—with the exception of those that we have already described as still active—have been cast aside, it is necessary to secure information from a great many individuals in order to obtain an accurate picture of the inside operations of the Communist apparatus from day to day. This task, however difficult and challenging, is by no means impossible. And if continued vigilance results in the elimination of a few subversive individuals a year from positions where they could do injury to our youth, utilize critical information for the benefit of the party, twist the thinking and activities of divisions of our State Government to the Communist Party line—then the effort is very much worthwhile. Indeed, there is no other medium through which responsible public officials can be kept reliably informed concerning these vital matters.

COMMUNISM AND THE LAW

The Supreme Court

No discussion of the fight against subversion can be complete without an understanding of the recent decisions of the United States Supreme Court—decisions that have provoked more comment than any since the same court declared the National Recovery Act unconstitutional in 1935. Dealing with problems of Communist activity, this series of decisions not only reflects a complete reversal of the high court's previous attitude, but they will seriously hamper the efforts to deal adequately with the constant challenge to our national security by subversive forces.

It is highly pertinent that we discuss these decisions here and at some length, and we do so for the reason that they directly affect conditions in this state. One of the cases resulted in the reversal of a jury conviction of California Communist leaders, and struck down the weapons that had been legally used by the F.B.I. to put them behind bars; another decision held that the California Legislature would thenceforth be powerless to pass sedition laws for the protection of the people within the borders of the state; a third opinion held that a committee of the California State Bar had no business to inquire of an applicant for the privilege of practicing law in this state whether or not he was then a member of the Communist Party. The other decisions, more than a dozen, all deal with problems of internal security and are of as much if not more practical application in California as elsewhere in the United States. We wish to make it very plain that we do not criticize the Supreme Court as an institution; we do not suggest, even by implication, that its powers and prerogatives be changed. We do disagree with the decisions in the field of internal security, and we know of no rule or decision, as yet, which would deprive us of exercising that right. It has been suggested that Congress pass legislation to whittle down the high Court's jurisdiction. We wish to make it clear, again, that we imply nothing of the sort in this portion of our report. We do wish to present the facts fully, and for that purpose we will refer to resolutions passed by the American Farm Bureau Federation, the Conference of State Chief Justices from the several states, and the American Bar Association. We also have included statements by Dean Erwin Griswold of Harvard Law School, and Louis C. Wymans, former President of the National Association of State Attorneys General.

The Communist Party of the United States was started at a Chicago convention in 1919. It thereafter affiliated with the Communist International and swore to be obedient to the mandates of the Kremlin. It has since carried on a continual program of infiltration of our schools, churches, cultural organizations, scientific projects and communications media—and it has placed its agents deep in the heart of our government. As federal and state legislative committees dug into Communist activity and disclosed the techniques whereby liberal dupes were attracted to front organizations, the people began to realize the nature of the very imminent threat to our continued security. The Gouzenko, Hiss, Remington, White, Ware, Wadleigh, Field, Silvermaster, Kramer, Glasser, Oppenheimer, Fuchs, Rosenberg, Gold, Sobel and MacLean cases, to name a very few, quickly dispel any doubt about the extent of the infiltration. The arrest of Col. Rudolf Abel of the Soviet Secret Police a few months ago should dispel any doubt about the present danger.

As we have said, as these disclosures increased, so did the activities of the F.B.I. and the legislative committees. Under the Smith Act Communist leaders were convicted and imprisoned. Deprived of its leadership, harried by the testimony of defectors and undercover operatives, exposed by legislative committees, the Communist Party was, by the middle of 1951, getting desperate. In August, 1951, the organ of the

National Committee of the Communist Party of the United States declared:

"It is evident that there is growing alarm voiced among progressives and in the labor movement, at the increasing onslaught against the Bill of Rights. The struggle against the Smith Act is today the link to the broadest anti-Fascist unity, around the dissenting opinions of Justices Black and Douglas. [Reference is to a decision of the U. S. Supreme Court upholding the constitutionality of the Smith Act, in which Justices Black and Douglas wrote a dissenting opinion.] The demand for a hearing by the Supreme Court on the appeal of the eleven Communist leaders and the defense of all others to be tried under the Smith Act are bound together as one struggle, and *must be the basis for an immediate broad mass campaign to restore the Bill of Rights.* (Committee's italics.)

The American peoples' love of democracy and their will to peace cannot be destroyed by McCarran Acts and Smith Acts. The forces of democracy and peace in our country are possessed of strength—a strength of which they must be made fully conscious. The full alerting to the conscious action of these forces in the United States demands the vanguard role of the Communist Party. *In that role the Communist Party will continue to function—and no Hitler-like legislation and police state hounding can halt it."* (Committee's italics.)

In the September issue of the same publication this appeared:

"A rehearing must be demanded by a mobilization of everyone who has ever spoken out on the Smith Act. *This demand must be heard decisively in Washington.* (Committee's italics.) It is the duty and responsibility of all progressive anti-Fascist, democratic forces to join in this crusade to save the Bill of Rights. Regardless of differences, it is the duty of the labor movement to unite against this forerunner of the Taft-Hartley Law, which is an abominable threat to the life of the labor movement today. We Communists, who are post-June 6th victims of the Smith Act, are resolute in our determination to expose the real conspirators against the historic freedom of the American people—those who constitute an actual clear and present danger to the freedom of our people, those who would substitute a Smith Act for the Bill of Rights." [68]

There were other articles, most of them equally critical and defiant.[69]

The declaration of war by the Communist Party against the Supreme Court of the United States in an effort to bring about a change in the judicial precedent that body had established, and to gain a breathing spell for the subversives, appeared in *Political Affairs* in March, 1952,

[68] "The Smith Act Strikes Again," by Elizabeth Gurley Flynn. *Political Affairs,* Aug., 1951, pp. 18 and 22.
[69] "What the Supreme Court Unleashed," by Elizabeth Gurley Flynn, *Political Affairs,* Sept., 1951, p. 28.

when a party official angrily denounced the court in an article commencing on page 15, which was entitled, "The Supreme Court Will *Not* Have the Last Word!" Here are some excerpts:

"The Supreme Court majority of Truman appointees has declared war against the peace aspirations of the American people. With flagrant arrogance it has provided the 'legal' framework for further Fascist onslaughts on the most elementary democratic rights of the people in a frenzied effort to intimidate into submission all opposition to the warmakers of Wall Street.

* * * Like the entire State apparatus of which it is a part, the Supreme Court is an instrument of the ruling class, and its decisions throughout the nation's history bear the imprint of that relationship, as well as the general alignment of class forces prevailing at each period * * *

These decisions make it compellingly clear that the Bill of Rights is in the gravest danger in our history. They shout from the housetops that the Supreme Court, far from being a defender of the Constitution, serves to acelerate monopoly's drive against Fascism and war.

But these decisions, drastic and sweeping as they are, cannot be held proof of the inevitability of Fascism in the United States. They prove quite simply that Americans cannot rely on the Supreme Court for the defense of the peoples' hard-gained rights and liberties"

*   *   *   *   *   *   *

"The actions of the Supreme Court and its onslaughts on civil liberties are directly associated with the bi-partisan war drive. They are directly associated with a tax on labor and the Negro people."

*   *   *   *   *   *   *

* * * The Communist Party must redouble its efforts on two fronts—on the one hand, to overcome passive or defeatist moves that may have been instilled in the labor progressive movements as a result of these new blows; on the other hand, to use these lessons to prove to the broad masses that their interests are vitally affected * * * *the Party can, in the development of these movements, help give shape and form to the organization of a powerful peoples' and anti-Fascist coalition.*

The Supreme Court will not have the last word. The people must and will take up the challenge." (Committee's italics.)

Whether or not this Communist campaign, announced in such clear and vehement terms, was successful, or whether it was pure coincidence that resulted in the stream of new decisions by the court that were eminently satisfactory to the party is an intriguing question. We know that such a campaign as the party announced was in fact launched; we know that the party's propaganda nationwide machinery was set in motion, and that the entire strength of the organization was alerted o bring pressure and influence to bear in strategic places. The party vas fighting for its very life, and this ambitious undertaking was for he avowed purpose of bringing about a change in the type of Supreme Court decisions that had so hampered the operation of the Communist onspiracy. It needed softer laws and more freedom to continue the vork of subverting our government.

During the last week of June, 1957, the Communist propaganda nachinery began to hail the Supreme Court as the saviour of the peoples' liberties. The praises swelled to ever mounting proportions vhen decision after decision was rendered by the court—hamstringing gencies of the government, and giving the Communists more freedom 'rom prosecution and exposure than they dared hope for. Completely reversing the position it had adopted for years, this is what the Supreme Court did within the space of two years: (The following summaries of the decisions are taken from the report of the American Bar Association, Special Committee on Communist Tactics, Strategy and Objectives, *American Opinion*, Dec. 1958, page 31 et seq.)

1. *Communist Party* v. *Subversive Activities Control Board.* The court refused to uphold or pass on the constitutionality of the Subversive Activities Control Act of 1950, and delayed the effectiveness of this act.

2. *Pennsylvania* v. *Steve Nelson.* The court held that it was unlawful for Pennsylvania to prosecute a Pennsylvania Communist Party leader under the sedition act of that state and indicated that the antisedition laws of 42 states and of Alaska and Hawaii cannot be enforced.

3. *Yates* v. *United States.* The court reversed two federal courts and ruled that teaching and advocating forcible overthrow of our government, even "with evil intent," was not punishable under the Smith Act as long as it was "divorced from any effort to instigate action to that end," and ordered five Communist leaders freed and new trials for another nine.

4. *Cole* v. *Young.* The court reversed two federal courts and held that, although the Summary Suspension Act of 1950 gave the federal government the right to dismiss employees "in the interest of the national security in the United States," it was not in the interest of the national security to dismiss an employee who contributed funds and services to an undisputed subversive organization, unless that employee was in a "sensitive position."

5. *Service* v. *Dulles.* The court reversed two federal courts which had refused to set aside the discharge of John Stewart Service by the State Department. The F. B. I. had a recording of a conversation between Service and the editor of the pro-Communist magazine *Amerasia* in the latter's hotel room, during which Service spoke of military plans which were very secret. Earlier the F. B. I. had

found large numbers of secret and confidential State Department documents in the *Amerasia* office. The lower courts had followed the McCarran Amendment which gave the Secretary of State absolute discretion to discharge any employee in the interest of the security of the United States.

6. *Slochower* v. *Board of Education, New York.* The court reversed the decisions of three New York courts and held that it was unconstitutional to automatically discharge a teacher, in accordance with the law of New York, because he took the Fifth Amendment when asked about Communist activity. On his petition for rehearing, the court admitted that its opinion was in error in stating that Slochower was not aware that his claim of the Fifth Amendment was *ipso facto* result in his discharge; however, the court denied rehearing.

7. *Sweezy* v. *New Hampshire.* The court reversed the New Hampshire Supreme Court and held that the Attorney General of New Hampshire was without authority to question Prof. Sweezy, a lecturer at the state university, concerning a lecture and other suspected subversive activities. Questions which the court said that Sweezy properly refused to answer included: "Did you advocate Marxism at that time?" And "Do you believe in Communism?"

8. *United States* v. *Witkovich.* The court decided that, under the Immigration and Nationality Act of 1952, which provides that any alien against whom there is a final order of deportation shall "give information under oath as to his nationality, circumstances, habits, associations, and activities, and such other information, whether or not related to the foregoing, as the Attorney General may deem fit and proper," the Attorney General did not have the right to ask Witkovich: "Since the order of deportation was entered in your case on June 25, 1953, have you attended any meetings of the Communist Party of the U. S. A.?"

9. *Schware* v. *Board of Examiners of New Mexico.* The court reversed the decision of the New Mexico Board of Bar Examiners and of the New Mexico Supreme Court which had said: "We believe one who has knowingly given his loyalties to the Communist Party for six or seven years during a period of responsible adulthood is a person of questionable character." The Supreme Court ruled that "membership in the Communist Party during the 1930's cannot be said to raise substantial doubts about his present good moral character."

10. *Konigsberg* v. *State Bar of California.* The court reversed the decisions of the California Committee of Bar Examiners and of the California Supreme Court, and held that it was unconstitu-

tional to deny a license to practice law to an applicant who refused to answer this question put by the Bar Committee: "Mr. Konigsberg, are you a Communist?" and a series of similar questions.

11. *Jencks* v. *United States.* The court reversed two federal courts and held that Jencks, who was convicted of filing a false non-Communist affidavit, must be given the contents of all confidential F. B. I. reports which were made by any government witness in the case even though Jencks "restricted his motions to a request for production of the reports to the trial judge for the judge's inspection and determination whether and to what extent the report should be made available."

12. *Watkins* v. *United States.* The court reversed the Federal District Court and six judges of the Court of Appeal of the District of Columbia, and held that the House un-American Activities Committee could not require a witness who admitted "I freely cooperated with the Communist Party," to name his Communist associates, even though the witness did not invoke the Fifth Amendment. The court said, "We remain unenlightened as to the subject to which the questions asked petitioner were pertinent." The court did not question the "power of the Congress to inquire into and publicize corruption, maladministration or inefficiencies of agencies of the government." The court did question the right of Congress to inquire into and publicize Communism and subversion, and suggested that this "involves a broadscale intrusion into the lives and affairs of private citizens."

13. *Raley, Stern, & Brown* v. *Ohio.* The court reversed the Ohio Supreme Court and lower courts to set aside the conviction of three men who had refused to answer questions about Communist activities put to them by the Ohio un-American Commission.

14. *Flaxer* v. *United States.* The court reversed two federal courts and set aside the conviction of Flaxer of contempt for refusing to produce records of alleged Communist activities subpoened by the Senate Internal Security Subcommittee.

15. *Sacher* v. *United States.* The court reversed two federal courts and set aside the conviction of Sacher of contempt for refusing to tell the Senate Internal Security Subcommittee whether he was "a member of the lawyers' section of the Communist Party." In the second Sacher appeal, the court again reversed the Court of Appeal and said that this question was not pertinent to the subcommittee's investigation of Communist witness Matusow's recantation. The court refused to hear any argument from the government lawyers representing this Senate subcommittee.

16. *Yates* v. *United States.* In the second Yates appeal the court reversed two courts and held that the refusal of Communist Party member Yates "to answer eleven questions about Communist membership of other persons" did not constitute eleven contempts. In the third Yates appeal, the court reversed two federal courts and held that Yates' contempt sentence of one year should be reduced to the fifteen days already served for this offense.

17. *Bonetti* v. *Rogers.* The court reversed two federal courts and held that, although the Internal Security Act of 1950 provides that any alien, who "at any time" after entering the United States shall have been a member of the Communist Party, is deportable, Bonetti, who became a Communist after entering the United States, was not deportable because he had re-entered after quitting the party. The dissenting judges charged that this construction reads "at any time" out of the act and the word "last" into the Statute, and "cripples the effectiveness of the act."

18. *Consul General for Yugoslavia* v. *Andrew Artukovic.* The court reversed two federal courts and held that Artukovic, an anti-Communist refugee from Yugoslavia who was living with his wife and children in California, could not claim political asylum in the United States but had to submit to an extradition hearing which would be based on Yugoslavia's political charges.

19. *Rockwell Kent* v. *Dulles.* The court reversed two federal courts and held that the State Department could not require every applicant for a passport to file a non-Communist affidavit.

20. *Dayton* v. *Dulles.* The court reversed two federal courts and held that the State Department had to give a passport to a research physicist whose passport application to accept a job in India had been denied for security reason. The Secretary of State had found that Dayton had lived for eight months with a person who "was involved in the espionage apparatus of Julius Rosenberg" and that Dayton was going to work in India with another Communist who "recently renounced his American citizenship."

Needless to say, the articles in *Political Affairs* assumed an entirely different tone after these decisions had come rolling down from the nation's highest legal tribunal.

One example of the enthusiasm with which the Communists have taken advantage of this abrupt and complete reversal of judicial precedent is to be seen in a recent editorial entitled, "Reds Now Travel on Their Subversive Errands—by Supreme Court Decree!" The editorial points out that during the 21st convention of the Communist Party of the Soviet Union, held last February at Moscow, Khrushchev completed his insulting and threatening remarks about the United States, and after a similar speech by Marshal Malinovsky, Minister of War, an American citizen addressed the assemblage. He was James E.

Jackson, a representative of the Communist Party of the United States. The editorial proceeds:

"How did Jackson get there? He got there openly and legally. And so did other U. S. Communist leaders who went to Moscow at the same time. These characters were present because the Supreme Court ruled last June that the Secretary of State had no right to withhold passports from members of the Communist Party.

Jackson had been convicted by a jury in a federal court as a conspirator against the United States. Last August the Court of Appeals reversed the conviction, on the grounds that the Supreme Court in a similar case had freed several convicted California red leaders. Thus Jackson was saved from prison.

Meanwhile the Supreme Court had issued its decision that the Communists must not be denied passports. President Eisenhower quickly sent a special message to Congress, urging legislation authorizing the Secretary of State to withhold passports from the supporters of communism. The bill was passed in the House, but when it came to the Senate it got tied up in a jam of legislation just before adjournment. So the Communist Party was free to send Jackson to represent it at the convention of the Soviet Communist Party.

Also present in Moscow was the best-known member of the C. P. U. S. A., Paul Robeson. He, too, had received a passport after the Supreme Court's decision. And who should show up in Moscow, almost immediately after Jackson, but Harry Bridges, President of the Communist-controlled International Longshoremens and Warehousemens Union? Years ago a split decision of the Supreme Court saved this Australian-born citizen from deportation.

A few days earlier, Khrushchev received Dr. W. E. B. DuBois, 91-year-old scholar, former professor and intellectual leader of the pro-Kremlin forces among Negroes in the United States. Both DuBois and his wife were identified long ago as members of the Communist Party. Although not a member now, he makes no secret of his devotion to the Communist regime. For years his efforts to get a passport failed. Then came the Supreme Court decision—and DuBois was free to go to Moscow. From Moscow, DuBois and his wife flew to Peking, defying the State Department regulation that United States passports are not valid for travel to Red China.

Another United States citizen in Moscow was George Morris, labor editor of the Communist Party's misnamed paper, *the Worker,* and member of the CP's Labor Commission. After months of delay, the State Department had unwillingly given him a passport.

Meanwhile, Dr. Alpheus Hunton, another identified Communist Party member, had gone to Africa. Hunton used to be the Director of the Council on African Affairs, which Attorney General Brownell called a Communist front.

The State Department has been forced to grant passports to scores of important Communists and fellow travelers. The department even felt obliged to give passports to a precious pair, one of whom on a previous trip abroad made speeches charging the United States with germ warfare! Who can check on what harm such people do to the United States abroad? Congress should adopt the bill that President Eisenhower urged last summer, unmistakably authorizing the State Department to deny passports to Communists and their 'willing instruments,' and to cancel every passport now in such hands." [70]

While the Communists were naturally delighted with these decisions, other segments of American life were not so pleased. The states were expressing resentment at what they deemed the big brotherly attitude of the court in substituting its own judgment for that of state agencies. The Department of Justice and the F. B. I. expressed resentment because of the edict that threw open their secret files to the scrutiny of the sort of lawyer who would defy state bar committees that inquired about his subversive affiliations in determining his fitness to practice law. School administrators were resentful because they were stripped of their power to fire teachers who refused to answer questions about their Communist activity. Administrators of the federal loyalty program were resentful because they were shorn of their authority to fire disloyal employees, no matter what sort of a job they held. Experience had indicated clearly that a non-sensitive position in government today might well become highly sensitive overnight.

Judging from the flood of editorials, magazine articles, resolutions, newspaper items and commentaries, the public as a whole is also resentful because the Communists were figuratively handed a license to pursue their subversive activities almost without restriction, while the agencies of the government—federal and state alike—charged with the duty of coping with the problem, were loaded with new shackles and new restrictions. On July 1, 1957, *Life Magazine* ran an editorial that put the sentiments tersely:

" * * * The Smith Act, the Congressional investigations, the Hiss and Rosenberg cases, the loyalty procedures, the internal security laws, are not only facts of life but wound stripes on an older, tougher and wiser body politic.

Instead of earning its own stripes by wrestling with the same problem, the court often displays the most lamentable virginity about Communism."

When, a few months ago, the House of Delegates of the American Bar Association adopted a resolution criticizing these decisions and recommending that Congress pass legislation to rectify matters, an immediate protest was heard from the Communists, their front organizations, and assorted liberals. They called the American Bar Association

---

[70] Editorial, *Saturday Evening Post*, April 4, 1959, p. 10.

old fashioned, conservative to the point of reactionism, and shrugged off the fact that the House of Delegates represented thousands of the most able members of the legal profession in the United States.

We have never seen any publication calling attention to the fact that the American Bar Association, although certainly the most persuasive organization that lifted a voice of protest against these decisions, is by no means the earliest or the only legal body that expressed such sentiments. On June 24, 1957, the President of the National Association of State Attorneys General, represented by delegates at a Sun Valley, Idaho, meeting declared that:

"The recent Supreme Court decisions have thrown the fight against Communism for a 25-year loss." He received a standing ovation from the assembled delegates.[71]

On August 20, 1958, the Tenth Annual Conference of State Chief Justices, representing 48 states, Hawaii and Puerto Rico, met at Pasadena. There they approved a report criticizing the decisions of the Supreme Court in a resolution that declared:

" * * * In the fields with which we are concerned, and as to which we feel entitled to speak, the Supreme Court too often has tended to adopt the role of policymaker without proper judicial restraint. We feel this is partially the case in the extension of the federal power and in the supervision of state action by the Supreme Court by virtue of the Fourteenth Amendment. In the light of the immense power of the Supreme Court and its practical nonreviewability in most instances, no more important obligation rests upon it, in our view, than that of careful moderation in the exercise of its policymaking role.

It has long been an American boast that we have a government of laws and not of men. We believe that any study of recent decisions of the Supreme Court will raise at least considerable doubt as to the validity of that boast."

Specifically mentioned in this report adopted at the meeting were three decisions concerning Communism: *Nelson* v. *Pennsylvania, Sweezy* v. *New Hampshire,* and *Konigsberg* v. *California.*[72]

Dean Erwin N. Griswold, of Harvard Law School, whom even the members of the National Lawyers Guild could hardly term reactionary, has criticized the court for basing its own opinions on grounds that were far too broad, and offered the Watkins case of 1957, which has effectively hampered Congress in its attempts to elicit information about subversion, as an example of the court's unwarranted generalizing of a narrow issue.[73]

Not only lawyers and judges have raised their voices in protest against this reversal of judicial precedent, but laymen as well. In December, the American Farm Bureau Federation held its fortieth annual

---

[71] *Los Angeles Times,* June 25, 1957.
[72] *Los Angeles Times,* Aug. 21, 1958; Sept. 12, 1958.
[73] *National Review,* Nov. 8, 1958, p. 292.

convention at Boston, Massachusetts, and passed a resolution which provided:

> "We are deeply concerned with respect with the tendency of the United States Supreme Court to enact legislation by judicial action."

And the resolution recommended that:

> "* * * Congressional action be taken prescribing the proper limits of court jurisdiction and correcting or conforming legislation in those fields where the Supreme Court has invaded the legislative field." [74]

No informed person could possibly entertain the idea that the Supreme Court Justices are subversive, or that any of them are pro-Communist. Earl Warren was appointed Chief Justice to fill the vacancy created by the death of Fred Vinson in 1953. He assumed office immediately, which brought a quick protest from certain professors of constitutional law who pointed out quite accurately that his action was somewhat premature, because he had neglected to wait until he was confirmed by the Senate. Since the flood of controversial and liberal decisions was commenced about the time Warren assumed office, there has been much speculation in the press and magazines and on the part of commentators about whether he was the ultra-liberal whose persuasiveness carried along the majority of the court.

It happens that Earl Warren is probably the only Chief Justice of the United States Supreme Court who, prior to assuming that position, had been questioned by a committee on un-American Activities. We referred to the occasion earlier. He appeared as a co-operative witness before our committee in San Francisco when he was serving as the State Attorney General on December 3, 1941. The circumstances were these: The press had recently announced the release on parole of three convicts who had been convicted by Warren when he was district attorney in Oakland. They had been arrested and prosecuted for the murder of an anti-Communist crusader named Alberts, and the Communist press and the propaganda outlets were most solicitous in their behalf and most uncomplimentary to Warren. He declared that at least two of the men were Communists. Culbert Olson was Governor at the time, and Warren charged him with playing politics by favoring the granting of the parole. That action, said Warren, "* * * was nothing more nor less than appeasement to the Communists for what he had done in signing the bill against them." Mr. Warren successfully opposed Olson in the next gubernatorial election.

During his lengthy testimony before the committee, Warren expressed his attitude toward Communism and state committees on un-American activities. He declared that such a committee could render service by *exposing* subversive activities—a fact that is stressed here only because he was to take the opposite view in one of the decisions

---

[74] *Los Angeles Times,* Dec. 12, 1958.

already referred to. His attitude toward legislative committees must have continued during his three terms as Governor, since he constantly called upon this committee for the purpose of ascertaining whether any of the persons he was considering for appointive positions had subversive records.

His testimony against Communism was positive, clear, emphatic, and unhesitating. To intimate that Chief Justice Warren is in any way subversive is simply foolish.

The Law Clerks

It has been pointed out that there are 18 young clerks who assist the justices in preparing their opinions.[75] They are selected from leading law schools on the basis of their outstanding scholarship. Their average age is 27 years, and six of them have never passed the Bar examination. None of them are subjected to a loyalty screening. Alger Hiss once served as a law clerk to one of the Supreme Court Justices. These young men submit their opinions concerning the law, prepare memoranda that form the backbone of the ultimate decisions, discuss the theory of each decision with their respective justices, and thus are obviously in a position to exert a tremendous influence on the general tenor of the court and its opinions.

Since the opinions of the Supreme Court are of such vital importance to the nation, it would seem that these influential young men should be required to have some experience in the practice of the law, and should be picked for stability and balance and loyalty and common sense—not simply because they made high grades studying legal theory in law school. Certainly they should be subjected to a loyalty screening like the other federal employees. The extremely sensitive nature of their jobs is amply demonstrated by the character of the decisions regarding our Nation's internal security that we have already discussed.

The article in *U. S. News & World Report* closes with this statement:

> "It is openly acknowledged in Washington, however, that the Supreme Court Justices lean heavily on the shoulders of their young assistants. It is unlikely, say observers of the Federal Courts' system, that the justices could wade through the 1,500 to 2,000 cases that confront them each term without benefit of the spade work done for them by their clerks.
>
> The question that is raised at this time, when the Supreme Court is deploying its power in fields formerly controlled by other branches of the government, is whether the influence of these young law clerks—some of them as yet not even admitted to the Bar—is reflected in court opinions."

Whether or not these clerks have a record of documentable affiliation with subversive organizations, it is manifest that if, while attending college and law school, they were subjected to a subtle dissemination

---

[75] *U. S. News & World Report*, July 12, 1957, p. 135.

of the party line, they could become infected to such an extent that they would act as ideological Typhus Marys—but we do not accuse any of these clerks with subversion, any more than such charges should be leveled at members of the court. The Communists called the court and everything attached to it a great many insulting things when the tide of decision was flowing against them, and characteristically reversed themselves at precisely the time the court began to reverse its opinions. It is our purpose in this portion of the report to simply point out the fact that a situation exists which should be brought to the attention of all persons interested in combatting subversion, and certainly to the members of the Legislature of this State where some of these decisions originated. We wish to emphasize the fact that the Communist Party of the United States did work to bring about exactly this sort of judicial change.

It is also significant to note that at a Communist Party meeting held in Seattle last year, spokesmen for the party who came from New York to attend the affair declared that the party had, indeed, announced its intention to spearhead a national crusade to bring about this change in the decisions that were causing it so much oppression, and that the party then and there claimed full credit for having been responsible for the recent stream of decisions that enabled it to go about its business with more freedom than ever before. This meeting was covered by at least three undercover informants, each of them made sworn and independent statements, and the committee not only has them in its files but also has a document giving us permission to refer to them in this fashion.

The Commission on Government Security, in the report heretofore mentioned, considered the problem of screening these law clerks, and made the following recommendation:

"The judicial branch of the government should take effective steps to insure that its employees are loyal and otherwise suitable from the standpoint of national security."

And the commission proceeded to give the rationale for its recommendation, in part, as follows:

"It is fundamental that there should be no reasonable doubt concerning the loyalty of any federal employee in any of the three branches of the government. In a judicial branch, the possibility of disloyal employees causing damage to the national security is ever-present. As an example, federal judges, busy with the ever-crowded court calendars, must rely upon assistance to prepare briefing papers for them. False or biased information inadvertently reflected in court opinions in crucial security, constitutional, governmental or social issues of national importance could cause severe effects to the nation's security and to our federal loyalty-security system generally.

There appears to be no valid reason why an employee of the judicial branch should not be screened, at least as to his basic loyalty to the United States. Certainly the judiciary proper and the public generally should have the assurance that the men and women who carry the administrative responsibilities of the courts or assist in the preparation of decisions are loyal, dependable Americans.

The Commission therefore recommends, as in the case of the legislative branch, that the judicial branch and the executive branch endeavor to work out a program under which adequate investigation or screening can be provided for all judicial employees.'' [76]

The American Bar Association special committee that rendered the report on which the Association's resolution was based, had this to say about the present Communist menace:

"The phrase 'remember Pearl Harbor' should remind us that we, people and leaders, were cocksure and complacent before the afternoon of December 7, 1941. The F. B. I. had warned of frequent messages from the Japanese Consulate at Hawaii to Tokyo telling of the presence and absence of American warships at Pearl Harbor. Dies Committee reports of Japanese espionage by fishing vessels were ridiculed as headline hunting. Capt. Laurance Safford, who was recently awarded $100,000 by a grateful Congress for his World War II coding and decoding inventions, had decoded all the Japanese pre-Pearl Harbor war messages for his superiors. Yet, the attack came as a stunning surprise.

Most persons who are informed on Communism think our country is now in greater danger than were the *Titanic* and Pearl Harbor. The thesis of J. Edgar Hoover's new book, *Masters of Deceit*, is: 'Communism is the major menace of our time. Today, it threatens the very existence of our Western civilization.'

In his speech to the 1957 national convention of the American Legion, Mr. Hoover warned: 'To dismiss lightly the existence of the subversive threat in the United States is to deliberately to commit national suicide. In some quarters we are surely doing just that.'

On July 6, 1958, Prof. J. Sterling Livingston, a Pentagon consultant, stated: 'The doctrine of pre-emptive war is definitely a part of Soviet strategy. The Russian's plan as part of their strategy to strike a forestalling nuclear blow against their enemies.'

The lawyer-author of the Gaither report to the President on national security recently told our Association: 'Our security is in unprecedented peril * * * The ultimate objective of international Communism is world domination, and the Soviet Union will

---
[76] Report of Commission on Government Security, pursuant to Public Law 304, Eighty-fourth Congress, as amended, June, 1957, pp. 106-107.

pursue this objective ruthlessly and relentlessly, employing every possible political, economic, subversive, and military strategy and tactic'.''

The Bar Association's special committee considered Communists in the legal profession such a serious menace to the nation's security, and so inconsistent with the standards of the profession that it has implemented its convictions with positive action. The report declared:

"In accordance with the resolution of the House of Delegates and authorization of the Board of Governors, our committee—on the request of the State Attorney for its co-operation—applied for and obtained permission to appear as *amicus curiae* in the appeal pending in the Supreme Court of Florida from the order of dismissal of the disciplinary proceedings against Leo Sheiner. Leo Sheiner had twice previously been ordered disbarred by the Circuit Court of Florida.

Our committee prepared and submitted a brief to the Supreme Court of Florida stating its views on the duty of the Bar and of the courts to cleanse its ranks of an unfit member. The committee further stated its concepts of an acceptable standard of fitness for attorneys and for the unfitness of any member of the Bar who, in appropriate proceedings, persists in refusal to answer pertinent questions concerning his activities in the Communist Party or Communist-dominated fronts on the grounds that his answers to such questions concerning his activities might tend to incriminate him. It is inconceivable to us that an attorney and officer of the court may continue in good standing while he pleads self-incrimination in refusing to answer questions relating to subversive activities.

The brief pointed out that, in other walks of life, labor union officials, teachers, government employees, and employees of private industry, there had been set a standard under which the individual might be safeguarded in invoking the Fifth Amendment to inquiries which might tend to incriminate him, but by so doing he forfeits his position of trust and responsibility. The Sheiner case is very important to the Bar as other states having such problem attorneys on their roles have been awaiting the final decision in this matter.

The appeal was argued before the Supreme Court of Florida on February 8, 1958. Julius Applebaum, a member of our committee, argued as *amicus curiae* for this association. On July 24, 1958, the court issued an order on its own motion requesting argument on September 5, 1958, and permitting supplemental briefs as to the application of three decisions. * * * rendered by the United States Supreme Court on June 30, 1958. Our committee is preparing such supplemental briefs in behalf of the association that will participate in the reargument. *Our committee is willing to appear in similar cases upon direction of the House of Delegates or Board of Governors.*'' *(Committee's italics.)*

It is most interesting to note, by way of contrast, that the Supreme Court of free Germany started to consider the legal status of the Communist Party in that country about the same time as our Subversive Activities Control Board did—each court taking evidence for a period of about five years. As we have seen, our Supreme Court not only reversed the board when it decided against the Communist Party and sent the matter back for more years of taking evidence, but has persistently refused to rule on the constitutionality of the Act of 1950, under which the board functions.

This is what the German Supreme Court held:

"The Communist Party of Germany is unconstitutional.

"The Communist Party of Germany will be dissolved.

"It is prohibited to establish substitute organizations for the Communist Party of Germany or to continue existing organizations as substitute organizations.

"The assets of the Communist Party of Germany will be confiscated in favor of the Federal Republic of Germany for purposes of the common weal." [77]

Hancock v. Burns

On August 10, 1953, the committee held a closed hearing in the City of San Francisco for the purposes of investigating the extent to which the Pacific Gas & Electric Company had been infiltrated by Communists. Among the witnesses subpoenaed were Patrick Thomas Hancock, Travis Lafferty, Joseph Chasin, and Holden Hayden. The press was not admitted to the hearing, and each of the witnesses was represented by counsel. When questioned about membership in the Communist Party and activities as Communists, the defendants all invoked the privilege of the Fifth Amendment and declined to testify on the ground that if they gave truthful answers to these questions they would subject themselves to criminal prosecution.

Other witnesses were called during the course of the hearing, and thereafter Senator Burns, as chairman of the committee, wrote a letter to the Pacific Gas & Electric Company in which he stated that the employees mentioned had invoked the Fifth Amendment and expressed his opinion that employees of public utilities in general who invoked the Fifth Amendment when questioned by official agencies under oath about their subversive affiliations were bad security risks. Thereafter, on August 14, 1953, after the committee had authorized the release of a complete transcript of the hearing, the Pacific Gas & Electric Company discharged the four employees mentioned.

On August 13, 1954, a matter of minutes before the statute of limitations would have barred the right of the employees to file a suit, a complaint was filed in the Superior Court of the State of California at San Francisco against Senator Burns, Senator Nathan F. Coombs,

---

[77] Judgment of the Federal Constitutional Court, Aug. 17, 1956. Translation by the Division of Language Service, U. S. Department of State.

the late Senator Earl D. Desmond, Senator John F. McCarthy and Senator John F. Thompson, both individually and as members of the committee, and against R. E. Combs, individually and in his capacity as counsel for the committee. The complaint alleged all of the facts heretofore stated, and proceeded to charge that all of the members of the committee and its counsel had wrongfully conspired to persuade the Pacific Gas & Electric Company to discharge the plaintiffs and asked for damages in the sum of $218,333.

The San Francisco Superior Court ruled that the plaintiffs had no case, and sustained a demurrer without leave to amend. An appeal was then taken to the District Court of Appeals for the first Appellate District of California, where a written decision was rendered by a unanimous court in favor of the committee. The plaintiffs then appealed to the State Supreme Court, and their appeal was rejected. Since the rendering of our last report, time for an appeal to the Supreme Court of the United States has elapsed and the case has ended.

It is to be noted that the attorney for the plaintiffs was also the attorney for the American Civil Liberties Union of Northern California, and was so designated on the complaint; and after he resigned from that position he was replaced by Attorney Albert M. Bendich, staff counsel for the American Civil Liberties Union of Northern California, and these attorneys were assisted by Rubin Tepper and Edward F. Newman. The committee was represented by the Attorney General of the State, then the Honorable Edmund G. Brown, through his Chief Assistant, Clarence A. Linn, by the Legislative Counsel Bureau and the San Francisco firm of Melvin, Faulkner, Sheehan & Wiseman.

So important and practically valuable to all legislative committees was the opinion rendered by the district court of appeal in our favor, that we quote briefly from it as follows:

> "While Senate Resolution No. 127 does not, nor could it, authorize the commission of tortious acts, nevertheless it does establish a committee of the State Senate authorized to act as an official adjunct of that body. Such committees are expressly authorized by our State Constitution in Article IV, Section 37. Therefore, by reading the resolution in conjunction with the complaint, it becomes apparent that the conjunctive pleading of respondents' status (as to respondents' having acted both as committee members and as individuals in doing the acts here complained of) must be grounded on reasoning that by going outside the legislative sphere the defendants were stripped of any legislative immunity and stand before the court as individuals.
>
> This theory of the evaporative quality of legislative immunity, by its very statement, discloses its own vice. If government, operating through the individuals who form it, is afforded immunity from private suit only when its actions are beyond any question, and loses that immunity upon mere allegation of improper motives or unlawful acts in a complaint seeking damages, then those per-

sons who form government are subject to the threat of personal liability in any matter in which their discretion is exercised.

The fact that a legislative committee erroneously exercised powers, in a mistaken belief that it has such powers, would immediately subject its members to the harrassment of litigation. What would a logical extension of this rule lead to so far as the judiciary is concerned? Would a judge who mistakenly assumed the jurisdiction in a proceeding be liable to personal suit by an agrieved party litigant who merely alleged willfulness, wrongfulness and malice? Would not such a rule require the examination of the motives as well as the propriety of all governmental action by our courts? We think so.

The basic principle of separation of power which is one of the bases for our entire form of constitutional government would be diluted to the point where the judicial branch, because of artful allegations in a complaint, would be required to re-examine every act of the executive and legislative branches which had an adverse effect upon any individual.

Granting that the courts have the privilege and the duty of protecting the personal civil rights of the citizens of this Country from abuse, nevertheless, when the enforcement of such personal civil rights results in an erosion of the government which alone can guarantee such rights, the obligation to society as a whole may dictate that the individual forego personal recovery for injuries suffered so that government may continue.

It has often been said that when elected officials so conduct themselves as to indicate a lack of essential obligation to their responsibilities, there are remedies available to the electorate which can correct these abuses; also the power of impeachment still exists. 'The Constitution has left the performance of many duties in our governmental scheme to depend upon the fidelity of the executive and legislative action and, ultimately, on the vigilance of the people in exercising their political rights.'

It will no doubt be argued that, by holding the action here taken by the committee as within the protection afforded by legislative immunity, the members of such a committee could commit any tortious act by claiming it to be within the same rule. The argument would, however, fail. Were the committee or its members charged with the commission of some bodily injury inflicted on another in the course of conducting their hearings, such acts could not reasonably be urged to come within the immunity here stated, as the mere recitation of the infliction of bodily harm is a statement of an act which by no reasonable means could be encompassed by the immunity.

The act here complained of was committed by the use of the ordinary means adopted by such committees in reporting their findings and conclusions: namely, the preparation and forwarding of a written communication.

One of the basic foundations of our constitutional government is to be found in the separation of powers. This doctrine has been recognized as essential to a free form of government wherein public officers may perform their duties untrammeled by fear of sanction in the form of personal liability if it transpires that their acts were unwise or based upon a misinterpretation of the law. Much has been written, commencing with Montesquieu in the Eighteenth Century, and continuing up to date, regarding the necessity or advisability of continuing the doctrine of the separation of powers. It has been said, 'The problems of government are complicated and difficult of solution. But must it not be apparent to everyone, as we gaze into the future, that we cannot hope to maintain the way of life which we call American without exercising every effort to preserve to each branch of government its proper sphere and the states and the union a due recognition of their proper function.' [78]

The rights here sought to be enforced are assuredly right to which a citizen of this country is entitled unless, in the exercise of those rights, the person committing the act is protected by some privilege or immunity. * * *

In view of our holding that the action of respondents here was protected by their legislative immunity * * * it is not necessary to discuss the other points urged by appellants. The immunity appearing on the fact of the complaint, it would be useless to allow amendments.

The judgment is affirmed. McMurray, Justice pro Tem; Peters, Presiding Justice; Bray, Justice.''

THE LIQUIDATORS

We have noted how the Communist Party found it necessary to declare war on the Supreme Court of the United States and launch a campaign to bring about a change in the type of decisions being handed down by that tribunal. We also noted how the Communists mounted the campaign and then claimed credit for the complete and sudden reversal of the Supreme Court's opinions and the issuance of a series of decisions that gave it more freedom than ever. Not content with having brought about this amazing situation, for which the party claims full credit, it is now engaged in an equally earnest and widespread endeavor to liquidate the state and federal legislative committees on un-American activities and to further stifle the activities of the Federal Bureau of Investigation.

---

[78] *The Doctrine of the Separation of Powers and Its Present Day Significance,* by Arthur T. Vanderbilt, p. 142.

In previous reports we have discussed in great detail the old cultural front, the Arts, Sciences and Professions Council. We also gave resumes of hearings involving its successor, the Citizens Committee to Preserve American Freedom. We have indicated how a great many of the leaders of the old Arts, Sciences and Professions Council are now to be found doing equally active work for the Citizens Committee to Preserve American Freedom. This organization, largely confined to the southern part of the state, although it has also been active to some extent elsewhere, is loosely affiliated with the Emergency Civil Liberties Committee, a nationwide organization established in 1957 for the same general purposes. Frank Wilkinson, a graduate of the University of California at Los Angeles, and formerly a top employee of the Los Angeles City Housing Administration, is probably the most active single figure in both organizations, being loaned back and forth between the two as the exigencies of the situation may demand.

Wilkinson was first brought to the attention of this committee when the former Attorney General of the State, now Governor Edmund G. Brown, together with the Housing Authority, requested us to conduct an investigation into alleged Communist infiltration, and which resulted in a closed hearing and the discharge of several employees, including Wilkinson.

It was also disclosed that Mrs. Wilkinson was employed as a teacher by the Los Angeles City Board of Education, and this led to the first of a series of hearings that ended with the discharge of more teachers, paved the way for the passage of the so-called Dilworth Act, and prompted the board of education to inaugurate a system by which it could keep itself currently advised concerning the subversive backgrounds of applicants for employment, both academic and administrative.

On the occasion of its last hearings concerning the Citizens Committee to Preserve American Freedom, and at hearings involving the former Communist front, the Arts, Sciences and Professions Council, the committee had intended to subpoena Dr. Murray Abowitz, who had been prominent as a member of the Medical Division of the latter organization. He appeared before the committee in Los Angeles on June 9, 1958, represented by his attorney, Robert W. Kenny.

The witness admitted that he was chairman of the medical division of the Arts, Sciences and Professions Council in 1952, and also recalled having attended several meetings of the organization over a period of several years, together with several meetings of the Citizens Committee to Preserve American Freedom.

It will be recalled that the Arts, Sciences and Professions Council was a Communist-controlled organization, described as such by several official agencies, but that it had dissolved itself shortly before Dr. Abowitz testified at the hearing in 1958. He had no hesitancy in testifying about his activities in that organization, but promptly invoked the Fifth Amendment when asked whether or not he was a Communist. The following question was then put to him:

> Q. (By Mr. Combs): Is it not a fact that you joined the Communist Party in Los Angeles in 1936, that you were attached to the physicians branch of the 13th Congressional District Section, that in 1938 your Communist membership book bore No. 78476, and that in 1939 your Communist membership book bore No. 1205?
>
> The Witness: I decline to answer to answer that, too, on the same ground.
>
> Q. Is it not also a fact that during the period of your membership in the Communist Party, commencing in 1936 and extending through 1939, you used the Communist Party name or alias of Thomas Wilson?
>
> A. I decline to answer that question also on the same grounds, but I would also like to point out to you, Mr. Combs, that I wasn't in California in 1938—'36.
>
> Q. Where were you in 1936?
>
> A. I was in medical school in Vienna, Austria.
>
> Q. Would that prevent your having been assigned to the Communist Party of Los Angeles County?
>
> A. I was just trying to help you with your records; I'm just trying to be helpful.
>
> Q. I am satisfied with it."

Dr. Abowitz admitted that he had attended meetings of the Civil Rights Congress, which was described by the United States Attorney General as a Communist front organization and by the witness as "a fine, worthy organization that defended many civil rights cases. * * * " The witness also stated that he had contributed to the Joint Anti-Fascist Refugee Committee, that he held a membership in the International Workers Order—both Communist-controlled organizations—and that he was on the Board of Directors of the Communist school in Los Angeles, the California Labor School, in 1948, and was affiliated with the American-Soviet Medical Society.

Dr. Abowitz has been identified as a member of the Communist Party by several witnesses, probably the earliest one being a former employee of this committee who declared under oath that she had known Dr. Abowitz and his wife as members of the Communist Party during the late thirties.[79]

A documentation from Communist sources and from various official agencies investigating Communist activities was recently published by Mr. George Robnett, of Pasadena. The booklet, entitled, "The Crusade

[79] See affidavit and testimony of Rena M. Vale, 1943 committee report; see, also, 1947 report, pages 54, 55, 70, 73, 210, 238, 241, 244, 298; 1948 report, pages 198, 239, 253, 254, 279, 308, 309, 355; 1949 report pages 421, 428, 433, 435, 436, 478; 1951 report, pages 255, 268, 275, 280; 1953 report, page 139; 1959 report, pages 86, 100, 105-109, 112, 114, 138, 208, 223, 267, 277, 287, 293, 295, 302, 303, 307, 308, 311-313, 315-318, 320, 338, 351, 357, 360, 367, 370, 374, 387.

Against Government Investigating Agencies, a Report on Forces and Processes," opens with this statement:

"What do you think would be the reaction in this country if a group of individuals were caught trying to destroy our Army, our Navy, or our Air Force, especially at a time when we were engaged in a life and death struggle with some enemy country?

How different would you consider this to be in principle from the present collaboration of certain individuals and groups whose clear purpose is to destroy our front line of security—defense agencies, when we are engaged in the deadliest 'cold' war that this Country has ever faced with an avowed enemy?

This latter reference is to an open and active crusade by certain groups to demolish the House Committee on un-American Activities, as well as to a campaign, not so openly declared but just as real, to discredit and dissipate the work of the Federal Bureau of Investigation and other security agencies."

The attack against the Federal Bureau of Investigation was kicked off on October 18, 1958, with a special issue of *The Nation*, edited by Carey McWilliams. The entire issue of 280 pages is devoted to an article by Fred J. Cook entitled, "The F. B. I." Our copy was purchased at the International Book Store, 1408 Market Street, San Francisco, California, where it seemed to be in great demand.

Mr. McWilliams has been the author of several books, many of them widely sold. He is the author of Factories in the Field, he appeared as a witness before this committee many years ago, and he has been listed as a member of practically every major Communist front organization that ever existed. McWilliams was active in California as Commissioner of Immigration and Housing in the early forties, having been appointed to that position by Governor Culbert Olson, and prior to that time he had been active in Labor's Non-Partisan League, the United Organization for Progressive Political Action, and with the Communist Party itself. During the late thirties McWilliams was collaborating with Dorothy Healey, who was then known as Dorothy Ray. We have already devoted some attention to Mrs. Healey, now Mrs. Philip M. Connelly, in her capacity as the Chairman of the Southern California Division of the Communist Party, and the target for considerable criticism on the part of the top functionaries in New York. In October, 1938, Dorothy Ray was sent to Bakersfield by the International of the United Cannery, Agricultural, Packing & Allied Workers of America, a Communist-dominated union, to handle a cotton strike in that vicinity. Two years thereafter a field workers' school was sponsored by that union at Chino, California, for the purpose of training its organizers. Among the instructors at the institution, with whom Dorothy Healey was then co-operating, were Revels Cayton, Amy Schechter, and Carey McWilliams.

Mr. McWilliams, contemporaneously with his elevation to a state position with some prestige and authority, ceased his intimate contacts with the Communist Party but continued to publish his progressive-type books, kept up his dues in front organizations, and essayed the role of a liberal. The fact is, however, that Mr. McWilliams did join the Communist Party, according to the sworn statements of many individuals who sat in closed party meetings with him. How long his membership continued we do not know, but we are quite aware of the fact that his Communist front affiliations have continued for at least 20 years, and that he is the editor of a publication that contains an attack against the Federal Bureau of Investigation that was considered so effective that it evoked high praise from the Soviet Union, as follows:

"It transpires from Cook's article and from press reports on big trials that the main task of the F. B. I. is the identification and liquidation, including the physical liquidation, of persons of whom the U. S. ruling circles disapprove for one reason or another." [80]

No stranger to the artifices and techniques of the Communist Party, especially in California, is Los Angeles County's new Sheriff, Peter Pitchess. While an F. B. I. agent in Los Angeles, one of Pitchess' duties was to deliver lectures to peace officers throughout the state. At the LaFayette Hotel in Long Beach last February 12, Mr. Pitchess told members of the Exchange Club that the Communist Party is conducting a "concerted drive to destroy public confidence in the F. B. I. That the Communist Party and its sympathizers and apologists whose hatred for the F. B. I. results from its effectiveness in carrying out its responsibilities and in protecting the internal security of America, had been accelerated to an extreme degree."

Sheriff Pitchess concluded his remarks by adding: "I must further express hope that the American public * * * will continue to demonstrate its faith in this great law enforcement leader, J. Edgar Hoover, by rejecting the foul spewings of the Kremlin's messenger boys." [81]

In contrast to the remarks of Los Angeles County's Sheriff, let us examine some comments by Elizabeth Gurley Flynn, charter member of the Communist Party of the United States and a member of its National Committee. Mrs. Flynn, herself a Smith Act defendant who was sent to prison, and who played a remarkably active role in the party's fight to bring about a change in the federal laws that were hampering its operations, was moved to comment about J. Edgar Hoover and his book, Masters of Deceit, which attained best-seller status. She said:

"* * * J. Edgar Hoover is today the undisputed czar of the F. B. I. The master of self-adulation, who continually publicizes himself on the radio, in the press and magazines, speaks to women's clubs, graduating classes, businessmen, the Legion, etc. If ever

---

[80] Radio Moscow, 1800 gmp. 22 December, 1958.
[81] *Los Angeles Examiner*, Feb. 12, 1959.

there was a shining example of the 'cult of the individual,' it is exemplified in this politically illiterate and conceited man, who has used almost unlimited power for the attempted suppression of the Bill of Rights.'' [82]

In Washington Congressman James Roosevelt introduced a measure which would have taken away the autonomous power of the House Committee on un-American Activities and stifle it to death by absorbing it in the Judiciary Committee. The House, however, voted $327,000 to enable the committee to function during the current year, and the Communist pressure has apparently been shifted to bring about a repeal of the McCarran Act, to undermine public respect for the F. B. I. The tentative moves have already been made, but, as was the case of the campaign to liquidate the House Committee on un-American Activities, the sniping is always made from concealed positions and frequently by individuals who have no formal connection with the party but are, nevertheless, most sensitive to its demands and responsive to its pressures.

An example of how some of these credulous liberals are utilized contemptuously by the Soviet Union appears in a book by Boris Morros, an undercover counter agent for the Federal Bureau of Investigation.

"Some time before, I had told Vitaly that I would be returning to the United States in the Fall. He had two assignments for me on this trip: he wanted me to find between 10 to 20 Americans who were loved and trusted throughout the United States, and to get them to come in a group to Moscow. These influential Americans could then see for themselves that the Russians truly wanted peace. Vitaly insisted that the Reds were willing to make concessions to such a delegation of Westerns. 'We do not want to talk to your comedian progressives,' he said, 'but to men who can go home and convince the people of America that another World War is the last thing the Kremlin wants!' I was to hear this plea a hundred times from the lips of other Communist officials and spies." [83]

Just as the constant program of exposure and vigilance caused the Communist Party to give up its major front organizations and to retreat to its underground sanctuaries, so has the program of public education and disclosure operated to shrink the supply of gullible liberals who could be wheedled into unconsciously carrying on the party's dirty work. It is not very difficult to distinguish between a sincere and dedicated liberal and one who is consciously or unconsciously imbued with the precepts of the class struggle and the Communist ideology to the point that they become almost a part of his sympathetic nervous system. The true liberal is interested in resolving conflicts, in fighting for advanced and really progressive reforms for the benefit of humanity. The Communist tool, on the other hand, is constantly striving to perpetuate the current party line, and instead of

[82] *Political Affairs,* May, 1958, p. 61.
[83] My Ten Years as a Counter-Spy, op. cit., pp. 142-143.

resolving conflict and problems he seeks to keep the class struggle going by complicating the old problems and creating new ones.

At least in California, there is encouraging evidence that liberals in the true sense of that much-abused term, are beginning to heed the phrase attributed to Vemelot, and which is so characteristic of totalitarians in general and Communists in particular: "When I am the weaker I demand liberty of you, because liberty is one of *your* principles; but when, one day, I am the stronger, I shall strip you of liberty because stripping others of liberty is one of *my* principles." [84]

There are other signs of encouragement in California, in this neverending battle against internal subversion. The committee has found during the last three or four years a rapidly increasing interest on the part of students and faculty members alike in obtaining accurate and objective information not only on Communist ideology and revolutionary history, but on practical problems on combating Communist subversion. We wish to particularly commend the Citizens for Political Freedom in Pasadena. Also the Women for America in Beverly Hills. The Pasadena organization, under the leadership of Mrs. Virginia Cassil, has just completed its third year as sponsor of a series of annual lectures at Pasadena City College's extended day program, entitled "How to Detect Communist Indoctrination." The popularity of this course has increased every year, it is well attended by students and teachers in addition to the public at large, and by arrangement with the State Department of Education, institute credit is given to teachers who attend all of the lectures. The lecturers are carefully selected, not only for their ability as speakers and their qualifications as experts in their respective fields, but because of their balance and stability in handling controversial topics.

Women for America, the organization in Beverly Hills, recently completed an outstanding program under the aegis of the extended day department of the Beverly Hills High School. This program, like the ones held in Pasadena, comprises lectures by the best experts the sponsors can obtain, each lecture running for approximately two hours including a period for questions and answers from the audience. Mrs. Morrie Ryskind and Mrs. Fred Bartman are to be congratulated on the time and effort they have devoted to making this Beverly Hills program an outstanding success.

The Fresno State College Chapter of Phi Gamma Mu, a scholarship honor society of faculty members and students, also sponsored a lecture on Communism in California in January of this year, and these programs are being duplicated by many schools throughout the state. We also note that the press is carrying an ever-increasing amount of reliable information concerning problems of internal Communist subversion, which is replacing a great deal of unreliable and sensational material that was being widely published a few years ago.

---

[84] Letter from Prof. William Roetke to the International Association of Political Science, 1958.

Such patriotic organizations as the American Legion, the Daughters of the American Revolution and the Los Angeles Chapter of the American Jewish League Against Communism have contributed greatly to public understanding of these problems by sponsoring citizenship and patriotism awards and holding programs that emphasize the necessity of understanding the problems that we face from Communism, and by encouraging the proper sort of educational programs on the widest possible basis. It is, of course, impossible to mention all of the schools and all of the patriotic organizations that are contributing to an educational program that will arm the public at large with the proper knowledge that will equip them to recognize these subtle subversive activities, to know the party line, to identify the front organizations, and to help in rendering completely ineffective the all-out Communist campaign which is now being waged to undermine public confidence in our official agencies.

THE INTIMIDATION OF VIRGINIA HEDGES

Virginia Hedges came to California from Terre Haute, Indiana, with her mother and stepfather in August, 1947. They lived at 5154 Sunset Boulevard, Hollywood, for about a year and a half, moved to La Canada for 18 months, then returned to their former residence in Hollywood. Shortly thereafter the mother and her husband separated, and Virginia lived with her mother at 1308 West 109th Street in Los Angeles for several years.

After graduating from high school, Virginia got a job with the telephone company in Los Angeles and had a phone installed under her own name—Virginia Hedges. This was in June, 1953.

For the purpose of clarifying a complicated set of circumstances, it is necessary to bear in mind that the hearing at which Frank Wilkinson was examined occurred during the latter part of October, 1952. In connection with the interrogation of Mr. Wilkinson we had received reports from several former Communists who had attended closed party meetings with him. These informants gave entirely separate and independent statements, and no one of them was aware that any of the others were cooperating with us. One of these informants was, by an amazing coincidence, named Virginia Hedges, although not related to and completely unknown by her namesake.

But this identity of names was only the first of a series of coincidences. Our informant had once resided in the same general vicinity as Virginia Hedges and her mother. And the latter bore a striking resemblance to our informant. Adding to this confusing situation was the fact that our informant also had a telephone listed in her name—Virginia Hedges, and when she moved her name was taken out of the directory, only to be replaced shortly thereafter when her namesake had *her* telephone installed. So, although there was only one Virginia Hedges in the book, after June, 1953, it was actually the name of a different person.

During the time that elapsed after we first questioned Mr. Wilkinson, he devoted more and more of his time to Communist activities, participating in many front meetings, especially the newly formed Citizens Committee to Preserve American Freedom. We received reliable information that he had also advised party members who had gone underground concerning security precautions, and he was obviously given an important assignment when he was sent east to assist the Emergency Civil Liberties Committee correlate its campaign to liquidate federal and state committees on un-American Activities and undermine the reputation of the F. B. I.

We consequently decided to contact our informants to secure any available information that might shed additional light on these developments. On January 23, 1958, a letter was accordingly directed to the only Virginia Hedges listed in the Los Angeles telephone directory and, of course, it was received by the informant's namesake.

Puzzled by the somewhat cryptic terms in which the letter was written, Miss Hedges consulted the Los Angeles Field Office of the F. B. I., described to them a series of experiences that had occurred to her, and was advised to contact us. This she did in a note dated January 28, 1958, and we then learned for the first time of the peculiar circumstances we have already described.

Conferences with Miss Hedges disclosed that she had been mistaken for our informant and subjected to a familiar harassment that commenced almost as soon as the telephone was listed under her name and continued until she appeared before us as a witness on June 10, 1958.

We have described this technique of Communist intimidation by telephone in previous reports. It is constantly used, now more than ever since there are more defections from the party than previously, to prevent former party members from cooperating with official agencies. Even after having testified openly and fully, informants are frequently subjected to this type of annoyance.

This final section of our report is being dictated on Saturday, April 4th. On the evening of March 5th, a representative of the committee visited with Paul and Marion Miller, who acted as undercover agents for the F. B. I. in the Communist Party. Mrs. Miller was active in the Los Angeles Chapter of the Citizens Committee for the Protection of the Foreign Born for five years, and then disclosed her experiences to the fullest extent by testifying under oath. Since that time the Millers have been subjected to precisely the same sort of telephone annoyance that were described by Virginia Hedges. On the evening of March 5th, an anonymous telephone call was made to the Miller home, and when one of their three children answered the telephone he was subjected to a tirade of vicious and unprintable abuse of his parents.

The Millers had expected to be subjected to this familiar pattern because they had been warned that it would probably occur, and they were more or less prepared for the barrage of false and defamatory statements on mimeographed leaflets that were anonymously distributed among their neighbors. But Virginia Hedges had never had any experience with any type of subversive groups, and was completely unprepared for the long harassment to which she and her mother were subjected.

She testified that her telephone would ring at 3 or 4 o'clock in the morning and when she or her mother awakened and answered they would hear someone breathing, then a click as the receiver was hung up and the connection was broken. Then, after an hour or more, the call would be repeated. This procedure continued for almost five years.

It seems rather odd that in cases where a former Communist has *already* testified, it is usual practice to subject them to a tirade of abuse during a short conversation before the connection is broken. But when it is desired to intimidate a former member who is only suspected of having given information, or whom the party wishes to *prevent* from doing so, the calls are ordinarily without conversation, the receiver being hung up after an interval of a few minutes.

This practice is described in many books by former Communists and by non-Communists whom the party seeks to scare into ceasing their anti-Communist activities. An officer of the Commonwealth Club of California was recently subjected to such calls for a period of many months. Virtually all ex-Communists who have really broken from the party have received this form of intimidation.

Finally, Virginia Hedges' mother noticed that she was being followed when she left her home in the afternoon. She saw the same person following her day after day, and finally complained to an attendant at the service station she usually patronized and he told her that he had also noticed she was being followed. Then came a call on January 24, 1958, that so unnerved the mother that she left California and returned to her former home in Indiana. Her daughter described the experience in a reply to the original letter intended for our informant, and written in January, 1958:

"Mr. Combs: In reference to the enclosed letter I'm sorry to say there must be a mistake. I've never testified. You must have the wrong address.

On the twenty-fourth my mother received a call for an unidentified person who said 'Tell Virginia Hedges she is going to get her throat cut.'

On Sunday there was a call from New York, too. I don't know who it was.

I am the only Virginia Hedges listed in the phone book. It sounds like she is in trouble."

Questioned by the committee in June, 1958, Virginia Hedges described the calls as follows:

Q. When did this telephone call threatening to cut your throat occur, and what time did your mother receive that call?

She answered the telephone, did she not?

A. Yes.

Q. What time of the day?

A. I am not sure.

Q. Was it a man or a woman?

A. It was a woman.

Q. Was there any noticeable accent?

A. She wasn't sure.

Q. She wasn't sure?

A. No.

Q. During all of these times the telephone would ring early in the morning, or any time during the two-year period, would you endeavor to find out who was calling and whom they wanted, and so on?

A. Well, several times I answered the phone and they would ask for Virginia Hedges.

Q. Yes?

A. And I would say, 'This is Virginia Hedges.'

Q. Yes?

A. But, for some reason they wouldn't say anything else.

Q. They would just hang up?

A. Yes.

Q. You haven't had a bit of trouble since you wrote me this note, have you?

A. No, sir.

Q. You don't know the other Virginia Hedges?

A. No.

Q. Virginia Hedges No. 1?

A. No.

Q. You have never had any connection with any Communist organization of any kind, have you?

A. No, sir.

Q. * * * Did you ever have any experience with telephone calls of this type before in your entire life?

A. No.[85]

Shortly after having received the note from Miss Hedges, and after having conferred with her at some length, representatives of the committee contacted the real informant who had moved several times and had changed her occupation. A supplemental sworn statement was taken from her, in which she described in detail the circumstances under which she affiliated with the Communist Party, her attendance at the Communist beginner's classes for a period of approximately eight months, the party textbooks and other material she was required to study in order to prepare herself for active party membership, and her assignment to a definite unit of the party.

---

[85] Vol. 66, Committee Transcript, pp. 156-158.

The informant gave additional information concerning Mr. Wilkin-
on and his identity as a Communist Party member, together with his
ictivities in the party unit to which he was assigned.

We wish to make it clear that our informant, Virginia Hedges, has
10 telephone, and has already given full and complete cooperation to
ill official agencies that have asked her to do so. In that connection she
.estified as follows on June 5, 1958:

Q. Have you ever been solicited by any party member to reac-
tivate your activities and rejoin the party?

A. No, I have not.

Q. Have you ever had any threats, either directly or indirectly,
about disclosing the information you gained during your party
membership?

A. No, I have not.

Q. It is a fact, is it not, Miss Hedges, that you have heretofore
given to this committee full and detailed information concerning
other people who were in the party with you, in addition to Frank
Wilkinson, and detailed information concerning your own activities while you were a party member?

A. That is correct.

Q. This is also true, is it not, that you flew to Sacramento several
years ago, at your own expense, for the purpose of conferring with
me about the general matters that are covered in this statement?

A. That is correct.

Q. And is it not also true that in addition to giving information
to this committee, that you voluntarily have given full and detail
information to federal agencies concerning your experiences during
all of the time you were a member of the Communist Party?

A. That is correct.

Q. And it is also true, is it not, Miss Hedges, that you are giving
this testimony pursuant to a subpoena served upon you by me,
which subpoena is a continuing subpoena to remain in effect until
such time as you are excused from appearing before the committee?

A. That is correct.[86]

It is clear to the committee that the reason our informant was not
)othered after she had cooperated with us in 1952 was because the
ndividuals responsible for the anonymous telephone calls had been
onfused by the series of coincidences outlined above and had spent
lmost five years intimidating the wrong person. During the 18 years
luring which the committee has been active, we have never experienced
ior heard of a case like this, and we include it in the report for the
iurpose of documenting still another example of the techniques that
re being used by the Communist Party in California.

Sworn statement executed by Virginia Hedges on June 5, 1958, taken by John B.
Hossack, Certified Shorthand Reporter, pursuant to the provisions of Senate Resolution No. 132, adopted by the California State Senate, at the General Session of
the California State Legislature in 1957.

The party had an excellent motive for endeavoring to frighten our informant so she would refuse to give information and the party was well aware of the fact that she did possess highly damaging knowledge about the Communist activities and stature of Mr. Wilkinson, who became an exceedingly active and important Communist figure after he was discharged by the Los Angeles City Housing Authority. There was utterly no reason whatever for the intimidation of the Virginia Hedges who actually received these telephone calls, since she never had the slightest connection with any sort of Communist organization, even an innocuous Communist front, and while to laymen this business of panting into a telephone then hanging up may seem somewhat melodramatic and silly, to people who have been members of the Communist Party for a number of years and who never know when they go to bed at night whether or not they will be awakened by the ominous ringing of their telephone at 3 or 4 o'clock in the morning, the implied threat is clearly understood, and after several years the intimidation becomes extremely annoying. Since the calls are usually made from either a pay phone or from sources that are changed from time to time, and since the conversation or lack of conversation only continues for a minute or so, the calls are virtually impossible to trace.

The official of the Commonwealth Club who was subjected to a period of similar early morning calls, was not particularly bothered at first because, having been extremely forthright in his anti-Communist activities, he had rather expected such occurrence. But he can testify most convincingly concerning the nervous tension that is produced in an individual who has been subjected to this technique for a period of several months.

We should add at this point that the party's attacks on former members who are suspected of being possible sources of information to anti-Communist agencies is incredibly vicious. The preservation of secrecy concerning all of its activities and the concealment of the identity of all its members is essential to the continued operation of the party, and it will go to any length to destroy the credibility of former members who presume to break through this elaborate screen of security. We have had informants who, while still in the party, were given the most responsible assignments, highly complimented for the caliber of their Communist work, regarded as extremely dedicated and capable comrades. The instant they defected and testified before us, however, the party attempted to destroy their credibility by circulating wild rumors of sexual perversion, mental instability, alcoholism, and resorted to every trick and device for the purpose of destroying their reputations.

This type of activity, as well as the espionage activities of the Communist Party, are carefully insulated away from most of the intellectual members of the party, who are usually convinced that the organization does not engage in this sort of thing. It is a source of neverending astonishment to us that American citizens can be lured into the Communist apparatus and indoctrinated to the point that they will believe only the things that originate from Communist sources, and soon come to distrust and disbelieve all statements issued by the capitalist press which they regard as propaganda from the class enemy.

In conclusion the committee wishes to again state that we do not believe it is now necessary to hold large-scale public hearings for the purpose of exposing individual party members who have been in the organization for a number of years. The indices of our various reports have listed such people from the middle twenties down to the present time, and we have learned from years of practical experience that very little good is accomplished by issuing subpoenas for indoctrinated party members, listening to them use the witness stand as a propaganda medium, having them clutter up the expensive shorthand report of the proceedings by monotonously invoking the Fifth Amendment over and over again, and indeed, very little real good is accomplished by prosecuting and convicting this type of witness for contempt. This type of fanatic cannot be cured by a 30-day jail sentence. He is eager to suffer for the cause, he furnishes propaganda ammunition for the party that regards him as a martyr, and he emerges from his cell as a proletarian hero who is more eager and dedicated than before. To parade a somewhat moth-eaten series of dedicated party members through a hearing and afford them the facilities of radio and television publicity while they castigate the committee has become in our view largely a waste of time. In earlier years public hearings were necessary —and are occasionally still necessary—for the purpose of exposing front organizations. And 10 years ago it was necessary to hold a good many public hearings for the purpose of breaking through public apathy and exposing Communist schools, Communist publications, and open party activities.

It is imperative that we obtain the cooperation of the utilities, the various agencies and departments of State Government, the trade unions, and organizations of all types for the purpose of keeping abreast of Communist tactics and implementing the enforcement of the laws that have been enacted to cope with the situation.

We believe that the preventive aspect of the problem is now paramount, that the work of a committee cannot be gauged by the amount of publicity it receives, and that the most effective weapon against internal subversion is an informed Legislature and an enlightened public.

INDEX

For Reports of
1943, 1945, 1947, 1948, 1949, 1951, 1953, 1955, 1957, and 1959:

The Committee on Un-American Activities believes a complete index of its reports will be of assistance for those engaged in referencing work on the activities and accomplishments of hearings conducted by the committee from its inception in 1943. This index identifies the person or subject, followed by the year in which the report was published, and the page number.

INDEX

Alameda County Communist Party, Special Section—Continued
232, 234, 235, 238, 241, 242, 243
Alameda County Communist Party, Special Section Organizer
1951—206
Alameda County Congress of Industrial Organization Council
1951—37, 50, 51, 76, 79, 173, 175, 176, 185, 186, 192, 193, 194, 198, 201, 203, 207, 208, 212, 213, 236, 254
Alaska Fishermen's Union
1947—92
Alba, Victor
1951—272
Albany Civil Rights Congress
1949—446
Albert, Bessy
1948—179
Albert, Lillian
1951—267
Albert, Sam
1955—386
Albert, Samuel
1943—60
Alberts Case
1959—15, 198
Alberts, Doris
1948—311, 314, 317
Alberts, George
1959—131
Alberts, George W.
1943—150, 177, 178, 182
Alberts, Sam
1947—238
1948—311, 314, 317, 355
Albertson, William
1948—213
Albrier, Mrs. Frances (Francis)
1948—194
1949—438
1953—284
Albritton, Clarence
1948—338
Alcalay, Helen
1947—73
Alderete, Nora
1949—438
Alert
1949—9, 614, 616, 631, 646, 651, 654
1955—106
Alesen, Dr. Lewis Albert
1955—85, 86, 87, 88, 89, 90, 91, 218
Alexander, Charlene
1959—42, 43
Alexander, Dr. Chauncey A.
1947—189
Alexander, Ed
1951—24
Alexander, Mrs. Elizabeth
1947—185
Alexander, George
1948—338
Alexander, Harmon
1947—185
Alexander, Dr. Herbert
1948—148, 310
Alexander, Hursel
1949—429, 432
1953—162, 253
Alexander, Leon
1947—74, 85, 89, 91
1949—425, 429, 431
Alexander, Mara
1947—89, 91

1948—185
1949—425
Alexander, Milnor
1955—318
Alexander, Raymond Pace
1949—449
Alexander, Robert
1947—238
1948—355
1949—480
1953—107, 103, 113
1955—319, 387
Alexander v. State
1949—254
Alexander, Dr. Will H.
1948—199
Alexandrov
1953—235
Alexeev, Alex M.
1948—268, 374
1955—390
Algase, Benjamin
1948—271
1949—468
Algren, Nelson
1945—121, 126
1948—274
1949—472
Aliard, John
1943—137
1947—67
1948—63, 280
1949—419, 437, 470, 688
Alkaw, J. M.
1948—383
All-American Anti-Imperialistic League
1948—67, 106, 107, 143, 145, 188, 273
1949—174, 268
All-American Slav Congress
1949—413, 414
Allan Rudak Studio
1948—104
Allan, William
1948—233, 343
All-Calif. Conference for Defense of Civil Rights and Aid to Labor's Prisoners
1948—107
1949—269
Allen
1957—116
Allen, Dr. Bennet M.
1948—171
Allen, Billy
1947—203
Allen, Rev. Carl
1948—106, 160, 161, 164, 358
Allen, Claude O.
1949—438
Allen, Fay
1943—137, 139, 195
1947—47, 67, 71, 96, 97, 129
1948—116, 183, 201, 328, 351, 375
1949—419, 422, 638
Allen, Harland
1948—323
1949—538
Allen, Dr. Harold B.
1948—185
Allen, Henry D.
1943—359
Allen, James Egert
1948—198
1949—449
Allen, James S.
1948—233, 343
1949—189, 621, 626
1957—106
1951—153

Allen, James T.
1948—15
Allen, Oliver S.
1949—480, 489
Allen, Dr. Raymond
1959—54
Allen, Dr. Raymond B.
1953—201, 202, 204, 206
1957—5, 6, 8, 9, 16, 18, 27, 30, 31, 32
Allen, Sam Houston
1955—309, 360
Allen, Shannon C.
1948—248
Allen, Ted
1948—226
Allen, Warren O.
1947—47, 67, 71, 96, 97, 129
1948—317
Allen, William
1948—164, 332, 340
1949—542, 547, 638
1951—267
1953—103
Aller, Elsa
1948—179
Alley, Raymond
1948—338
All-Harlem Youth Conference
1948—75
1949—269
Alliance, The
1953—23
Alliance of Certain Racketeer and Communist Dominated Unions in the Field of Transportation
1959—109
Alliance of Social Revolutionaries
1953—22
Allied Labor News
1948—168, 181, 280
Allied Labor News Service
1948—49, 224
1949—269, 381, 460, 461
Allied Printing Trades Council
1947—80
Allied Voters Against Coudert
1943—38, 96, 146
1949—269
Allied War Relief Rally
1948—216
All-India Kisan Sabha
1953—231
All-India National Congress
1953—214, 215
All-India Trade Union Congress
1953—225, 226, 230, 231, 233, 242
Allis-Chalmers
1949—440
Allison, Elmer T.
1948—243
Allison, Tempe
1947—89
1949—425
Allister, Mona
1948—355
Allister, Wm.
1948—355
All-Slav Congress
1949—413
All-Union Society for Cultural Relations With Foreigners
1948—107, 383
1949—269
Allsberg, Dr. Martin
1959—125

Carroll, Dr. Vincent F.
  1948—16
Carroll, Wm.
  1948—94
  1949—554
Carse, Robert
  1948—189
Carson, Allan
  1953—79, 120
Carson, Jules
  1947—71, 78, 89, 90, 91,
    101
  1949—422, 424, 425, 429,
    430, 432
Carson, Mimi
  1948—358
Carson, Saul
  1949—480, 486, 499, 509,
    510, 513, 515, 537
Carter, Alan
  1949—480
Carter, Dyson
  1948—226
  1949—633
Carter, Edward C.
  1947—321
  1948—169, 170, 357
  1949—412
Carter, Mrs. Edward C.
  1948—131
Carter, Elmer
  1951—267
Carter, James
  1948—206
Carter, James C., Judge
  1955—298
Carter, Justice
  1955—51
Carter, Marvin
  1943—153, 164
Cartwright, Jack
  1943—157
  1949—177
Carus, Dr. Clayton
  1948—171
Carvajol, Jose
  1948—16
Carver Club
  1948—214, 259, 280
  1957—26
Carver Cultural Council
  1948—392
Casals, Pablo
  1948—311
Casden, Norman
  1949—499
Case and Comment
  1959—177
Case, Clair
  1951—280
Case, Fox
  1945—116
Casetta, Mario (Boots)
  1949—542
Casey, W. B.
  1949—437
Cash, Vernon
  1948—16
Caso, Alfonso
  1951—272
Caspary, Vera
  1947—179, 189
  1948—97
Cassidy, Harry M.
  1948—352
Cassidy, Mary Ann
  1948—215
Cassil, Virginia
  1959—212
Castelhun Dorothy
  1948—341
Castle Lodge, Temple Israel
  1948—280
Caston, Rev. J. L.
  1948—333
Castro, Oscar
  1949—438

Catacklill, Bessie
  1948—377
Catholic Daughters
  1948—15-17
Catholic Inter-Racial
  Council
  1948—147
Catholic War Veterans of
  the U. S.
  1948—15-19
Catlett, Elizabeth
  1949—546
Cattell, J. McKeen
  1948—248
Caughlin, John
  1951—263
Cave, Jack
  1948—311
Cavett, Thomas L.
  1943—7, 61
Caya, Al
  1948—257
  1949—688
Cayla, Florence
  1948—251
Cayton, Ethel
  1947—90
Cayton, Revels
  1943—87
  1945—139, 140
  1947—70, 90, 163
  1948—162, 218, 283, 290,
    303, 305, 307, 375
  1949—421, 688
  1953—102
  1959—209
Cazden, Norman
  1949—480, 508, 513, 536
CEC
  1949—163
Cedars of Lebanon Hospital
  1955—78, 82, 86, 98, 100,
    105, 107, 108, 114,
    127, 134, 135, 167,
    221, 223, 224, 225,
    226, 236, 308, 309,
    310, 311, 359
Cedars' Shame
  1955—109
Celebration of 15 Years of
  Birobidjan
  1949—288
Celebration of 15 Years of
  Birobidjan, Soviet
  Union Colony
  1953—173
Celler, Emanuel
  1947—247
Celler Radio Bill
  1947—134
Cena, Loco
  1943—301
Censored
  1948—130
Censored News
  1948—5
Centenary of Marxism, The
  1951—153
Central Committee of the
  Communist Party
  1948—135, 158, 385,
  1949—398
Central Council of American
  Croatian Women
  1949—288, 289
Central Council of American
  Women of Croatian De-
  scent
  1949—288, 289, 338
Central Intelligence Agency
  1951—3
Central Labor Council
  1947—48-50, 52, 70, 176,
    188, 192, 261

Central Labor Council of the
  American Federation of
  Labor in Los Angeles
  1949—421
Central Panchayat
  1953—216
Central Plan Branch of the
  Communist Party
  1948—215
Central Trades and Labor
  Council
  1953—143
Cerda, Frank
  1947—91
Cerney, Ed
  1947—89
  1949—425
Cerney, Isobel
  1947—89-91
  1949—428
Centro Anti-Communista
  1943—201
Cervantes Fraternal Society
  1949—466
Cestare, Frank
  1948—186
  1949—562
Chabot, Joseph
  1947—73
Chadwick, John E.
  1943—176, 191, 192
Chadwick, Martha B.
  1948—266
Chaffee, Zachariah, Jr.
  1948—198, 320
  1953—175
Chakin, Alfred
  1948—179
Challenge
  1947—225
  1948—260
  1957—73
Challenge Records
  1948—392
Challman, Dr. Robert C.
  1949—480, 499, 504, 507,
    512, 513, 518, 532
Chalmers, Mrs. Allan
  Knight
  1948—320
Chamber of Commerce
  1948—171
  1949—613
Chamberlain, Ernest R.
  1943—109, 110
Chamberlain, Howard
  1948—356
Chamberlain, Howland
  1943—135, 145, 147, 150,
    164
  1951—83
  1955—306
Chamberlain, Rowland
  1948—315
Chamberlain, Mrs. Selah
  1948—144
Chamberlin, Rev. Mark A.
  1949—480
Chambers, Pat
  1943—37
  1951—135
Chambers, Tom
  1953—259
Chambers, Whitaker
  1945—119
  1948—266
  1949—2, 678
  1951—90, 183
  1953—7, 175
  1955—401
  1959—167, 183
Champion
  1949—383
  1955—88

McTernan, Katherine
1947—71, 72, 78, 79
1949—422, 424, 689
McTernan, Kay
1955—392
McWilliams, Carey
1943—87, 129, 149, 156,
158, 159, 163, 203,
210, 217
1945—127, 128, 137, 139,
141, 193-195
1947—34, 47, 54, 55, 67,
97, 98, 116, 126,
130-132, 138, 170,
179, 188, 189, 208,
209, 235, 236, 239,
242, 348, 349, 354
1948—4, 106, 109, 114, 116,
146, 160, 162, 176,
179, 184, 193, 198,
199, 201, 208, 226,
233, 235, 239, 244,
249, 254, 258, 265,
267, 268, 272, 273,
279, 308, 309, 327,
328, 330, 332, 341,
344, 346, 351, 354,
355, 358, 359, 375,
376, 382
1949—146, 147, 419, 435,
436, 448, 449, 455,
464, 471, 478, 481,
488, 490, 498, 501,
502, 503, 504, 505,
506, 508, 510, 511,
512, 513, 514, 516,
517, 518, 521, 523,
526, 527, 532, 536,
537, 542, 547, 689
1951—63, 56, 57, 58, 59,
60, 65, 92, 93, 235,
255, 263, 264, 271
1953—131, 139, 151, 172,
176, 177, 281
1955—329, 383
1959—209
McWilliams, Mrs. Robert
1947—79, 89, 93

N

NAACP Youth Council
1948—338
Naboisek, Herbert
1953—255
Naboisek, June
1948—215
Nacht-Express
1951—41
Nadir, Moishe
1945—125, 126
1948—194
Nadji, General
1949—555
Nagata, S.
1943—337
Nagle case
1919—246
Nagy, Ferenc
1949—114, 115, 116, 654
Nahem, Joseph
1949—442
Nalditch, Jack
1953—79, 99, 121, 124,
125
Naileben
1948—225, 261
1949—393
Naked City
1948—131
Naked God, The
1959—85, 147
*Nakedness of Howard Fast,
The*
1959—147

Nance, Merle
1948—343
Naranjan Singh
1953—218, 219
Narodna Volya
1949—181
Narodna Wola
1949—467
Narodni Glasnik
1948—225, 269
1949—181, 393, 467
Nasatir, Esther
1947—239
1948—355
1955—318
Nash, N. Richard
1948—210
Nash, Naomi
1948—378
Nashburn, Mrs. Genevieve
(Same as Mashburn)
1955—32, 40
Nassau County (N.Y.) Con-
ference for Human
Rights
1949—446
Nasz Swiah
1949—181
Nathan, Dr. Otto
1949—482
Nation, The
1947—313
1948—246
1949—620, 621
1955—185
1959—186, 209
National Action Committee
1957—65
National Advertising
Council
1949—660, 673, 676
National Antiwar Week
1949—334
National Archives
1959—174
National Association for the
Advancement of Colored
People
1947—241, 293, 294, 304
1948—43, 149, 254, 338
1949—435, 438
1951—289
1957—26, 27, 60, 96, 99,
100, 104-125
National Association of
Manufacturers
1951—46
National Association of
Mexican-Americans
1955—391
National Association of
State Attorneys General
1959—188, 197
National Board of the
Young Communist
League
1949—409
National Book Agency
1953—229
National Book Mart
1943—232, 233
National Broadcasting Co.
1947—364
1948—263, 264
National Chinese
Government
1949—311
National Citizens Political
Action Committee
1947—101, 184, 188, 196,
209, 233, 236, 237,
241, 369
1948—38, 115, 116, 217,
254, 334-336

1949—315, 351, 352, 435,
477, 512, 628, 705
1955—364, 365
National Citizen's Political
Action Committee,
Southern Calif. Chapter
1951—248
National Civil Rights
Federation
1949—335
National Committee Against
Censorship of the The-
atre Arts
1948—52, 130
1949—335
National Committee for
Browder and Ford
1948—196
National Committee for
People's Rights
1948—61, 122, 155, 156,
364
1949—335, 336, 440, 453
1959—140
National Committee for the
Arts, Sciences and Pro-
fessions
1949—623
National Committee for the
Defense of Political
Prisoners
1948—61, 112, 122, 155,
364
1949—335, 512
1959—137, 140
National Committee of the
Communist Party of
the United States
1948—10, 94, 95
1949—394, 441
National Committee of the
International Labor De-
fense
1948—93
National Committee to
Abolish Poll Tax
1947—45
1948—319, 320, 334-336
1949—336
National Committee to Aid
Victims of German Fas-
cism
1948—324
1949—336
National Committee to De-
fend Political Prisoners
1949—348
National Committee to De-
fend the 12 Communist
Leaders
1953—247
National Committee to Win
the Peace
1948—124, 197, 318, 354
1949—336, 373, 467
1955—88
National Communist Party
—see Communist Party
National Conference for
Democratic Rights
1949—448
National Conference on
China
1948—218
1949—105, 505
National Conference on
Civil Liberties
1948—61, 335
1949—336, 440
National Conference on Constitutional Liberties in
America
1948—112

o

L-4361 4-59 5M   *printed in* CALIFORNIA STATE PRINTING OFFICE

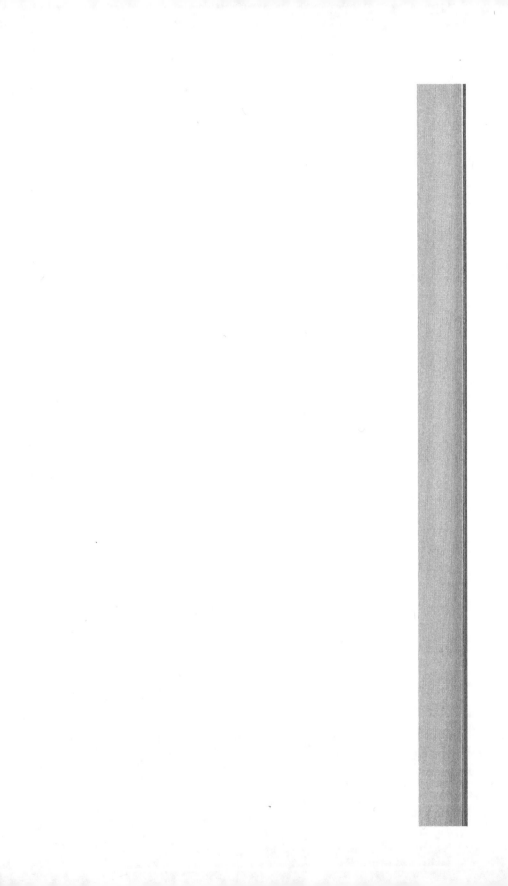